START YOUR OWN
eBAY
BUSINESS

Additional titles in **Entrepreneur's Startup Series**

Start Your Own

Entrepreneur.
MAGAZINE'S

.::: STARTUP

START YOUR OWN

eBAY
BUSINESS

THIRD EDITION

YOUR STEP-BY-STEP GUIDE
TO SUCCESS

The Staff of Entrepreneur Media, Inc. & Christopher Matthew Spencer

Entrepreneur Press®

Publisher: Entrepreneur Press
Cover Design: Andrew Welyczko
Production and Composition: Eliot House Productions

Library of Congress Cataloging-in-Publication Data
Names: Spencer, Christopher Matthew, author.
Title: Start your own eBay business : your complete guide to success / by Christopher Matthew
    Spencer and the staff of Entrepreneur Media, Inc.
Description: Second edition. | [Irvine, CA] : Entrepreneur Press, [2020] | Series: Entrepreneur
    magazine's startup | Includes index. | Summary: "Start Your Own eBay Business, Second Edition,
    gives readers a nuts-and-bolts look at the ever-growing, ever-changing business of selling on
    eBay. What once began as a simple way to unload unwanted items online is now a booming
    business model for online retailers. Author Christopher Matthew Spencer, along with the staff
    of Entrepreneur Media, shows readers how to source products, create sales listings, establish an
    eBay storefront, create a loyal customer base, and make profitable sales on the eBay platform"
    -- Provided by publisher.
Identifiers: LCCN 2020008131 (print) | LCCN 2020008132 (ebook) | ISBN 978-1-59918-670-2
    (paperback) | ISBN 978-1-61308-427-4 (ebook)
Subjects: LCSH: Internet auctions. | eBay (Firm)
Classification: LCC HF5478 .S643 2020 (print) | LCC HF5478 (ebook) | DDC 658.8/777--dc23
LC record available at https://lccn.loc.gov/2020008131
LC ebook record available at https://lccn.loc.gov/2020008132

Printed in the United States of America

25 24 23 22 21   10 9 8 7 6 5 4 3 2 1

Contents

Chapter 2
What It Takes to Succeed on eBay 25

Chapter 3
Planning and Organizing Your eBay Business 45

Chapter 4
Researching Products and Pricing 57

Chapter 5

Preparing Your Products Before Listing. **69**

Chapter 6

Setting Up Your eBay Listings **87**

Chapter 8

Communicating with Buyers Pre- and Post-Sale 143

Chapter 9

Packing, Shipping, and Delivering to Buyers 155

Chapter 13

Handling Unexpected Challenges Like a Pro 217

Chapter 14

Keeping Your Finances in Order for Tax Day 231

Chapter 15

Connecting with the eBay Community 237

Foreword

I encourage you to read this book once thoroughly and then keep it close by as a reference guide. It will be instrumental in opening new doors and in closing big deals. The sage advice that you will uncover in these pages is evergreen, and while inflation may warrant adjusting a figure—or perhaps a screenshot may look unusual in the future due to eBay's evolution—every concept, tip, and methodology presented will stand the test of time.

On August 5, 2019, my curiosity was piqued by a help-wanted ad on a quest for fact-checkers. It was for a book project—not just an ebook, but a physical treasure made from ink and paper. I'm a small-town suburban teenager from Kent, Washington. Needless to say, the opportunity to participate in something so useful to millions of entrepreneurs had me jumping out of my skin. I devour books with a laser-sharp focus on business and career improvement.

Christopher Matthew Spencer and I enjoyed an hours-long initial phone call, and I was one of only two individuals under consideration out of hundreds of applicants. Christopher Matthew and I became fast friends. He dispelled my misconceptions about business and about a teenager's ability to score big-time in the capitalist world. I was stunned to learn that Christopher Matthew incorporated his first business at the same age as me: 18 years old.

Being able to assist a published author is exhilarating. I never imagined that this opportunity would include mentorship power sessions. Christopher Matthew's internship included the opportunity for such excellent mentorship in business—an opportunity for guidance that I seized instantly.

Christopher Matthew asserted that meaningful fact-checking also includes testing the techniques and theories. So that's exactly what I did: I started my own eBay business.

As I write these words, I am operating a successful eBay "empire" selling vintage video games and consoles. I've become a local "mogul," known as the resident revival doctor resurrecting the early video game movements. Christopher Matthew and I debated brand names to no end, and eventually we landed on "PIXLBasket" because retro video games display graphics that are relatively basic and pixelated.

I certainly was scared out of my pants to get started: What would happen if I failed? Would I live up to the expectations that I set for myself? Would I disappoint my "Jedi Master" in the process? Above all else, would I be able to build a profitable eBay business from scratch and fire my current boss? These concerned inquiries proved themselves to be needless ramble. I have found a tremendous amount of success already thanks to the help of Christopher Matthew and the techniques in this book. My eBay business is thriving and profitable. All my previous reservations have dissipated.

I moved out of the house three days after my eighteenth birthday. Prior to launching my eBay crusade, serving food at Red Robin was my sole source of revenue, but now I pay my own rent with my eBay income. I'd been looking for a mentor in the field of internet retail (since I had a couple of failed starts with drop-shipping), but finding a suitable role model is no easy feat. Without meaningful mentorship, I was concerned with the reality that I might end up being a worker drone.

The entire experience of fact-checking *Start Your Own eBay Business, Second Edition* has been sublime. I was the first person to read every iteration of this new version. I am tremendously grateful and deeply honored to have been invited by Christopher Matthew to participate and to write this foreword.

I'd like to add a shameless plug (as this book advises) and encourage you to reach out to me if you'd like help selling your retro video games or consoles (or anything of value you'd like to consign).

My email: PIXLBasket@gmail.com

—Ben Akrish

Preface

"I wanted to throw it out—it was so ugly. And, of course, I thought it was worthless," she said.

"And I," her husband said, "almost dropped it—right out there." He nodded towards the Burbank, California, sidewalk in front of my store. "But I talked her out of trashing it."

The young couple and I peered down at what they had just brought to my eBay consignment store. There on my counter was a porcelain figurine of a whimsical nude woman sitting on a pear. The item, standing about ten inches high, was in mint condition and well-marked with "Lenci," the date 1930, and the artist's name. It didn't look like much. The three

FIGURE P–1: **An Extraordinary Garage-Found Treasure**

of us gazed at it with a mixture of skepticism and wild hope—it was an odd piece (see Figure P–1).

"I figured maybe $100," the young man said, referring to what I might be able to get for it on eBay on their behalf.

The young man's father had recently passed on, leaving a Burbank garage crammed with the fruits of 40 years of collecting with a very interesting eye. The couple was moving to Oregon and wanted to give me the entire contents of the garage to list for them on eBay.

I listed the Lenci figurine on eBay with a starting bid of $9.99. In a spectacular example of eBay magic, seven days later, it brought $17,100 and went to a collector back in Italy where it was made.

The contents of their garage brought a total haul of $74,330.60.

I'm not going to say that this was just another day in the life of an eBay seller. That garage was an extraordinary treasure. But if you decide to become an eBay seller, I guarantee that every day there is surprise, gratification, and good old-fashioned creative work.

And my simple eBay business has made me a millionaire.

Not only have I created a successful business for myself on eBay and made lots of money in the process, but I have also taught thousands of people all over the world how to make money easily on eBay. And with this book, I will help you learn this kind of entrepreneurialism. This can lead you on the path to financial freedom and a better life filled with interesting, fun, and profitable surprises.

Being your own boss is fun. If you have a connected device and a way to capture photos, you can easily set up shop as an eBay seller today.

How Pokémon Started It All

I started selling on eBay in the summer of 1998. While I was visiting my brother, Buck, and his family one evening, my nephew, Matt, proudly showed me his Pokémon trading card collection. Pokémon was quite popular at the time, and Matt had acquired these fun collectibles on a relatively new website called eBay. His father was helping him learn the art of using this innovative new online service, and Matt was simply thrilled by the whole experience—the eBay experience. Even on a sluggish dial-up connection, eBay was cool, and Matt was thrilled to be using this neat site to do something really awesome: connect with people in a safe and social way to trade nifty stuff.

This little random event changed my life forever—it gave me an idea for a new and exciting business venture.

Starting as a teenager, I had held various sales jobs and worked in public relations and special events production, and by 1998, I had become a very successful personal manager of actors. The money was fantastic, and I was good at making it. But I am a person in constant need of mental stimulation, and being a personal manager had become routine. Though I worked in the heart of the entertainment industry and was in constant contact with celebrities, I was in a rut. I wanted to be the master of my own destiny—not a well-paid drone to the whims and demands of my clients.

The little Pokémon incident at my brother's house made the wheels start turning in my head and made me think about what else could be sold on eBay. My best friend in the world, Mike Richards, was a Beverly Hills antique dealer (may he rest in peace). I started working for Mike straight out of high school as an intern for his company, writing letters, running errands, and handling his accounting work. It was my first office job! By 1998, I knew that his business—the antiques business—was on the verge of dramatic changes.

For many years, I had tried and failed to get Mike interested in using a computer for his company. I actually forced him to buy a personal computer in the early 1990s, but this state-of-the-art device quickly turned into an expensive doorstop. By now the internet had really taken off—its growth could only be described as explosive.

Shortly after learning about eBay from my nephew, I suggested to Mike that we try selling a few of his antiques on the eBay website. He handed me six nondescript war medals in rather poor condition to photograph and list on eBay. They were just a few bones that Mike threw me as a completely risk-free test case.

At the time, I owned a cool Sony Mavica digital floppy disk camera. Though very expensive then and with a resolution of 800,000 pixels, my camera was a mere toy by today's standards. I took several pictures of each medal and listed them on eBay. A week later, I returned to Mike with my findings. I had sold all the medals for between $60 and $80 each.

Mike was stunned.

But Mike soon became a believer. He promptly prepared another 60 items for me to photograph and list on eBay. Between actor and client phone calls and my regular business meetings, I handled the 60 eBay auctions: answering email questions from prospective buyers, collecting payments, and shipping orders. Quickly, this hobby turned into a real enterprise, and Mike, my only client, was bringing me between 100 and 400 items to list on eBay each week.

By 1999, I was shipping well over $30,000 in merchandise that I had sold on eBay on a monthly basis. This was getting serious. I was now selling a wide variety of items for many new clients besides Mike, and I was getting paid commission. Most of these clients came to me by word of mouth.

One day, while I was busily handling my eBay hobby—that was still the way I thought of it, though it was certainly becoming a lucrative hobby—I got an email from one of my eBay buyers who said that a relative of hers was a writer for *Time*. The magazine was preparing an internet-themed edition with some stories about selling online, my buyer told me, and the writer wanted to interview me. Frankly, I thought this email was a joke, but I played along. The next thing I knew, my entire office was taken over by a *Time* photographer who set up lights and tons of equipment to photograph me for this story. The writer, Sally B. Donnelly, conducted a very pleasant interview, and a few months later, the phone was ringing off the hook.

People I hadn't spoken to since grade school were calling to congratulate me on being in *Time*. At that moment, I realized I had really started something precious, wonderful, and amazing.

The phone rang, and it was a man named John Slocum. John had written a computer program called Auction Assistant Pro—a listing management tool for eBay that automated and facilitated multiple auction listings. John knew that I had been using his program for my eBay business. He told me that someone from eBay would be calling me shortly because they were looking for a substitute instructor for a class on Auction Assistant Pro at an event called eBay University. My fellow eBay University instructors and I were prominently featured on the eBay University page (see Figure P-2 on page xxii). One of their instructors had fallen ill, and they knew that I was an avid user of eBay and this listing tool. Eventually, I found myself speaking in front of hundreds of eager students who yearned to learn eBay.

This convergence of events happened for a reason. Fate (or something) was making a major change in the course of my life. Next came quitting my job as an actors' manager and selling on eBay full time with a new, second job of teaching regular seminars for eBay University. Today, I have successfully listed more than 200,000 items on eBay and have spoken in front of tens of thousands of students at eBay University events. I have authored so many eBay-related educational presentations, technical manuals, and produced instructional videos that I have lost count. I have a trusted staff that helps me run my eBay business, and they are my invaluable allies. I've been so successful on eBay that I now donate most of my proceeds to my favorite nonprofit organization: Dreams to Reality Foundation.

My eBay business started with zero personal investment. I did not have to quit my day job, although I wanted to and eventually did. The money earned from my eBay sales enabled me to purchase investment properties such as apartment buildings, houses, condos, a motel, a hotel, a bar, and a restaurant. My eBay business has generated great wealth for me and given me the freedom to do whatever I want, whenever I want—and it can do the same for you.

If you're wondering if you're starting too late and that eBay has already matured—nothing could be further from the truth. This book could be your passport to financial freedom. Online retailing is still growing impressively,

> **fun fact** ☺
>
> As of August 2019, there are 182 million active buyers on eBay who purchased $95 billion worth of goods. The opportunities for eBay sellers are not only extraordinary, but are growing every year.

FIGURE P–2: **eBay University's** *Meet the Instructors* **Page**

and you're seizing this opportunity at the perfect time. If you compare the internet to the auto industry, we are still in the "Model T" years. There will be plenty of business out there for you. With some determination and patience, you will reap the rewards of selling on eBay, and you can be as successful as I have been. You will reach the level of success that you choose because you now have the tools to achieve it.

Nuts and Bolts: What to Expect in this Book

I'm a nuts-and-bolts kind of guy. I wrote this book for anyone interested in starting their own eBay business. Maybe you're thinking of starting at your kitchen table. And maybe flipping through this book, you saw a chapter heading that confused you and made you think, "This book's not for me—too complicated." Or, "Employees? You have to be kidding!" Well, this book *is* for you. In fact, I wrote it just for you and everyone else interested in selling on eBay. Whether you have never been in business or are already running a large company, eBay can offer you endless opportunity and wonder.

This book is all about nuts and bolts—a nitty-gritty blueprint for running an eBay business. It takes you step by step through the entire process of setting up your business and making it a fantastic success. If you think you're already an expert on what's covered in any particular chapter, feel free to skip that chapter. It's all here—the nuts and bolts of starting and running your own successful eBay business. So have a seat, whether at your kitchen table or the desk in your 4,000-square-foot warehouse, and read on.

In this book, you will find:

▶ Profiles and case studies of the most profitable eBay sellers, both homebased and brick-and-mortar

▶ Proven, step-by-step techniques for planning, starting, and executing a successful, profitable eBay business

▶ Great ideas for researching just the right products to list on eBay

▶ Clear direction on how to launch and manage your items on eBay

▶ Recommendations for safe and secure packing and reliable shipping

▶ Master tips for sourcing profitable items

▶ Step-by-step, screenshot-accompanied instructions for launching an eBay Store

▶ A wellspring of ideas for selecting great employees when you need them

▶ Recommended routines to streamline day-to-day operations

▶ A roadmap for going from little to big without growing pains

▶ Cautionary advice on avoiding trouble along the journey

▶ Proven methods for elevating your eBay sales by networking with other eBayers

This book is a wellspring of eBay knowledge that's been distilled down from my two decades of eBay experience as well as ideas shared with me from other eBayers along the way—and industry insights from the team at Entrepreneur.

I welcome you into my circle of friends. Please feel free to write me with your very own tips, ideas, and personal success stories. Please know that I am accessible. I welcome interaction with you. Not only can you find me on social media @borntodeal, but you are always welcome to email me at borntodeal@gmail.com.

You have begun a unique and fascinating journey, and I'm honored to be your guide through this valuable educational experience. We'll have plenty of fun working together as I show you the ropes. With your enthusiasm and a bit of patience and determination, you too will be trading online with your very own eBay empire. You will become your own boss. It is time to claim your piece of this growing opportunity.

Remember that Lenci I sold for $17,100? Those deals are really out there, and you can grow rich making mega-bucks on items like that. It's one of those business success stories that has already become a legend in its own time: eBay, the hottest way to buy and sell new, everyday items as well as rare and unique goods.

The Nickel Tour–
Understanding the eBay Ecosystem

My goal with this book is to guide you through a learning path. I'll share meaningful, practical advice on how I successfully picked a lot of low-hanging fruit off the eBay tree. I've sold millions of dollars' worth of *everything* on eBay. As you look around, I'm sure you'll discover many things that no longer serve any purpose in your life: an orphaned power supply or a something-or-other, a bottle of fragrance that you bought but didn't quite like, or an old vinyl record collection you never listen to anymore. Sell them on eBay!

There is no one-size-fits-all approach to success on eBay. The platform itself is so customizable that it works within *your* lifestyle and how *you* want to do business.

Selling items on eBay is simple. You can grab and sell a few of those unneeded items around your home or office, and you'll be off to the races. You can earn substantial profits now and in the future. While you can grow an eBay business without the necessity of a book, I wrote this text as an antidote for trial-and-error. Have the courage to try something new and be creative with your eBay business. Nothing would be more gratifying than to know that you took my eBay tips and tricks and advanced them with your own ideas. If you aspire to do a whole lot more than simply re-home your old phone, then you'll need an education on how to run a profitable eBay business.

You'll be traveling light. All you need to start this journey is a way to capture photos and get on the internet to access the eBay site. Don't worry about where to find stuff to sell. Everyone you know has unwanted items lying around. If you can't find items of your own right away, then you can start by asking family members, friends, and coworkers. After all, this will be one of the primary ways you will get business for your new enterprise—by asking people.

To begin, this chapter will teach you everything you need to know about eBay and how it began. More importantly, you'll gain some insight into some of the basics of selling on eBay.

eBay: A Brief History

In 1995, Pierre Omidyar, the founder of eBay, spent Labor Day weekend at home developing computer code for a site he called AuctionWeb. He wanted to connect buyers and sellers in an "honest and open marketplace" (see Figure 1–1 on page 3). Pierre's first sale was a broken laser pointer acquired by Canadian Mark Fraser, a tech geek who figured he could fix it.

Within a year of opening AuctionWeb, Pierre hired his first employee, Chris Agarpao, to help him stay on top of this rapidly rising business. By 1996, $7.2 million worth of goods had been sold on the site.

In September 1997, AuctionWeb was officially renamed eBay, which stands for "electronic bay," a nod to the South Bay area where Pierre launched the company.

Pierre quit his day job and hired Jeff Skoll as eBay's first president. They moved the company from the bedroom to the boardroom and opened a small office in San Jose,

Auction Web

[Menu] [Listings] [Buyers] [Sellers] [Search] [Contact/Help] [Site Map]

Welcome to today's online marketplace...

Welcome to our community. I'm glad you found us. AuctionWeb is dedicated to bringing together buyers and sellers in an honest and open marketplace. Here, thanks to our auction format, merchandise will always fetch its market value. And there are plenty of great deals to be found!

...the market that brings buyers and sellers together in an honest and open environment...

Take a look at the listings. There are always several hundred auctions underway, so you're bound to find something interesting.

If you don't find what you like, take a look at our **Personal Shopper**. It can help you search all the listings. Or, it can keep an eye on new items as they are posted and let you know when something you want appears. If you want to let everyone know what you want, post something on our wanted page.

If you have something to **sell**, start your auction instantly.

Welcome to eBay's AuctionWeb.

Join our community. Become a registered user. Registered users receive additional benefits such as daily updates and the right to participate in our user feedback forum and the bulletin board.

Please **read on** about the AuctionWeb vision...

From the founder:

February 26, 1996

I launched eBay's AuctionWeb on Labor Day, 1995. Since then, this site has become more popular than I ever expected, and I began to realize that this was indeed a **grand experiment** in Internet commerce.

By creating an open market that encourages **honest** dealings, I hope to make it easier to conduct business with strangers over the net.

Most people are honest. And they mean well. Some people go out of their way to make things right. I've heard great stories about the honesty of people here. But some people are dishonest. Or deceptive. This is true here, in the newsgroups, in the classifieds, and right next door. It's a fact of life.

But here, those people **can't hide**. We'll drive them away. Protect others from them. This grand hope depends on your **active** participation. Become a registered user. Use our feedback forum. Give praise where it is due; make complaints where appropriate.

For the past six months, I've been developing this system single-handedly, in my spare time. Along the way, I've dealt with complaints among participants. But those complaints have amounted to only a handful. We've had close to **10,000** auctions since opening. And only a few dozen complaints.

Now, we have an **open forum**. Use it. Make your complaints in the open. Better yet, give your praise in the open. Let everyone know what a joy it was to deal with someone.

Above all, conduct yourself in a professional manner. Deal with others the way you would have them deal with you. Remember that you are usually dealing with individuals, just like yourself. Subject to making mistakes. Well-meaning, but wrong on occassion. That's just human. We can live with that. We can deal with that. We can still **make deals** with that.

Thanks for participating. Good luck, and good business!

Regards,

Pierre

[Menu] [Listings] [Buyers] [Sellers] [Search] [Contact/Help] [Site Map]

eBay Internet

FIGURE 1–1: **The AuctionWeb Homepage in 1995**

California, which is now known as Building 6 on the current eBay campus. Just two years after Pierre's brainchild hatched, over one million items had been sold on eBay.

The business genius Meg Whitman joined eBay as President and CEO in February 1998. Meg was one of my first customers and bought my Army Corps of Engineers compass on eBay. I also had the pleasure of sharing a table with Meg for lunch one day when I was onsite to teach for eBay University, and the conversation was inspirational and amazing. (I worked for eBay University from 2001 to 2008, spreading the good word to eager eBayers, and helping them with selling tips through over 200 eBay road shows and events.)

Meg stayed on as the fearless leader of the eBay team for 10 years, and under her guidance, eBay's success was without comparison.

While many things have changed since I worked at eBay, the company has remained resilient and consistently profitable, both for sellers and shareholders. Since its humble beginnings, eBay has faced ferocious competition in a hypercompetitive industry. That said, as of 2018 there were 179 million buyers and over 1.2 billion items listed on eBay, with $95 billion worth of goods sold.

Unlike other online commerce sites, eBay executives have always refused to compete with eBayers. They have never sold "house brands" and they do not list items for sale (other than shipping supplies). The fundamental philosophy of supporting third-party sellers is what improves value and selection.

Pierre wanted online sellers to have a level playing field where Grandma's chances of selling her wares would be on par with a big company's. eBay initially focused on the auction-style listing format where sellers set a starting price that would rise when at least two eBayers placed bids in competition with each other. The high bidder would receive the prize. Online auctions are ubiquitous now; however, it was a novel idea when Pierre first conceived eBay. The online auction-style listing format is an opportunity to score more profit from a potentially high-demand or rare item. It didn't take long for entrepreneurs across the globe to latch onto this fantastic opportunity. Today's eBay sellers are soccer dads and CEO moms; full-time store owners and one-time sellers. The makeup of the eBay community is as diverse as the products they sell. The eBay family of companies allows anyone virtually anywhere to sell almost anything through an auction-style listing at a fixed price or through a classified ad. Plus, eBay works on your time. Jump in and jump out whenever you feel like selling. Take a long vacation sipping your Mai Tai by the beach, and when you return home, you can start right back up again.

The fine folks at eBay encourage sellers to call them with questions about selling. The toll-free support number (for sellers on the U.S. eBay site) is (877) 322-9227.

Selling on eBay: How it Works

Let's take a basic look at the makeup of a traditional eBay listing process (which we'll dig into more later). eBay is a marketplace platform where buyers and sellers trade. The transactions are somewhat private; however, eBay will mediate if things go awry or if course corrections are required. As a marketplace, eBay acts as a meeting place where buyers and sellers can trade among themselves—eBay does not buy or sell the items.

In this chapter, I'll go over the registration process, selling formats and options, eBay's Money Back Guarantee protection program, how privacy works, the benefits of an eBay Store, charitable giving on eBay, and the member feedback system. There's a lot to learn and we'll cover a lot of ground very quickly—connecting all these dots in detail throughout the book.

FYI, while I'll be talking about a warehouse full of terms and eBay web pages, don't worry about getting lost. At the top of every eBay page is the "Help & Contact" link or at the bottom of most eBay pages is the "Site Map" link. From these two places, you can find nearly every resource you need. For your convenience, I'll be providing handy QR codes that you can scan with your mobile device. Android users need to install a QR code reader; iPhone users can point their camera, and the QR code will launch. Here's the first one, which you can use to be magically transported to eBay's Site Map (see Figure 1–2).

FIGURE 1–2: **QR Code for the eBay Site Map**

Register as a Seller

Don't worry, registering on eBay is fast and free—and always free for buyers. Sellers only pay to list and sell items. There is no monthly charge unless you open an eBay Store (and

I'll talk about Stores in-depth in Chapter 11). eBay is free for buyers, and sellers usually pay a fee to list items and another fee when the item sells. You'll need to be at least 18 years old because eBay transactions are legally binding contracts. What are you waiting for? Get registered today. As shown in Figure 1–3, simply head over to http://www.ebay.com and click on the Register link in the upper-left-hand corner of the browser viewport.

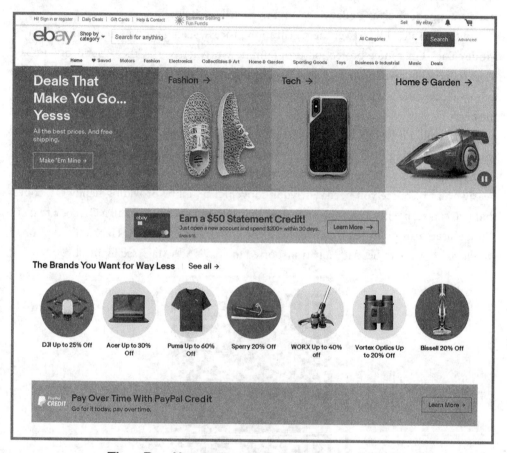

FIGURE 1–3: **The eBay Homepage with the "Register" Link at the Top-Left Corner**

Both individuals and businesses can register to sell on eBay. When signing up, you can choose the type of seller you wish to register as. The process for listing and selling merchandise is the same. Businesses must fill in a few other fields, such as the organization's name, type, and address. Registration can be accomplished using an email address or a social media account, such as Facebook or Google. Virtually all eBay sellers accept payment through PayPal, so you'll want to register for an account at http://www.paypal.com as well.

You'll be linking your eBay and PayPal accounts using your email address, so it's ideal if they are the same on both sites. Trying to sell on eBay without offering PayPal will be hard. I'm sure it's possible, but you'll definitely lose sales. Buyers love the safety and security that PayPal offers. They can pay you without revealing sensitive card or bank account information.

High-volume sellers may wish to organize their listings by genre so that similar merchandise is presented together. This can be accomplished by having multiple eBay accounts. I have 11 of them. You'll need a unique email address for each one, and they will have different user IDs. Having multiple eBay accounts can be incredibly useful. For example, perhaps you'd like to conduct your virtual garage sales on a different account than your new goods. If you decide to launch an eBay Store, it can be themed. For example, you may want to keep your intimate apparel shop separate from your hunting and fishing gear store.

Selecting your user ID is a nontrivial matter. eBay provides suggestions, but give this some careful thought before you proceed. Don't put yourself into a box. The user ID "glasswarebycms" is very narrow. (I'm using C.M.S, my initials, here.) A better choice would be "curiositiesbycms." Don't pick something embarrassing or offensive, even if eBay doesn't put the kibosh on it. Your user ID should be relevant, trustworthy, simple, and memorable. As your business changes, so can your eBay user ID. You can only change your eBay ID once every 30 days. A change icon will appear next to your ID for 30 days after you rename it.

> **tip** ⓘ
>
> Never reuse passwords between websites. Use a password manager to generate safe, secure passwords and remember them. Apple has Keychain. I'm an iPhone user; however, most of my eBay business is conducted on a desktop. I use LastPass to generate, store, and manage my passwords. With the LastPass mobile app, I'm able to instantly find my passwords and get them right the first time. No messy guessing. Find LastPass at https://www.lastpass.com.

eBay's Gospel

Common sense isn't as common as you may have heard (or experienced firsthand). When was the last time you actually read all that wonderful legalese that you're asked to "agree" to when you register to use a website? If you said "never," then you're in the majority. I'm among the guilty. I'd like to share a few points with you that I feel are critical to be aware of when you're using an eBay account. It's a situation that's analogous to "you don't know what you don't know," if you know what I mean.

Accessibility

If accessibility matters to you, it would be prudent to explore this information, which is a link you can find at the bottom of most eBay pages by clicking Accessibility. eBay's accessibility policy page talks about *MIND patterns* and *OATMEAL testing methods*. No, they aren't tampering with your private thoughts or stuffing your mouth full of oatmeal raisin cookies. These are acronyms for e-commerce web components and accessibility testing methods. MIND stands for Messaging, Input, Navigation and Design; while OATMEAL refers to Open Accessibility Testing Methods for Experts And Layfolk. On the accessibility page, you'll also learn how eBay addresses subjects such as improving the site's experience for people with disabilities and providing visually hidden text for ambiguous links and buttons. Diversity and inclusion are very important to these fine folks, as is their compliance with industry standards for such web technospeak as HTML, WAI-ARIA, CSS, and JavaScript. If anything about the eBay site isn't working well for you, feedback is not only welcomed, the company provides a dedicated email for feedback relating to the accessibility of their products. That email address is accessibility@ebay.com. Let's take a look at some other important sections of the site.

User Agreement

As you continue along this journey of reading, you would be wise to review the User Agreement, which can also be found as a link at the bottom of most eBay pages. The User Agreement is very concise and remind us that eBay is not our business partner and is merely a marketplace for trade. We are allowed to use eBay "as-is" and at our "own risk." The User Agreement also reminds you that your access to eBay's platform is a privilege, not a right, and that privilege can be taken away at any time. If you run across any problems, violations, or iffy conduct, you can report it to ebayinc@ebay.com.

Speaking of legal issues, accepting the eBay User Agreement means that in any legal dispute with eBay (not with other eBayers), you agree to arbitration of those claims. *Arbitration* is a legally binding means of settling disputes without the involvement of a court (including class action lawsuits, which you are also agreeing never to file). The silver lining in eBay's arbitration clause is that eBay agrees to cover all costs of arbitration for claims of $10,000 or less—and disputes can be resolved by telephone arbitration. You can opt out of arbitration, but you must complete and postmark the Opt-Out Notice Form (found on the User Agreement page) within 30 days of your first use of the eBay site. I'm not sure why you would want to opt out because taking your gripe with eBay to court could prove to be a very expensive proposition. Not only is arbitration cheaper, but eBay also pays the initial costs to file the *de minimis* dispute. Frankly, I prefer to stay out of trouble and just follow the "eBay rules" to the best of my ability. Like most people, I prefer love, not war; and I love eBay—I have had a great experience so far, and I have high hopes for eBay for many years into the future. That said, the User Agreement limits your financial recovery in any legal action against eBay to $50 in any legal action.

Privacy Policy

Next, let's discuss eBay's Privacy Policy. eBay collects some personal information about you that they require in order to register you as a user of the site—and to ensure safe trading (nothing nefarious here, just common sense). When you click on the Privacy link (also at the bottom of most eBay pages) you can explore eBay's User Privacy Notice. eBay can only know what you allow them to know. So, what little "data bits" can eBay become privy to? Here's a list:

▶ Personally identifiable information such as your name, address, phone number, email address

▶ Financial information (e.g., credit card and account numbers, payment details)

▶ Bid and purchase data (and habits) as a buyer

▶ Sales data related to your activity as a seller

▶ Taxpayer ID

▶ In some cases: age, gender, country of birth, nationality, employment status, family status, interests and preferences

▶ Location data

▶ Computer and connection information, such as IP address, access times, browser history data, language settings, and blog information

▶ Data from public sources, credit agencies, and data providers (so that eBay can look at your demographic data and interests stored by third parties in order to market to you)

▶ Access to your social media activity when you sign on to eBay through a social network (e.g., the content you have viewed, ads you clicked, videos you watched, etc.).

You are most certainly allowing the company access to some pretty private information, so it's important that you hand out only as much as you're comfortable with a total stranger knowing. I'll talk in more detail about protecting yourself further along in this chapter.

AdChoice

Finally, let's talk about AdChoice (indeed, a link that is also at the bottom of most eBay pages). This is eBay's bespoke advertising methodology that uses your tidbits of activity data curated from eBay to tailor-make ads that you might find interesting. Personally, I am not bothered by ads. I simply ignore them virtually all the time (there's that one-in-a-million ad that Svengalis me, and I cannot resist the temptation to click it). To decide which ads to show you, eBay uses stuff like search terms you enter, information you've provided to eBay, as well as data collected by third parties and queried by eBay. You may opt out of the personalized ads if you feel creeped out by how accurately they know what strikes your fancy (I find it a bit unnerving and way too seductive), by using the opt-out button towards the top of the AdChoice page. No one will be offended and if you decide to leave the party, you'll see some (probably irrelevant) ads that will have you scratching your head.

Choose a Selling Format

Sellers may select from a variety of eBay listing formats. Hummel dealers will agonize over pricing their precious figurines, while a fashionista knows Banana Republic pricing like the back of their hand. Collectibles may have uncertain prices, while commodities have very well-known values. Selling formats need to accommodate both the type of item a seller is offering and the urgency of the transaction. A rare car warrants a carefully-planned auction-style listing while a buyer of AA batteries needs them as soon as possible. The wonderful people at eBay give us options of both auction- and fixed price-style listings; there are also some special format variants for certain categories. You should plan according to the type of item that is for sale.

Auction-Style Listings

Auction-style listings allow you to receive competitive bids from multiple people and sell to the highest bidder. You can list one or multiple items, and your listing can be featured in up to two eBay categories. Categories are analogous to departments in a store. You can list auction-style with durations of one, three, five, seven, or ten days. If you sell real estate, you can run your auction for 30 days. There's a feedback rating system in which both the seller and buyer can leave each other feedback comments, but only the buyer can leave a negative or neutral remark. Sellers can only leave positive feedback for buyers. Auction-style listings are ideal for items that are in demand or rare, such as collectibles and hard-to-find merchandise. For example, while a classic roadster warrants an auction, a new car probably does not.

A low starting price for an auction-style listing will encourage bids, but there's a real probability only one person may bid on an item. It takes two to tango! The price of your auction-style listing will only rise if at least two eBayers place bids. With millions of listings on eBay every day, only high-demand merchandise is likely to receive many bids—a low starting price means you could lose money. You can set a secret *reserve* price for your item on eBay's back-end when you launch the listing—the lowest price you're willing to accept. I'm not a fan of using a reserve because many bidders dislike and are frustrated by them. You can, and probably should, start your item with a minimum bid amount that represents the lowest you would accept without pulling your hair out if only one person bids. If you launch an unsuccessful listing, just relist it with a lower starting price.

Fixed-Price Listings

Fixed-price listings satisfy a buyer's urge for immediate gratification. There is no bidding. The buyer doesn't have to wait until the end of an auction. You can add a Make Offer option that permits buyer haggling. Think of Make Offer like a backward auction. Fixed-price listings can have one or many of the same product and can be listed in up to two categories. There is only one duration, which eBay refers to as "Good 'til Cancelled." These listings automatically renew every month until all quantities are sold or you end the listing. The seller and buyer can also leave feedback for each other. This listing format is ideally suited for commodities that are readily available and can be replenished or for items that have a clearly understood value. Best Offer permits you to enter both a value at which eBay will automatically accept an offer as well as a floor price, below which eBay will reject an offer. This sidesteps the annoyance of low-ball offers. I should point out that you can always add a buy-it-now price to an auction-style listing for an added possibility of an immediate sale.

Classified Ads

The *classified ad* format is a way to advertise where the seller and buyer complete the transaction off eBay. It's a bit more private with the caveat that eBay won't mediate disputes if things go south. Ads can run for 30 days, and there is a very limited number of eBay categories that offer this feature. Real Estate classifieds can be posted for a term of either 30 or 90 days. Because these ads allow buyers to contact you outside of the eBay website to complete a sale, eBayers are not permitted to leave each other feedback. Scan the QR Code in Figure 1–4 on page 12 to access eBay's article *Selling with Classified Ads* for a deeper dive into this.

Motor Vehicle Listings

While selling a train on eBay is allowed, it's more likely you'll want to sell a vehicle. *eBay Motors* listings let you re-home cars, trucks, motorcycles, power sports vehicles, boats, planes, trailers, and other vehicles. eBay Motors is a special shopping destination where vehicles and vehicles parts and accessories are bought and sold. eBay Motors can be

FIGURE 1–4: **Selling with Classified Ads**

accessed from the URL https://ebaymotors.com. Sellers in the Motors section of eBay can use auction-style, Buy It Now, and Best Offer formats. Auction-style vehicle listings can be launched with durations of three, five, seven, or 10 days. eBay Motors vehicle fixed-price listings can be launched for three-, five, seven-, 10-, or 30-days or Good 'til Cancelled, whereas eBay's core site only permits fixed-price listings to run with the Good 'til Cancelled option. There are more duration options when listing vehicles; however, vehicle parts and accessories follow the same durations as items listed on the core eBay site. To help streamline the process of listing a vehicle, eBay offers a handy checklist as a foolproof guide for selling on eBay Motors. Scan the QR Code in Figure 1–5 to access it.

Selling a vehicle on eBay is ideal if your car is collectible or in high-demand. Buyers typically pick up their spoils or pay for the transportation costs after a successful sale, so

FIGURE 1–5: **eBay Motors Checklist**

the price-to-value ratio or rarity would need to exist for a buyer to be motivated to buy a vehicle online. Licensed vehicle dealers can call eBay for special pricing. For easy reference, the eBay Motors team can be reached at (866) 322-9227. As of December 2019, eBay says there are 7.4 million unique visitors a month looking for cars on the site. Is your engine revving yet?

Handle Dissatisfied Customers

The *eBay Money Back Guarantee* protects eBayers from faulty or damaged merchandise or instances when an item doesn't match what was represented. The buyer gets their money back. Once an issue is reported, a seller has three business days to make things right. If the buyer remains dissatisfied, the case can be escalated, and eBay will make a decision within 48 hours. The eBay Money Back Guarantee only protects eBayers when the seller hasn't handled things correctly. eBay will not help with buyer's remorse.

Return options are up to the seller. You can sell items on a no-returns basis, which *maybe* makes sense for a very limited number of things. Anytime a buyer opens a claim under eBay's Money Back Guarantee, it will generally result in an uphill battle. The phrase "no returns" is a turn-off for most online purchasers. Those days are long gone. Buyers want great selection, excellent prices, a simple shopping experience, and an opportunity to examine the merchandise. For example, my eBay return rate is 1.95 percent.

I recommend you accept returns. eBay's listing form displays the option to accept returns within a window of either 30 or 60 days. You can inform buyers if you offer free returns—where you pay the return shipping—or if they'll have to foot the bill.

The best way for you to protect yourself against returns is to do your homework. Create a listing that is in the best category at the price level you want to achieve with clear photos and a candid description. The selection of listing format may require some further study on your part. With so many product categories, there is no textbook answer on what works best. Auction-style listings offer the potential of selling for more than you may have predicted, but a low starting price may leave you with an unfavorable outcome. You can use reserves to protect your investment, but many buyers dislike them. The days of starting an item at a dollar and always reaching the market price are over because eBay is really competitive. Proceed with common sense and caution, and protect yourself against losing money by using a listing format and pricing strategy that's sensible.

Consider Listing Privately

We've all peeked under the Christmas wrapping paper or given our Hanukkah present a little shake thinking, "I wonder what's inside."

Making your eBay buyer anonymous is as elegant and simple as ticking off a checkbox, as shown in Figure 1–6. Doing so will hide eBayers' usernames from other members viewing the listing and can only be viewed by you. Aside from precious privacy, there are a few other reasons to use the private listing option. Private listings avoid:

tip

For an added layer of privacy and security, get a mailbox from the U.S. Postal Service and then sign up for the free, optional Street Addressing Service. This convenient program allows you to use the street address of the USPS location for your mailing address in addition to your PO Box number.

- ▶ Spamming of your customers by other eBay sellers
- ▶ Prying eyes knowing what your buyers have purchased, such as for "gifty" goods and high-value merchandise
- ▶ Embarrassment when your buyer has purchased adult, health, medical, or pharmaceutical products
- ▶ Transparency of pricing when you're selling wholesale to other eBay sellers
- ▶ Nosy competitors getting intel on your business practices, prices, and customers

---

Selling details

"Format ⓘ   Auction-style ▾

"Duration ⓘ   7 days ▾

                     ◉ Start my listings when I submit them
                     ○ Schedule to start on ($0.10) -   ▾   12 ▾   00 ▾   AM ▾ PDT

Price   *Starting price   Buy It Now price   Reserve price (fees apply) ⓘ
                     $ $ $

                     Best Offer ⓘ
                     ☐ Let buyers make offers. Being flexible with your price may help your item sell faster

Quantity   1

                     ☐ Sell as lot ⓘ

Private listing ⓘ   ☑ Allow buyers to remain anonymous to other eBay users

♟ Make a donation ⓘ ☑ Donate a percentage of your sale to the charity of your choice and we'll give you a credit on basic selling fees for sold items
                     Donation percentage 100% ▾
                     ◉ ♟ Dreams to Reality Foundation
                     Or, select another nonprofit you love
                     Your donation will be paid through the PayPal Giving Fund within 45 days. By donating, you agree and accept the eBay for Charity Terms & Conditions.

"Payment options   ☑ PayPal
                     Email address for receiving payment: info@dreamstorerealityfou
                     ☑ Require immediate payment with Buy It Now ⓘ

                     Additional checkout instructions (shows in your listing)
                     Please complete payment within 24 hours of purchase or win. We gladly combine items. Unpaid items will be managed by eBay's automated system. New items must be returned sealed/unopened in the same condition as shipped to you.

FIGURE 1–6: **Private Listing Setting in "Selling Details" of a Listing**

Why not simply make all your eBay listings private? That makes good sense to me. Nearly everyone cherishes their privacy, and your buyers will appreciate your sensitivity to theirs. But there is a caveat. The buyer on a private listing can still leave feedback. Many eBayers will mention what they acquired from you in the feedback comment.

For example, a buyer might leave a comment like, "Thanks for the gorgeous diamond ring." Perhaps you don't want the world to know you have a home or office filled with pricey, luxury goods. Be safe and don't make yourself a target. In that case, you can either ask customers to avoid mentioning what they purchased in their feedback remark, or you can make your entire eBay *Feedback Profile* private, which I'll explain in the next section.

eBay Superpowers

Now, before you don that mask and slip into your super suit, cape and all, please consider that eBayers will usually find your listing by searching keywords. Savvy buyers browse categories to uncover listings with misspelled titles or listings with inadequate keywords.

There are a lot of listings on eBay. Billions of items are listed, in fact. How do you stand out? Don't get caught up in the temptation of adding all the optional listing enhancements. Go easy on all that hot sauce, for goodness sake. You might be fine without it. Here's why: eBay has a fancy computer algorithm that's called *Best Match*. The Best Match technology intuitively displays relevant listings to potential customers based on these factors:

- ▶ Item popularity
- ▶ Your compliance and track record as an eBay seller
- ▶ Your price
- ▶ Listing completeness
- ▶ Your returns policy and shipping time
- ▶ The quality of your listing photos, descriptions, item specifics, and other factors
- ▶ The buyer's search terms as compared to your listing

Scan the QR Code in Figure 1–7 on page 16 to access eBay's article *Optimizing Your Listings for Best Match* to discover how to ensure your listings take full advantage of eBay Best Match.

tip

You may have heard that scheduling your listing to start and end on a particular day, such as Sunday, yields the highest price for auction-style listings. While this could be true for certain categories, keep in mind that offering international shipping, which I do, will change the dynamic of your customer demographics. Many countries thirst for American goods, so you should experiment with different timing and tally the results.

FIGURE 1–7: **Optimizing Your Listings for Best Match**

Other than the scheduling and complimentary Gallery Plus in select categories, I'd suggest you save your money for now. Promoted Listings are beneficial, and I use them sparingly as well. If you are in it for the *long game* and aren't in a hurry, then try listing your wares without the bells and whistles. See how it goes first. You can always experiment with the enhancements after you've become a true eBay "Jedi Master."

The True Cost of Selling on eBay

Selling on eBay involves fees. There's an *insertion fee* for listing an item and usually a *final value fee* when the item sells. There's no final value fee for unsold items, so you're off the hook if your item stays on your virtual shelf. Understanding eBay fees can save you a lot of money. For example, adding a reserve to an auction-style listing will add a fee, while simply starting the auction at your bottom-line price will not. Every month, eBay will gift you 50 zero-insertion-fee listings—even more if you subscribe to an eBay Store. Insertion fees are:

▶ Non-refundable for unsold listings
▶ Assessed per listing and per category
▶ Charged again when you re-list your item
▶ Charged only once per listing for listings that have multiple quantity of the same item

Final value fees are only assessed when an item sells. They vary by product category, and there's no final value fee for the Classified Ad listing format. Certain eBay categories don't have final value fees, but there are still costs when you've scored a buyer. When you sell real estate, you'll pay a *notice fee* once the sale occurs, and when you sell vehicles on eBay Motors, you'll pay a fee referred to as the *successful listing fee*. The language can be confusing. These wacky semantics are most likely due to legal restrictions on how fees are charged. For example, both the Real Estate and automobile dealer industries are highly regulated. Commissions (such as final value fees) can only be charged by licensed entities.

Optional listing upgrades will layer on costs, too, and if eBay discovers that you're using their site as a lead generator to trade off eBay, you may be surprised by a bill for additional final value fees for violating the policy of buying or selling outside of eBay.

There's a wonderful listing enhancement I find very valuable—*Promoted Listings.* Promoted Listings allows you to place your items ahead of everyone else when someone is searching for keywords that relate to your eBay item. This placement is valuable because buyers are more likely to purchase the items they see first. Elevating your listing to stand out from the crowd is easy with Promoted Listings. All sellers who are in good standing can use this service to improve the chances of landing a sale. The cost is a percentage, set by you, at the time you list or revise your listing. The fee, set by you, is paid only if the item sells. You'll see this option pop up when you list a new item or revise an existing listing. While Promoted Listings isn't viable for low-margin goods, it's a home run for profitable items and when you have deep inventory available.

> **tip** ⓘ
>
> Land a 10-percent discount on final value fees by earning the *Top Rated Seller* status. You'll qualify if you've been on eBay for at least 90 days, stay in eBay's good graces, and have at least 100 transactions and $1,000 in sales in a year.

Receiving money through PayPal or other payment processing services, such as eBay's *managed payments program*, will also add costs to each transaction. eBay and PayPal fees have changed over time. They look very different today than on my first day on eBay, way back on June 4, 1999, when I registered my eBay ID "borntodeal" and listed my first item. Scan the QR code (Figure 1–8) for a comprehensive list of eBay fees:

FIGURE 1–8: **eBay Fees Page**

FIGURE 1–9: **PayPal Fees Page**

You can scan the QR code in Figure 1–9 for the latest PayPal fees:

eBay Stores

You'll notice a tiny blue door icon next to an eBayer's user ID. This means they have an eBay Store. Once you hit the "big time" on eBay, you'll want to open a store. An eBay Store provides all these benefits and more:

▶ A branded, dedicated URL where your customers can shop

▶ Free listings and up to a 60-percent discount on final value fees

▶ A sellers' toolkit loaded with sales-boosting tools to help optimize and promote your listings

▶ A vacation hold feature so you can pause sales without ending your listings

▶ Access to a special, dedicated white-glove customer service team

▶ Complimentary access to world-class pricing research on the Terapeak website

▶ Unlimited insertion fee credits for successful auction-style listings

▶ Free eBay-branded shipping supplies

Check out Figure 1–10 on page 19 for an overview of eBay Store subscriber benefits.

tip

Don't struggle with designing your own eBay Store graphics. Hire a freelancer. There are plenty of freelancers to be found online—ask around for recommendations! If you see a company with awesome branding, ask them who produced their graphics.

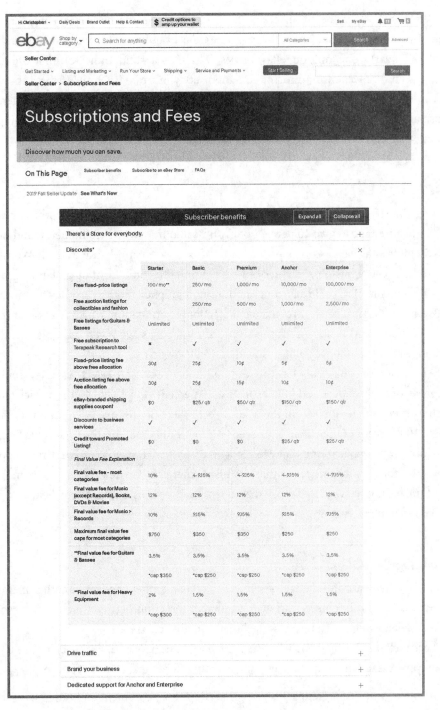

FIGURE 1–10: **Store Subscriber Benefits**

When you subscribe to an eBay Store, you can use the basic branding that eBay offers, or you can primp your Store with custom branding for your own unique look. There are nearly one million eBay Stores, which is a solid indicator that Stores are working. To discover more information about eBay Stores, visit https://stores.ebay.com. Do you own or work for a physical store? Great. Your local eBay Store customers can peruse and purchase your inventory online and pick up purchases in person, saving you packing time and avoiding shipping costs for them.

eBay for Charity

My long-time friend, mentor, and client, Kathy Ireland, supports many philanthropic causes and has inspired me to give 10 percent of my time and money to help homeless and under-served children as well as other people in need. Her company, kathy ireland® Worldwide requires that every business partner of hers commits to some form of philanthropy. And yes—I do that on eBay. I sold a Peyton Manning autographed football on eBay for more than $900 to benefit a great cause, Providence Educational Foundation, which is an organization that both Kathy and I support. Kathy arranged for a backstage meet-and-greet with Janet Jackson, which I sold for $25,000, also benefiting Providence.

Any seller on eBay can tick off a simple checkbox and select an eBay-approved nonprofit of their choice and give as little as 1 percent (for eBay Motors vehicles) or as much as every single dime from the sale. Direct sellers of approved eBay nonprofits who donate 100 percent of their item's proceeds receive a full credit on the final value fees.

Nonprofit organizations that are recognized by the IRS as tax-exempt may apply to be on eBay for Charity's roster so that any eBay seller can donate proceeds to them. Using eBay for Charity, I have raised more than $1 million for causes close to my heart.

To learn more, visit https://www.ebayforcharity.org.

Feedback on eBay

Feedback is the heart of the eBay system. Each eBay member can leave another member a feedback comment in connection with an eBay transaction between them. eBay requires that all feedback relate to a business deal that actually occurred.

Feedback on eBay is straightforward and easy to understand. Feedback is an easy way for eBayers to exchange experiences. When posting feedback, eBayers receive:

► +1 point to your feedback score for each positive comment and rating left for you
► 0 points to your feedback score for each neutral comment and rating left for you
► –1 point to your feedback score for each negative comment and rating left for you

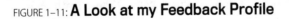

Hi Christopher! ▾ | Daily Deals | Gift Cards | Help & Contact   Love These Labor Day Deals   Sell   Purchases   My eBay   🔔 22   🛒

ebay   Shop by category ▾   Search for anything   All Categories   ▾   Search   Advanced

Home > Community > Feedback forum > Feedback profile

Feedback profile

Report a buyer

borntodeal (31866 ☆) me 🔲   [Top Rated: Seller with highest buyer ratings] ?

Duncan Realty

Positive Feedback (last 12 months): 100%
[How is Feedback percentage calculated?]

Member since: Jun-04-99 in United States

View your Seller Dashboard
View items for sale
View seller's Store
View ID history
View eBay My World
View About Me page

Recent Feedback ratings   ?
(last 12 months)

	1 month	6 months	12 months
Positive	135	554	1081
Neutral	0	0	0
Negative	0	0	0

Detailed seller ratings   (last 12 months)   ?

Criteria	Average rating	Number of ratings
Item as described	★★★★★	729
Communication	★★★★★	753
Shipping time	★★★★★	746
Shipping and handling charges	★★★★★	732

ebay - MONEY BACK GUARANTEE
Get the item you ordered or get your money back.
Learn what's included

Feedback as a seller	Search seller feedback	Feedback as a buyer	All Feedback	Feedback left for others

34,243 Feedback received (viewing 1-25)   Revised Feedback: 34   ?

Period: All ▾

Feedback	From Buyer/price	When
⊕ 5 STAR eBayer -- great communication + very fast delivery - Thank You!!	zog10 (1835 ☆)	During past month
--	--	Private
⊕ 5 STARS Great Seller -- Very Fast Shipping -- Item exactly as described	zog10 (1835 ☆)	During past month
--	--	Private
⊕ Livraison rapide, contenu impeccable, transaction idéale, je recommande	zog10 (1835 ☆)	During past month
--	--	Private
⊕ Livraison rapide, contenu impeccable, transaction idéale, je recommande	zog10 (1835 ☆)	During past month
--	--	Private

FIGURE 1–11: **A Look at my Feedback Profile**

Figure 1–11 is the feedback profile for my eBay account "borntodeal."

Buyers of high-value items will put your feedback under a microscope. Selling lower-value items will be your solution for a glowing feedback profile when you're just getting started. Let's try to get you to 100 before selling anything too valuable. Do you remember eBay's Top Rated Seller program requirements I mentioned earlier in this chapter? That's the significance of the number 100.

Not all eBayers automatically give feedback comments following a transaction. While it is important to communicate with your buyer after the sale, there are different schools of thought about asking for feedback. I do not ask buyers to leave me feedback. Clearly, maintaining a good relationship with your trading partner is important as a seller (and buyer) during the transaction, so feedback is the natural result of a successful trade. If you start pushing and prodding for feedback, you may receive an unfavorable one. Many people don't want to bother with returns or fiddle with complaints about items that didn't delight them. Silence is often their way, but if you push too hard, you'll raise the tiger in them and be flamed with an unexpected negative or neutral comment. Be warned.

Your feedback score is the sum of all the positive comments you receive from unique eBay members, less the sum of all the negative comments. Neutral feedback can be seen but does not count towards your score. It's also important to note that each member can only affect your score by one point, even when they make several transactions.

Trade honestly, be fair, and offer liberal returns, and your voyage will remain a smooth one. The possibility always exists that another member may give you negative feedback. You can't make everyone happy all of the time. The key here is that you have to make sure most of your trading partners are happy with you. Only buyers can leave a negative comment for sellers. Sellers can never leave a negative feedback for a buyer.

As an enhancement to the buyer's ability to rate you, eBay offers buyers an optional area to leave *detailed seller ratings*, known as DSRs for short; check Figure 1–12 on page 23 for an example of DSRs. DSRs are anonymous; however, they do tally up on your profile in the following areas:

- ▶ Item as described
- ▶ Communication
- ▶ Shipping time
- ▶ Shipping and handling charges

Tend your eBay garden because if you do, you'll be rewarded with a cornucopia of profits. If you slack off on listing practices, fall behind on shipping, or aren't the best with customers, your feedback will suffer. If things get ugly enough, eBay will step in with a warning, or even worse, an account suspension.

That concludes the nickel tour of the eBay site. In Chapter 2, we're going to look at some powerful eBay sellers and how they garnered their success.

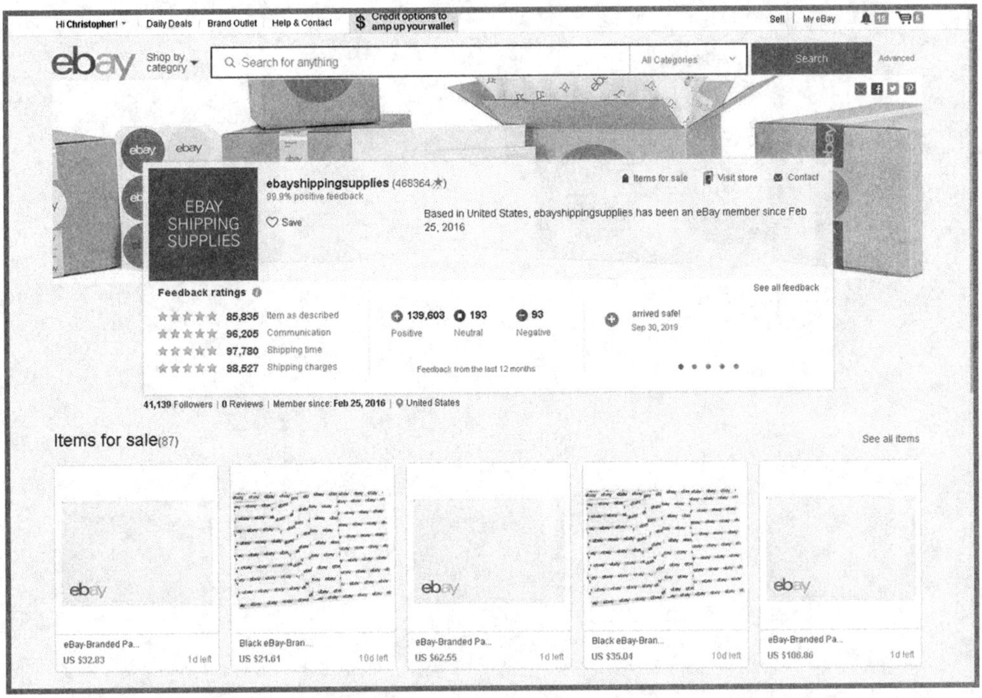

FIGURE 1–12: **Detailed Seller Rating Summary for the Official eBay Shipping Supplies Store**

What It Takes to Succeed on eBay

There are some common traits that I have identified in successful eBay sellers (and businesspeople, in general) over the years, and they are:

► A positive attitude

► Adventurous

► Lots of drive

► Perseverance and passion (I refer to this as simply "grit")

▶ A love for customers
▶ The willingness to learn what it takes to run a business
▶ Common sense
▶ An obsession for excellence

A book on business that will genuinely help someone get started and head towards success must rely on the wisdom of the author, but must also show proof that the author's contentions hold water. So, I have the privilege of being able to share some incredible seller success stories with you. I do not traffic in fantasies and pipe dreams—there are oodles of fantastic claims being made online. I can assure you that short of picking winning lottery numbers, there are no get-rich-quick secrets. The truth about business is that there are very few secrets. Before you lay out money for any system or program of education alleging to offer a sure-fire method of generating millions in passive income without having to lift a finger, please study the journey of those before you. For example, I read shareholder letters for public companies that I admire, including eBay. The founders of the greatest companies in the world will reveal (at no cost to you) the intimate inner-workings of successful businesses within their annual reports. Success isn't easy. The world isn't in debt to you, and there is a ton of competition. None of these facts should discourage you because simply staying on the journey dramatically improves your chances of success (and only you can define the meaning of "success").

All that said, extraordinary claims require extraordinary evidence. In this chapter, I will share some extraordinary evidence—these eBayers who achieved extraordinary things with their eBay businesses. I think you'll find that, after reading their success stories, you can take the reins of your own eBay dream and make it a profitable business for the long term. And who knows—maybe you'll see some of yourself in these eBay superstars and get inspired to make your eBay dream a reality!

Meet Ben Akrish–PIXLBasket (eBay ID: pixlbasket)

At 18, Ben Akrish responded to my help-wanted ad for a fact-checker for this very book. Ben enrolled in college majoring in business administration, and he feared that, without proper mentorship, he would end up working manual labor jobs. When I first spoke with Ben, he mentioned that he moved out on his own and worked nights as a server at a Red Robin restaurant to pay his rent, tuition, and living expenses.

After our first telephone conversation, I was immediately inspired to help Ben start his own eBay business, something he expressed a desire to do *right away*.

Ben and I had an initial "power session"—lasting for hours—where we discussed his past experience. While he had traded on eBay in the recent past, we brought laser focus to his goals. Ben's lifelong passion for vintage video games would be the foundation for his eBay business. From this, "PIXLBasket" was born (Figure 2–1). Ben decided to sell vintage video games and consoles under this eBay ID and general merchandise under a second user ID, which is "itemadopt."

The most credible *extraordinary evidence* that this book can help you start your very own eBay business exists in Ben's success. Ben faithfully followed my advice, and within the first 60 days, he listed 213 items and generated $1,200.51 in sales. Ben's success results from consistent application of proven methods. He is open-minded, curious, and willing to take action to get things accomplished. For a young man barely out of high school, attending college, and working a night job to sell so much working a few hours per week from a folding table in the corner of his apartment, Ben Akrish is an incredible success story. Ben is the very person for whom I took the time out of my busy life to write a book on how to

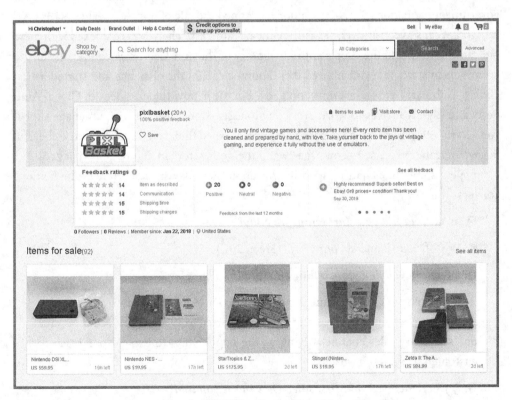

FIGURE 2–1: **Ben's PIXLBasket eBay User Profile**

become a successful eBay entrepreneur. I am honored to be able to send the elevator down to someone as worthy as Ben Akrish.

Meet Bonnie Sugawara–Global Auto Parts (eBay ID: globalautodistributors)

Each of the next three exceptional eBay sellers, including Bonnie Sugawara, received the prestigious eBay Shine Awards recognition for their inspirational eBay journey and achievements on the marketplace. Their stories represent the millions of sellers harnessing the power of technology and eBay's global marketplace to support and grow their small businesses while also strengthening their local economies.

Bonnie's dad Henry Sugawara started selling brand name and aftermarket car parts in 1977. He worked very hard to grow his Global Auto Parts business by taking care of his customers with superb service, excellent selection, and fair prices. Bonnie joined the family business and brought Global Auto Parts to the world of ecommerce as a result of restrictive government regulations. By 2009, California banned the sale of non-self-sealing R134a AC refrigerant cans to consumers, but sadly, Global Auto Parts' shelves were stocked with these old cans. Bonnie sold the shop's entire inventory of the non-California compliant cans to customers in states that still allowed them. Bonnie caught the eBay bug and started listing Global Auto Parts' entire inventory on eBay. Bonnie is now the president of Global Auto Parts and eagerly arrives to work every day to assist store customers and manage Global Auto Parts' eBay business. eBay has really supercharged their sales. Check out the cheerful Sugawara team in Figure 2–2 on page 29 and their eBay store in Figure 2–3 on page 30.

I spent some time chatting with Bonnie about her eBay success. Here's a look at our conversation:

Q: What year did you start selling on eBay?

A: We officially launched our eBay store in 2010.

Q: What did you do before selling on eBay?

A: I was doing exactly the same thing I'm doing on eBay: selling auto parts. Global Auto Parts is a family business that my father started in 1977. In 2010, eBay became our secondary sales channel, giving us the opportunity to expand our reach to customers around the world.

Q: If you remember your first sale, what was it you sold?

A: I don't remember exactly, but it was either a Honda crank pulley holder tool or a bottle of Castrol Hydraulic Mineral Oil for Jaguar vehicles.

FIGURE 2–2: **Henry and Bonnie Sugawara at their Family's Global Auto Parts Store in Stockton, California**

Q: *What was the coolest item you've sold on eBay?*

A: The coolest item I sold was a funky-looking thermostat for a classic, air-cooled 1963 Volkswagen Beetle. It was a one-of-a-kind, new-old-stock, discontinued part. I listed it for $135, and it sold just a few days later. It's funny to think that part had been sitting on our shelf for 25 years, and it finally sold on eBay. Thank goodness auto parts aren't perishable.

Q: *If you had a time machine, what would you do differently?*

A: If I could travel back in time, I would've listed a whole lot more items on eBay from the get-go. We have so many items that sell well in our retail store, which became top-movers on eBay. On the other hand, we've had a number of rare, slow-movers that unexpectedly sold quickly after listing them on eBay with many happy buyers as a result.

Q: *Is eBay your full-time gig, and if not, what is your other job?*

A: I consider it a full-time gig since it's so well integrated with my daily job of running a brick-and-mortar retail auto parts store. In a given day, I juggle walk-in customers and phone calls with responding to buyer emails, packing and shipping orders, and listing new items.

Q: *What excites you about selling on eBay (or being your own boss)?*

A: What excites me about selling on eBay and being my own boss is the opportunity to experience so many different facets of small business—from customer service

FIGURE 2–3: **Global Auto Parts eBay Store**

to inventory management, purchasing to accounting, photography to social media marketing—all in a flexible environment where I can do what I want at any given moment. It's nice to grow my business skills and learn something new from customer interaction every day. Plus, I enjoy playtime breaks at work. If I want to play ball with my dog, it's nice to know I won't be fired for doing so.

Q: How many seller accounts do you manage?

A: Only one. I keep it simple.

Q: How much time per week do you spend on eBay?

A: I'm on-call for eBay tasks during our retail store hours, which are 9:00 A.M.—6:00 P.M. Monday through Saturday. I'd say it amounts to about 12 to 15 hours per week on eBay-specific activities.

Q: How many items do you sell a month?

A: Currently, we sell about 750 to 1,000 items per month.

Q: Can you share any helpful tips you feel readers might benefit from learning?

A: A few tips come to mind. One thing that's always worked for me is being a responsive communicator. Buyers expect quick answers to their inquiries, both before and after the sale. The second tip involves shipping speed. Based on buyer feedback, it seems virtually everyone appreciates a seller who ships fast and gets an order delivered as promised. Finally, I believe it's important for sellers to carve out some time for themselves every day. Be it a hobby, a sport, or quality family time, recharging and refreshing one's body and soul goes a long way.

I love that Global Auto Parts ships orders received by 3:00 P.M. the same day, six days a week with 30-day free returns—to any address in the world. That is superb customer service.

Meet John Macris–Philadelphia Candies (eBay ID: philadelphiacandies)

The next seller case study involves a product that has wooed lovers across the globe, and millions of pounds of the stuff are sold each year—chocolate. John Macris (Figure 2–4 on page 32) opened an eBay Store (Figure 2–5 on page 34) for his family's 100-year-old specialty chocolate factory, and it has turned a sweet profit. Philadelphia Candies makes their candy

FIGURE 2–4: **John Macris Hand Making Chocolate Centers at the Philadelphia Candies Factory in Mercer County, Pennsylvania**

by hand using timeless, old-fashioned family recipes. John is the third generation to work the family business.

The Macris family is inspired and gratified by creating jobs and delighting customers—the not-so-secret ingredients for their delicious success. Mercer County, Pennsylvania has been enveloped in the aroma of Philadelphia Candies chocolate crafting since 1919. Every single candy center is scratch-made using only the finest ingredients—over 100 varieties of chocolate—shipped to anyone with an address and an eBay account. Philadelphia Candies is breaking eBay records; they ship tons of chocolate to loyal eBayers who insist on the Philadelphia Candies boutique, high-quality brand.

Here's my Q&A with John whose company is also a recipient of the esteemed eBay Shine award:

Q: *What year did you start selling on eBay?*

A: I launched the eBay store for Philadelphia Candies shortly before eBay Open (a live eBay-sponsored user conference) in summer 2017. On a personal level, I've been buying and selling on eBay since 2002.

Q: *What did you do before selling on eBay?*

A: I've always been invested in the family business since I was a kid. During the holidays, I spent time with my mother, Georgia Macris, in our factory retail store helping associates pack chocolates and wait on customers.

Q: *If you remember your first sale, what was it you sold?*

A: My first sale on eBay was a one-pound box of milk chocolate covered assorted creams to a buyer in Detroit, Michigan. Creams are a traditional, soft-center piece made from scratch in our kitchen. We specialize in cooking all of our centers using old-fashioned copper kettles and finish on a marble slab. It's 20th-century craftsmanship being performed on a routine basis.

Q: *What was the coolest item you've sold on eBay?*

A: Solid chocolate Easter eggs are becoming incredibly hard to find in local stores. We manufacture a variety of eggs each year between January and April. We've received countless stories from eBay buyers young and old who find a personal connection with our brand.

Q: *If you had a time machine, what would you do differently?*

A: To be honest, I've been fortunate to have few regrets on how I've spent my time or grown the company. Entrepreneurs should understand a key component of success is being yourself and differentiating from the competition. The best method is your own method.

Q: *Is eBay your full-time gig, and if not, what is your other job?*

A: Yes and no. eBay is a full-time responsibility; however, our chocolate shop is a traditional retailer with an omnichannel presence. When I'm not working directly on eBay, I'm investing time in our retail stores and factory, spending time with employees, and volunteering in the local community.

Q: *Tell me what excites you about selling on eBay (or being your own boss)?*

A: Each day can be truly different and unique, in both positive and negative ways. If I'm able to complete half of the goals I set for a given time period (day, week, month, even year), I consider it a success. There are definitely pros and cons to being an entrepreneur, including the unexpected and unknown. Of course, ultimately, one hopes the wins more than make up for the losses.

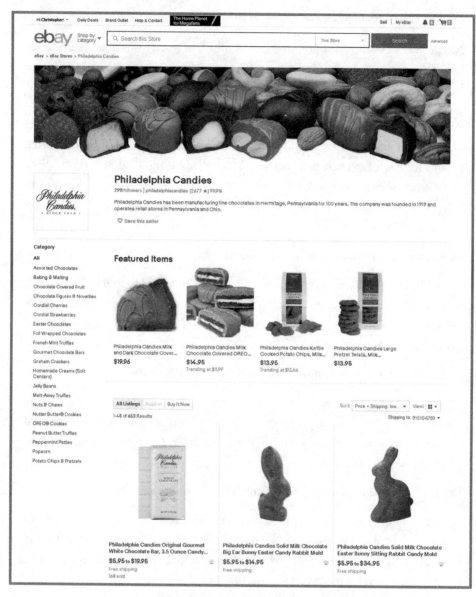

FIGURE 2–5: **Philadelphia Candies eBay Store**

Q: How many seller accounts do you manage?

A: Two seller accounts. In addition to representing my family's 100-year-old chocolate brand, I maintain a personal seller account where I sell hard-to-find items, including "pro stock" tennis racquets and inventory, which I source from outside the U.S.

Q: How much time per week do you spend on eBay?

A: eBay is a great partner in that one can commit a minimum amount of time to maintain status quo or choose to invest themselves to really grow on the platform. In a given week, I can spend anywhere from two hours to upwards of 20. The most basic task is ensuring positive communication with customers, including prompt attention to buyers' inquiries on eBay Messages.

Q: How many items do you sell a month?

A: The chocolate and confectionery business is highly seasonal; however, eBay helps us reach new customers during historically slow periods. Our main selling season includes Christmas and the entire month of December, Easter, Valentine's Day, Halloween, Thanksgiving, and Mother's Day. Our number of items sold has grown to 5,000+ in the last 12 months, an increase of over 100 percent from the prior year.

Q: Can you share any helpful tips you feel readers might benefit from learning?

A: I'm a firm believer in the idea that the biggest risk is simply not taking one at all. The modern economy rewards those willing to assume some degree of uncertainty in their decision making.

My interview with John was very inspiring for a number of reasons—I am both very fond of chocolate and deeply involved in philanthropy. Philadelphia Candies is a national supporter of the American Heart Association, and their 72-percent bittersweet dark chocolate bar was designed in coordination with Cleveland Clinic guidelines. According to Cleveland Clinic, 3 ounces of dark chocolate per day improves blood flow, protects arteries, and promotes healthy cholesterol.

Shipping chocolate poses some challenges—it's perishable, melts easily, and can become damaged when handled roughly. Philadelphia Candies has mastered the art of packing these fragile consumables and, when needed, even uses cold packs to prevent a disastrous meltdown. Without a doubt, John is the sweetest of our eBay seller case studies, and I am confident that the Macris family will be serving up little bites of heaven for another 100 years and beyond.

Meet Elijah McCloskey–Madison Freewheel Bicycle Cooperative (eBay ID: freewheel_bikes_madison)

Elijah McCloskey (Figure 2–6 on page 36) and I share some things in common—we were both homeless at 16, and we are both deeply passionate about philanthropy and helping

FIGURE 2–6: **Here's Elijah McCloskey in the Madison Freewheel Bicycle Cooperative Store in Madison, Wisconsin**

people in need. Madison Freewheel Bicycle Cooperative (Figure 2–7 on page 38) supports charitable bicycle programs by selling one bike on eBay and using the funds to give two away for persons in low-income groups. Madison Freewheel Bicycle Cooperative's mission is rooted in three beliefs: that transportation is a human right, education empowers social-economic justice, and things are made to be reused. An eBayer since 2011, Madison Freewheel Bicycle Cooperative received formal recognition as a 501(c)(3) nonprofit public benefit organization in 2017. Madison Freewheel Bicycle Cooperative gives away thousands of bicycles and provides essential training to its employees so they can mend bicycles with issues—supporting low-cost, sustainable transportation for the under served.

Here's my Q&A with Elijah, whose company is another worthy recipient of the venerated eBay Shine award:

Q: What year did you start selling on eBay?

A: I started selling on eBay in September 2011.

Q: What did you do before selling on eBay?

A: In 2006, a small group of bike-loving friends in Madison, Wisconsin founded Freewheel as a neighborhood bike shop. We provided hundreds of bicycles to people in need in the Madison area and gave people access to the shop space, tools, and knowledge they needed to repair their own bicycles.

I'm lucky to be one of the people who benefited from Freewheel's good work: as a teenager, I ended up homeless. I met up with Freewheel and learned to build my own bike, which helped me get a job. From there, I got housing. Now, I've graduated from the University of Wisconsin–Madison with a business degree, and I've taken on the position of Executive Director within Freewheel.

For the first five years of its existence, Freewheel's revenue consisted of money from donations and memberships. We're a charity with very low overhead and plenty of donated bikes and parts to give away, so this income carried us through our first five years.

But when we pivoted to selling our higher-quality bikes on eBay, we quickly learned how this revenue stream could transform our organization. With our proceeds from eBay, we've dramatically expanded our reach. As of late 2019, we estimate that we've given away over 13,000 bikes to people in need and taught bike repair to 6,000 people.

Q: If you remember your first sale, what was it you sold?

A: It was an XXXL vintage Raleigh road bike. An XXXL bike is HUGE: it's designed to fit someone who's about 6'8." It sold for about $400.

Q: What was the coolest item you've sold on eBay?

A: The coolest sale I ever made was with a guy who bought a vintage 1981 Trek. It's a high-quality bike, handmade in the U.S., but it's the story rather than the bike that makes this sale special.

Years ago, this customer owned this model of bike, and he rode it for 20 years. Eventually he moved and chose to sell the bike.

Then, 15 years later, he became nostalgic for his old bike. He went on eBay, and found the same make and model through our store.

We list the serial model for every bike we sell. I guess he had a hunch—and he had the old bike's serial number, too. When he checked the serial model we listed against the number he had, he realized we were selling the exact same bike he used to own.

He bought it in a heartbeat, and paid a little extra for us to do a full custom rebuild on it. It was a spectacular, once-in-a-lifetime coincidence that left everyone feeling incredible.

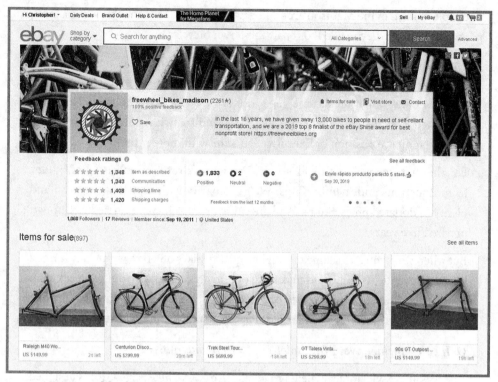

FIGURE 2–7: **Madison Freewheel Bicycle Cooperative eBay Store**

Q: If you had a time machine, what would you do differently?

A: If I could change anything, I would have pushed harder on ecommerce far earlier on. At first our eBay store was just something we focused on during our off-season, and I didn't take it very seriously. But as I kept exploring, I realized that eBay was potentially a huge untapped stream of revenue for our charity.

A lot of retailers (as well as banks, investors, and wholesalers) believe that brick-and-mortar establishments are more serious and legitimate than online retail. It's only recently that people have begun to change their minds about ecommerce. I wish I'd been willing to buck the trend earlier.

Q: Is eBay your full-time gig, and if not, what is your other job?

A: Selling on eBay is a big part of my full-time gig, but it's far from all I do in my work. I'm the Executive Director of Madison Freewheel Bicycle Cooperative, a charity that's dedicated to helping people learn how to build, repair, and maintain their own bicycles.

In addition to our educational work, we take donated bikes from around the Madison area and refurbish them. Some of these bikes we sell on eBay or to local buyers, but others we give away to people in need around the Dane County area. We also ship many of our recycled bikes to Africa. In developing countries, transportation access can have a radically positive impact, allowing more children to go to school, carry water further, take more goods to market, and have access to a wider range of potential jobs. All this really creates ground-up economic development and empowerment.

Q: What excites you about selling on eBay (or being your own boss)?

A: eBay has transformed how I do business. Selling on eBay means I can set my own schedule and work anywhere. All I need is an internet connection.

This has freed me up to travel and see the world. I've traveled across the U.S. as well as Europe and South America, all while managing my shop on-the-go and providing stellar customer service. This simply isn't possible with a traditional brick-and-mortar retail model, and it has greatly expanded my world and improved my quality of life.

Q: How many seller accounts do you manage?

A: I just manage one account.

Q: How much time per week do you spend on eBay?

A: Managing our seller account is full-time work.

Q: How many items do you sell a month?

A: We sell about 1,000 items every month. All our profits go toward supporting our charitable work, including classes, bike giveaways, and bicycle advocacy.

Q: Can you share any helpful tips you feel readers might benefit from learning?

A: Good research drives sales, gains buyer trust, and ensures repeat business. Develop a niche, gain expertise, and only sell items that align with your store's focus. Provide the best information possible about the items you list, especially high-dollar, high-margin items. Typically these items will be vintage or hard-to-find.

Enthusiasts will seek out and recognize your expertise and trust you more for it. If you don't know, try to learn. If you make things up or fudge details, people will figure it out, and you'll lose their trust.

Offering add-on services is a good way to improve the quality of your customer service. By refurbishing or repairing items you'd normally sell as-is, providing custom modifications, or offering custom-order related products, you'll see more customer interest and push your margins higher.

Having an eBay store doesn't mean you can't have a brick-and-mortar shop, too. There's good synergy in having a brick-and-mortar store. It allows you to access wholesale accounts, which help you provide better products, in larger, more reliable volume, and with better net margins. Your brick-and-mortar store doesn't need to be open all the time, and it doesn't have to be in a nice part of town. Just having one will go a long way toward increasing buyer confidence and sourcing opportunities.

Always stick to your shop's niche. This drives upsells, increases loyalty, and showcases your expertise. For maximum success, offer related items that vary in sales price, margin, sell-through rate, and other characteristics. This way, you'll offer items for a variety of buyers and budgets, showcase your expertise, and reduce sales volatility.

Don't try to compete on price. You'll lose every time. Big sellers can always undercut your prices. Focus on your items' quality, your expertise, and customer service. These will ensure high margins on high-price items, and others will have a hard time competing with your unique total customer value package.

I am so incredibly inspired by Elijah and the team at Madison Freewheel Bicycle Cooperative. These folks are doing good and truly changing the world. eBay is a mighty partner, not only supporting ecommerce, but noble causes that are agents for change like the work done by Elijah and his team.

eBay for Charity enables nonprofits to leverage the power of the eBay marketplace for the better good. Certified nonprofit organizations raise hundreds of millions of dollars on eBay using the eBay for Charity program—nonprofits can sell directly or receive a portion or all of the proceeds of sales from other eBay sellers. For details and to activate your cause today, visit http://charity.ebay.com.

Meet Todd and Tom Hallada–2Bros Sports Collectibles, LLC (eBay ID: 2bros788)

Todd and Tom Hallada (Figure 2–8) are the two "bros" who started 2Bros Sports Collectibles, LLC in May of 2003. When Todd was only 16, he faced challenges securing summer employment due to the physical limitations caused by muscular dystrophy. Todd and his older brother Tom were both diagnosed with the disease at an early age. Inspired by the brothers' shared love for sports, Todd wanted to launch a sports-card trading business. He noodled Tom into opening an eBay account (since eBayers have to be 18 or older), and the rest is for the history books.

For this interview, I sat down with cofounder Todd Hallada to talk about his experience as an eBay seller. Here's my Q&A with Todd:

Q: What year did you start selling on eBay?

A: I started selling on eBay in 2004.

Q: What did you do before selling on eBay?

A: eBay was my first job. I later worked in a corporate position for five years but gave that up to restart my eBay business with my brother.

Q: If you remember your first sale, what was it you sold?

A: The very first item I sold was a Sega Genesis game called NBA Jam. After that, I started selling sports cards.

FIGURE 2–8: **eBay Shine Award-Winners Todd and Tom Hanging Out with Their Dad Tim Hallada at 2Bros Sports Collectibles Retail Store**

Q: If you had a time machine, what would you do differently?

A: Early on, I prioritized sales over shipping speed. In hindsight, it is actually more to our benefit long-term if we focus on shipping speed and customer satisfaction above sales numbers.

Q: Is eBay your full-time gig, and if not, what is your other job?

A: Tom and I have made selling on eBay our full-time jobs.

Q: What excites you about selling on eBay (or being your own boss)?

A: I definitely enjoy making my own decisions. With that said, much of the time making your own decisions actually requires much more work than being told what to do, but it is far more rewarding.

Q: How many seller accounts do you manage?

A: One.

Q: How much time per week do you spend on eBay?

A: I work 60 to 100 hours per week, depending on the week.

Q: How many items do you sell a month?

A: We are selling as many as 30,000 sports cards monthly.

Q: Can you share any helpful tips you feel readers might benefit from learning?

A: Owning your own business is very rewarding, but be prepared for the workload involved, especially if you are trying to do something at scale. Everything from preparing eBay listings to shipping and customer satisfaction is in your control and something you have to manage on eBay. In addition, as you add to your workforce, managing those people increases your responsibilities.

Todd and Tom opened a gorgeous store selling autographed sports memorabilia in Blaine, Minnesota's Northtown Mall near their home. The Blaine store enhances the eBay business through cross-pollination—the in-store customers enjoy perusing the eBay inventory and buying from their favorite, trusted seller, and local eBay bidders can stop by the store to pick up their winnings. These industrious two bros have listed a whopping three million sports cards on eBay, and they love working and watching sporting events together. International shipping has expanded their business opportunities in unique ways—overseas fans have different tastes depending on the region, and the brothers tapped into soccer and hockey fans across the globe to move the inventory that's slow to

FIGURE 2–9: **The 2Bros Sports Collectibles, LLC eBay Store**

sell in the U.S. Todd and Tom have shunned the corporate cubicle to become the largest eBay sellers of new release sports cards. Today, 2Bros Sports Collectibles, LLC (Figure 2–9) has six full-time employees, and every member of the brothers' immediate family is involved in the business. Way to go, bros!

Planning and Organizing Your eBay Business

As with any business endeavor, you will quickly realize that when you start your eBay business planning and build a bridge from where you currently are to where you want your business to be, and there are a lot of little intricacies involved in this process. If you don't already own a business, it's essential to identify the necessities for keeping things running smoothly. You can avoid spreading yourself too thin by focusing on a niche. Being a generalist is harder and requires greater study and experience. Become an expert on what you're selling before adding new product categories. It's also crucial to start thinking about naming your business as well as ensuring you are complying with applicable laws and regulations.

If you don't plan to open a brick-and-mortar store, you will most likely conduct your new business from home. If you live with others, this means being in sync with everyone at home. What may seem like a harmless venture to you may be viewed as an annoyance by roommates or family members who don't share your vision (or your profits). You will want dedicated space to handle storage of items for safekeeping and protection from accidental damage. Be sure your family or housemates have given their blessing.

It is a rookie mistake to imagine eBay as a digital yard sale. You don't want to sell junk. Today's eBayers are savvy and demand quality merchandise at a fair price. Unsold merchandise piling up all over the place is the result of leaping before looking.

In this chapter, we'll be discussing suggestions for determining your mission and developing a business plan, tips for identifying your niche, the best way to brand your new company, how to stay on track with business structure and "legal stuff," and gathering up the essentials you'll need to get things started.

Mission and Business Planning

A mission statement helps you and others understand what your company does and why you're in business. This can be as simple as a brief written statement of who your customers are, what you sell, and whether you conduct business locally, nationally, or across borders. For example, there are eBay sellers who only offer local pickup and who sell big items; in these cases, the cost of shipping could be so expensive that most buyers wouldn't want to pay the freight. The company that sells commercial kitchen ranges to restaurants, schools, and local government agencies will focus on local buyers and skip the hassle of dealing with complicated and expensive shipping. Most eBayers sell to buyers across the nation because what they sell is practical to ship. More experienced sellers ship globally. A clear mission statement becomes more valuable when you add employees—it is important that your team's mission statement is ever-present in the way you conduct business. It embodies the essence of your goals and the reasoning behind them. Your mission statement also helps to share your vision not only with employees, but also with customers, vendors and the community.

The easiest way to develop a mission statement is to study other companies' statements, which can inspire you with ideas for yours.

Here are some of the questions to ask yourself while you sit down to write your mission statement:

▶ Why are you in business?

▶ Who are your customers?

▶ What differentiates you from your competition?

▶ What is your public image?

Avoid the hype of a meaningless mission statement that could describe any company. Vague, high-sounding ideas do not propel you forward. Focus on realistic and meaningful goals that genuinely relate to you and your business.

Let's see this in action. Here, I've prepared a sample mission statement for the fictional eBay seller of vintage shoes, "nothingdusty":

At Nothing Dusty, we offer a unique selection of rare antique and vintage footwear that is fully restored and ready-to-wear. Even though what we sell is very old, everything looks factory-fresh. We gladly ship to anyone on the planet and our prices are fair as are the wages we pay our employees. A percentage of every sale we make goes to help with global environmental causes. We are extremely loyal to our employees, and we obsess about our customers.

In addition to a mission statement, you can develop a business plan to help you become incredible at running your business. Does a business plan sound too formal for you? Not at all! A business plan can be as simple as a mental plan for making things happen or as precise as a well-developed documental roadmap for guiding your company from startup to ongoing management. There's no right way to write a business plan, and you don't need to spend a wheelbarrow full of money hiring a business plan "guru." Business plans can take on many different forms. A business plan is a helpful tool for starting a new business or applying for loans, but a superior business plan also provides direction and clarity for operating an existing business. It can be as short as a single page or as long as your heart desires. When researching business plans, you'll discover terms like "traditional" and "lean startup." A traditional business plan is robust and dives deep, while a lean startup plan is sharply focused and only contains summary key points. The perfect business plan is the one that works best for you. The Small Business Administration (SBA) recommends that a traditional business plan include these nine sections:

1. An executive summary
2. A description of the company
3. A market analysis

4. An explanation of the company's legal and management structure

5. A description of the product (or service), the customer value proposition, planned intellectual property and product development, and research and development strategies

6. The company's marketing and sales plan

7. Funding requirements (if the business plan will be shared with investors or banks)

8. Financial projections

9. An appendix (for supporting data and documents, credit histories, resumes, product images, reference letters, or other matters that don't fit elsewhere)

Scan the QR code in Figure 3–1 for the SBA's business plan development guide.

FIGURE 3–1: **The U.S. Small Business Administration's Guide** *Write Your Business Plan*

Narrowing Your Niche

If you're asking in your mind right now, "Can you tell me how to make a lot of money on eBay?" I would reply with, "Yes—through hard work doing what you love."

There is no scientific evidence that guesswork and random chance will beat out hard work and experience. The people who are most successful are those who are doing what they love. I genuinely believe that you are far more likely to succeed by selling merchandise on eBay that you're passionate about. Wanting simply to become rich is a foolish starting point. I am very rich, and I always knew I would become rich for a very simple reason: I love to work hard, and I love what I do.

I enjoy variety in my life, and what I sell on eBay reflects my varied interests, from collectibles to vehicles and everything in between. I find the entire process fascinating. I enjoy staying up-to-date on technology just as much as delving into old books to learn about museum-quality artifacts. I love to feel finely made fabric and admire master works of art. I am afforded the opportunity to see so many truly fascinating items because of my eBay pursuits.

Perhaps you love people and enjoy helping others. Try selling items for family and friends. The joy of helping other people brings a tremendous sense of accomplishment. Look to your hobbies for the possibilities. While you're dreaming of landing a lucrative agreement with a major wholesaler, that same company has been listing their wares with multiple other online firms. Do you struggle figuring out where to source goods? Most factories already sell on eBay. You may find it far easier and more profitable to start with secondhand goods rather than new items. The margin for new merchandise is generally lower because there's a tremendous amount of competition for new goods. Unwanted, used items tend to be in ample supply. Just look around you for profitable items you can sell today.

Here are some product categories that do well on eBay:

- ▶ Antiques, collectibles, and vintage items
- ▶ Cameras
- ▶ Designer clothing, shoes, and accessories
- ▶ Dolls
- ▶ Electronics
- ▶ Event tickets
- ▶ Excess inventory
- ▶ Housewares
- ▶ Jewelry
- ▶ Laptops
- ▶ Musical instruments
- ▶ Mobile phones
- ▶ Sporting goods
- ▶ Toys and games
- ▶ Vehicles and vehicle parts

tip ⓘ

Check out http://www.terapeak.com for clues on the hottest-selling eBay merchandise. This service comes complimentary with an eBay Store subscription. There you'll find insights on what to sell. You can also seek pricing guidance by looking at eBay's sold items.

I need to qualify the above list by reminding you that good stuff sells and junk collects dust. You'll want to sell items that will fly out the door. Brand-name goods tend to do the best; however, as you venture into antiques and collectibles, unbranded items can do very well if they're interesting. There are occasions where you'll stumble across a Spanish galleon of riches. For example, I was helping someone clear out their mother-in-law's apartment and took home two bags of early 1980's Apple computer software. Do you remember floppy disks? As it turns out, these are highly collectible. In ferocious bidding,

I sold one of the programs for $2,500, and the two bags generated tens of thousands of dollars. Can you believe they were headed for the trash? I share more ideas for product sourcing in Chapter 10.

Naming Your Business

You read about selecting your eBay user ID earlier, but let's take a deeper dive into naming your business. Everyone talks about branding, but what does that really mean? A company name must be memorable. Coming up with a fantastic business name is a crucial step toward building and growing your brand. A memorable name connects with customers and sticks with them. Before you become stressed, relax; this is long-term thinking. When you're just selling your mom's Barbie collection or packing up your dad's unwanted hand tools, branding isn't going to make or break your eBay business.

As you become more established, though, how you brand your company will become important. Here's the dilemma for small business owners: hiring a pricey business-naming firm or branding company isn't realistic. You have to figure out the perfect name for your company without the help of a big-budget advertising agency. And even if you spend a mint to develop a company name, there's no assurance that customers will embrace it.

FedEx is a terrific example of crowd-sourced branding. Founded in 1973, the goal of this powerful and respected brand was to provide a service that was needed in the pre-fax business community: overnight document delivery. Originally named Federal Express, the company was not affiliated in any way with the government. Perhaps its original intent was to suggest that it was an arm of the post office and somehow "federally" associated. This may have been its first naming error. Customers eventually found it easier to simply call it "Fed Ex." The name stuck. In 2000, the company bowed to its customers' higher wisdom and made the nickname the new brand name. Smart move for FedEx! It's a true success story. Do you think it would have dominated the market with a name like "AAA Shippers"?

Choose your eBay name wisely. Selecting the best name for your business can prove to be a daunting process. You'll invest a lot of time and effort promoting your online dynasty. Here are some suggestions:

▶ Don't copy other people's brands. Imitation is not flattery; it's stealing someone else's great ideas.

▶ Consider the domain name. As you grow this eBay dominion, you'll want a website with a URL that matches your eBay ID.

▶ Keep things simple. Your name should be easy to pronounce, spell, and remember. If folks have a hard time remembering your eBay ID, it's not a great one.

▶ Avoid puns, politics, and poking Protestants (or any religion, for that matter). Goofy names, those which evoke controversy by touching on politics or religion, are a no-no.

▶ Stay away from names that are too trendy or may require a rebranding later. If you sell PEX plumbing supplies, you'll be limiting your future growth if the word "PEX" is part of your brand name. You sell plumbing supplies. PEX just happens to be the largest part of your business. When a better technology comes along in five, seven, or ten years, you'll have to rebrand.

▶ Company names should not offend. That's not to say pop culture is completely off limits. For example, the term "wicked" has become synonymous with awesome, cool stuff. And as such, it's pretty positive in the minds of people. Wicked Skatewear, Wicked Brew, Wicked Donuts, Wicked Lashes, and a plethora of other brands include the word "wicked." If a name is over-the-top (e.g., a parody or hyperbole), it's not likely to be offensive.

A great business name tells your customers what you do. Brand confusion occurs when you're selling things that don't seem relevant to your company name or eBay user ID. If you're advertising expensive antique furniture and selling it under the (fictional) eBay user ID "modern_day_ephemera," don't you think your customer might pause before considering placing a bid on your item?

Are your customers getting blurry vision, or is your brand as clear as mountain spring water? What image does your brand portray in the mind of your customer? How will they benefit from a transaction with you?

Is your brand sneakers or cuff links? Ties or bolos? What's the voice you'd like your customers to hear? A consistent brand message will help grow your business.

Consider the eBay seller "betterworldbooks." Here's the text on their eBay profile: "At Better World Books, we love books. We also love the environment and helping people learn to read. That's why every single purchase from us helps fund literacy around the world." The name works because customers can see the direct connection between what they sell and what they hold as core values.

> **tip** ⓘ
>
> Check your proposed eBay ID on the website http://www.namechk.com to make sure that the name hasn't already been registered as a domain name or used on the most popular social media, video, or blogging sites. If you're in the clear, you'll want to register on these sites even if you're not actively using them (the free ones, of course) to ensure that you are doing as much as possible to protect your cherished fledgling brand.

Would you believe that as of this moment, they have 2,829,146 books listed on their eBay Store? Amazing.

It is true that you can change your eBay user ID, and I know what you're thinking: *If that's true, why does all this brand mumbo-jumbo matter?* Developing the trust that's associated with your eBay business is priceless, and brand building takes time and hard work. Every time you change your eBay member ID, you lose that instant recognition that buyers have associated with your business on eBay.

Keeping Things Legal

Considering your legal structure can be a conundrum. For some reason, the government has the ability to make even the most law-abiding citizen feel like they're in an interrogation room. Audit? The very word causes people's palms to break out into a clammy sweat.

That said, these concerns should never be a roadblock to getting started.

Let's take a look at various legal structures that businesspeople use to operate a company. If your aunt is a CPA or brother-in-law is a tax attorney, you can skip this section and bend their ear over lunch. (Just be sure to pick up the tab.) Otherwise, please read on.

A *sole proprietorship* is the most common business structure for someone just getting started in business. You'll be considered a sole proprietorship if you don't register any other form of business entity. You can use your existing bank account. The funds you receive from customers will generally be paid with PayPal, and you can transfer the money to your personal bank account.

> **tip**
>
> Post a legal question at http://www.avvo.com, and a licensed attorney will respond with a legal opinion. Seek out professional opinions about the proper legal structure for your business.

Consider keeping a separate bank account for your eBay business if you voyage beyond being a casual seller.

A *partnership* is the simplest way for two or more people to own a business together. Partnerships are a good way to manage a business when you aren't the only owner, and you'd like to test things out before advancing to a more formal business structure.

A *limited liability company* (LLC) protects you from liability in most situations in the event of lawsuits or business failures. This is not something that's very common with an eBay business.

Corporations are legal entities that are separate from their owners. Most corporations issue stock, are taxed separately, and can be held legally liable for the corporation's actions while shielding the stockholders and management from lawsuits, in most situations. There are different flavors of corporations. For example, I run an S corporation, which is a special type of legal structure that avoids double taxation because all income flows to me personally while still affording me legal protections. If what you do benefits the public, you can form a tax-exempt corporation to avoid business income tax because you are helping with a cause.

If you're just an itty bitty home-based casual eBay seller, you'll fall into the category of being a sole proprietorship.

Gathering Necessities

There are a few essentials to tuck into your eBay toolbox. Your mobile phone is all you really need to photograph and list items. But what happens after the sale? You'll need shipping supplies, too. And then there are the virtual tools you'll need, like various banking and communications accounts.

The tools you'll need to get started on eBay are:

▶ A PayPal account in good standing

▶ A bank account

▶ An email account

▶ A way to capture photos, such as your phone, a tablet, or a camera

▶ A way to list items, such as the same phone or tablet, a laptop, or a desktop computer

▶ An internet connection

▶ A backdrop or background for photography

▶ Good, indirect natural light or lighting equipment

▶ Packing supplies, such as boxes, tape, a tape dispenser, and bubble wrap or void fill (I'll discuss packing and shipping in-depth in Chapter 9)

▶ A way to print shipping labels, such as an ordinary printer or a dedicated label printer

▶ A postal-compliant shipping scale with a capacity large enough to weigh your biggest item and the ability to weigh as little as 1 ounce (I paid less than $20 for mine.)

▶ A cheap tailor's tape measure (more on this later)

tip ⓘ

It is absolutely essential that you replace a computer's spinning hard drive every three years or a solid-state hard drive every ten years. You can do this yourself (if you're computer savvy) or hire someone—but don't wait until it's too late. Hard drive failure will be a catastrophe to your eBay business when critical photos and other files are lost if you don't have a current backup.

Don't sink a wheelbarrow of money into fancy equipment. If you are a newbie to eBay, work with what you've got. You can improve your toolbox over time. Pictures captured on today's phones are excellent—today's phone cameras produce stunning images.

Perhaps you only want to sell a few items. Your success is measured by you, not me. If you love your job and have no interest in quitting, this eBay hobby is a great way to try something fun, interesting, and new.

If you've set your sights on big things, an investment in equipment would make sense, particularly if you have the clarity and confidence to know what size eBay enterprise you'll be launching. Selling on eBay is a lucrative and relatively low-cost proposition when compared to many other business opportunities out there.

Start contemplating how you'll safely store your items for sale. Fragile things will need to be out of harm's way while valuables must be locked up. The last thing you want is to find that a very expensive painting has a big yellow stain from your faithful dog or to come home and discover that a pricey Ming vase has been knocked over by your precocious pussycat. Don't you cringe at the very thought of hearing an antique vase shattering into a million pieces? Maybe you have a spare room, a spot in your basement, a corner in the garage, or some other suitable place for item storage. When guests visit, you'll have more than just looky-loos; family and friends will want to pick things up and have a look at them—creating the opportunity for damage. When entertaining large groups of people, there's a real possibility that a stranger can take something home that doesn't belong to them. So, store your eBay items wisely.

Dropping the Breadcrumbs

Tracking a lot of inventory is a daunting task. I was having a delightful conversation with a fellow eBayer—a big-time seller—and at some point in our entertaining banter, it came to light that he had no specific method for tracking individual items. I was astonished by this revelation because his eBay business was by all reports an extremely successful one. "How do you locate the item once you've sold it," I asked. "I just know where it is." With thousands and thousands of items, this answer didn't really track for me, but apparently, he possessed the uncanny ability to remember the locations of things.

I am very regimented and orderly—not because I was in the Navy for eight joyous years, but because I'm terrified by the possibility that I'm going to misplace something and have to face a very unhappy (or possibly downright hostile) customer. eBay allows you to enter a custom label to help with inventory management. You can enter anything you want in this field, which I will explain in more detail in Chapter 6. I have two bits of data that I enter for every item, which are the item location and the item stock keeping unit (aka the SKU). Here is an example: 42/14225. The number 42 is the shelf number, and 14225 is the SKU. In my inventory management system, I never use the same SKU twice except for replenishable items (items I sell over and over again).

The ideal moment to consider how you'll handle organizing and labeling your inventory is on *day one* of your business. It is far easier to work with a well-thought-out system that grows than to address the subject when it becomes a problem down the road.

When mentoring someone who has never owned a business, this is the point where I see eyes glaze over. It's OK. Relax. Do not allow yourself to become overwhelmed by all the legal considerations. Just remember to think about these key points moving forward:

▶ What you want to sell
▶ Your branding (c'mon this is part of the fun)
▶ Your legal structure
▶ What tools you'll need (you probably already have them)
▶ How you will store and organize your merchandise

If you can wrap your brain around these things, you'll be set up for long-term success.

Preparing to Pay the Piper

As with all business endeavors, making eBay deals requires that thing most of us dread—paperwork. My mother used to say, "If you don't mess up your room, there's nothing to clean." Mother knows best, and these days I stay on top of my eBay business by planning ahead and staying well-organized. One business associate tells me, "You're the most organized person I know." She didn't know me way back in my teens when my room was nothing but clutter.

My general recordkeeping guidance is to retain customer and eBay emails until the returns grace period expires, or if you're working out some issue with a customer, then 90 days after you resolve that issue. While the federal and state tax collectors might one day come knocking on your door, what you need to know from the income side of things is stored safely on both eBay and PayPal's servers. PayPal has made tax reports a breeze to generate (from the income side). eBay and PayPal don't track your cost of goods or expenses.

On the expense side of things, the IRS requires you to keep most records for three years so that you can prove the veracity of your reported deductions (and income). I manage my bookkeeping in QuickBooks, which also has a handy feature that lets you attach photos of receipts. I love being paperless because it keeps life uncluttered. American Express lets me upload pictures of my receipts, too, so I use their card for virtually everything business-related. I've been liberated from my paper prison.

I'll cover packing and shipping in a meaningful way in Chapter 9; however, shipping records and proof of insurance should be kept until you receive positive buyer feedback or sufficient time has passed that it is unlikely anything went awry. Before shredding those records (never put sensitive records in the trash), check to make sure the parcel was delivered. Even better, contact your buyer and ask if everything arrived in good shape. Once positive feedback is received, I trash those records immediately. If no feedback arrives, I keep them for 90 days.

Consider this—you don't always have to give a cut of your eBay bounty to the IRS (or to the state). Here's what the IRS says: "Income resulting from auctions akin to an occasional garage or yard sale is generally not required to be reported. However, there may be exceptions. If an online garage sale turns into a business with recurring sales and purchasing of items for resale, it may be considered an online auction business." If Justin Bieber threw you his sweaty stage-worn concert t-shirt and you score $5,000 for it on eBay (because you had a video of The Bieb throwing it to you), then you probably have to let the government know (and pay the tax).

Just how much recordkeeping you'll need to maintain in fulfilling your eBay sales depends on whether you are a casual seller, a hobbyist, or a business seller. Ask your tax professional for guidance. Most tax advisors will give you a few tips for free because they hope that you'll lean on them for tax prep come year-end. Keep purchase receipts for items you resell because the profit is the difference between what you sold it for and what you paid. Without a receipt, you may be held to pay tax on the entire sale, even if you sold it for less than you paid. Losses are usually deductible against your profits. Don't think it matters much? Someday soon you'll be making big bucks. In 2020 the federal tax rate for unmarried persons earning over $207,350 amounts to 35 percent. In my home state, they tack on an additional 7.6 percent which adds up to 42.6 percent in income tax. I hope that will get you motivated to save your purchase receipts. Deductions are the best cure for big tax bills.

Now, treat yourself to a nice cup of coffee or tea and let all of this brew in your mind a little bit. Work on bite-size goals and just do it. You're well on your way to earning the extra money you always dreamed of.

Researching Products and Pricing

It's impressive just how many buyers and sellers trade on eBay. Remember that there are 179 million *active* eBay buyers! What's truly glorious is that you can connect with these eager spenders while typing in your robe and bathroom slippers. (Shh. It's our little secret.) What's equally amazing is the extraordinary transparency to be discovered in the data available on eBay from pricing to sales lead time to reviews and ratings. All those sold and unsold items tell a clear story of what works and what doesn't.

Price research is one of the best ways to research products before you list and a primary indicator of a product's appeal on eBay. If you have talent with research and organizing things, then price research comes naturally. Please enjoy the information, but don't allow yourself to be ruled by it. A rare military button from the Civil War will have a less predictable value than last year's Reeboks.

Studying pricing involves greater understanding than just the information displayed on the screen. It also means being pragmatic, practical, and patient. Commodities can be priced using eBay search data or tools such as Terapeak, which is complimentary with an eBay store subscription.

Items that occur on eBay infrequently require more study. As incredible as it may sound, there are "eBay rarities." One of my customers was gloating because he scored an exceptional deal on a Loetz vase that I sold him. It was apparently worth many times what I charged for it. I didn't realize it was Loetz and listed it as a nice "antique" vase. A few quick pictures posted up on eBay's discussion boards at the eBay Community (which you can access using the QR code included below in Figure 4–1) would have revealed the true value of the piece. I stumbled upon the buyer's blog entirely by accident, where he was not only bragging about the low price he paid, but was using my picture on the blog. He had even asked me to offer a discount on the sale, which I had foolishly agreed to. I was clueless of the vase's high value. The gall of that guy!

But the pendulum swings in both directions. I have also realized incredibly high prices for items that I felt were essentially overpriced. The auction-style listing format is ideal for generating the excitement and competition needed to raise prices to lofty levels.

FIGURE 4–1: **The eBay Community**

When you're scratching your head about value, your instincts are probably saying, "Use an auction."

In this chapter, we'll be looking closely at how to research items and how to decide on the ideal price. We'll also see how you can start to develop a knack for discovering opportunity in price research.

Pinpointing Product Value

How in the world do you sift through all those eBay listings and settle on the value of what you're selling? Would you believe that eBay used to post the actual number of listings on their homepage? I remember when it was less than 800,000.

eBay uses a proprietary search program called Best Match that determines the default way that eBay presents listings. Best Match may present what eBay interprets as relevant to you, but you might want a different way to dive into this pool of products.

When you conduct an eBay search, Best Match is the default view—the way that eBay first displays the search results to you. You can sort by time ending soonest, newly listed, lowest price, highest price, or nearest to you. A plethora of filters allow viewing by format, condition, item specifics, distance, whether or not sold, and a multitude of other ways. In estimating value, sellers are generally interested in viewing completed, sold listings sorted by highest price. The search results page offers optional filters to bring clearer meaning to the sold item data.

In order to fully understand search, you need to comprehend listing best practices. Become a master of eBay's search tools so that you're optimizing your own listings for maximum buyer visibility. Add robust information and complete the item specifics on eBay's item to catalyze a more favorable position when eBay uses their Best Match protocol.

Item specifics are fields within the eBay listing form where you enter data that goes beyond the title and description. Item specifics vary by item category. Some information within item specifics may be prefilled. The eBay site also stores and recalls data from their catalog for certain categories, and the use of the catalog data is mandatory on some products. eBay knows that some things sell better when consistent information about those items is shown to buyers. eBay allows users to find merchandise by browsing and typing in keywords, but also by searching for a product using a part number or a Global Trade Item Number (GTIN), such as the Universal Product Code (UPC), International Article Number (also known as European Article Number or EAN), or International Standard Book Number (ISBN).

When a product has a unique identifier such as these, sellers may be required to list those items from the eBay catalog database—the online library of details and images for products in a wide range of categories. This requirement benefits everyone because it streamlines the buyer experience and provides sellers with timesaving stock photos, item titles, thorough product descriptions, and pre-filled item specifics. Here's a further explanation of these identification numbers:

▶ *Manufacturer's part number (MPN).* An identifier of a specific part design used to provide a pinpoint reference to that part that is unique to the manufacturer. Examples include products such as vehicle parts, hand tools, heating and air conditioner system replacement parts, and many millions of other products across thousands of industries. Because an MPN is only unique to the manufacturer and that same number may be used by other manufacturers, buyers will use the MPN in a search along with the brand name, e.g., "Acme 6789." If the MPN is truly unique, the product can be found by searching for just the MPN.

▶ *Universal Product Code (UPC).* A barcode system used in the U.S. and Canada, as well as some other countries, for tracking merchandise in stores. The package or product hangtag has the UPC barcode and the UPC number printed on it.

▶ *International Article Number, also known as the European Article Number (EAN).* In the world of retail sales, the UPC and EAN are the two primary barcode formats used on products. The EAN is used virtually everywhere that UPC is not used.

▶ *International Standard Book Number (ISBN).* Every published book is assigned an ISBN number. The ISBN identifies a book's edition and publisher. A modern book will usually have either a UPC or EAN as well as an ISBN number.

eBay integrates the Terapeak research tool into the *Seller Hub*, allowing access to years of real-world sales data. The tool allows searches by keyword(s), MPN, UPC, EAN or ISBN. I'll discuss the use of the Seller Hub in-depth in Chapter 7. Researching items by a unique identifier greatly increases accuracy.

I've noticed some sellers embellishing their item titles and descriptions with spammy keywords that they use as clickbait to attract more eyeballs on their listings. This can confuse people and may simply be counterintuitive. I believe the practice reduces buyer trust and hurts sales. It also makes product research more challenging because unrelated items will pop up. When conducting research, consider the quality of the sellers' work with titles, product images, shipping and handling practices, etc. A listing with misspelled or too few keywords, poorly-lit and out-of-focus images, and excessive shipping charges does not serve as a good comparison because you won't be making those rookie mistakes.

Let's practice searching for products. Using the simple search phrase "Blacklist Blu-ray" will return the results of all listings with *Blacklist* and *Blu-ray* in the title in any order— and in the description if you selected the option for eBay to search the item description. See Figure 4–2 on page 61 for the results of this search. There are filter options just above and to

FIGURE 4–2: **The Search Results Page for the Keywords "Blacklist Blu-ray"**

the left of the search results. The filters are dynamic and change depending on the category of merchandise in the results page. A common mistake is to add too many keywords into the search, making it less likely to discover what you want. Start with few keywords and embellish more words as you refine and reduce the number of results. Making the search very specific provides a more digestible list of results as well.

Include the model number in searches when the product has one. For example, type "Samsung RF28HDEDBSR" vs. "Samsung refrigerator." The model number narrows things down. For a unique model number like that, you won't need to enter the brand name.

Use these additional tricks to improve your searches:

▶ As a seller, you'll want to see what sold, so limit your searches to the sold items option, which is available on the left side of the search results (you'll probably have to scroll far).

▶ Drill down to the condition you want, new or used, to cut down the clutter in your search.

▶ Filter your results to view only auctions if you're sourcing product on eBay to resell back on eBay or if you'd like to evaluate if auction-style listings generate a better price for what you're selling.

▶ Try using the price range feature (to weed out low price accessories or high-value wholesale lots that match your search terms).

▶ Filter by category to see items only in a specific category. The exception to this would be when you're hunting for seller mistakes and want to discover those misplaced bargain items.

Once you master the basics of the search engine, you will save lots of time and effort searching for products, whether for purchase or for research. Though the search engine can be used effectively with this knowledge alone, there are some additional searching tricks that are available to you.

If you're a techie or just want to act like one, try the Boolean search operators; these are cool ways to search using simple tricks that expand the power of your eBay search capabilities. Remember that eBay searches are not case sensitive. Let's walk through a few ways you can use Boolean operators to maximize your search capabilities on eBay.

The Minus Sign

Placing a minus sign in front of any word acts as the NOT operator, which means that the word is excluded. The search "-faux pearl necklace" will omit the results with the word "faux" and only return pearl necklaces.

Parentheses

Placing parentheses around a group of words acts as an OR operator. The search "sterling (pin,brooch,necklace,pendant) –gold" will return all listings that have the word "sterling" and any of the words in the parentheses, but not the word "gold" since I excluded it.

Minus Sign with Parentheses

You can place the minus sign in front of the parentheses search to tell eBay to look for listings that do not including a group of words, like this: "–(platinum,gold)." A search keyed in this way "necklace –(platinum,gold) will return a list of necklaces that are not made from platinum or gold. In another example, you'd key in "sweater –(polyester,wool)" to find sweaters that don't contain polyester or wool.

Quotation Marks

Adding quotes around a set of words changes the search quite a bit. Placing quotes like this: "floor mat" will search only the words in that sequence. This may be critical when you're searching a person's name, "Marilyn Monroe," or a make and model, "Samsung Galaxy". All of the above examples will return massive search results, which you'll need to cut down even further with filters.

The Asterisk

An asterisk is the way to search wildcards. A wildcard search is a magical tool that will expand your search. When you use an asterisk after the beginning of a word, the eBay search engine will automatically complete the word without regard to spelling or other factors. For example, I'm fond of fossil sharks teeth, and the eBay community hasn't quite fully mastered the spelling of megalodon, the largest of the extinct shark species. Listings with misspellings tend to fetch lower prices. Try this search . . .

meg* (shark,sharks,shark's) –replica

. . . which will find the misspelled examples and will weed out replicas. The meg* means that the search results will locate any word starting with "meg" will be included along with "shark" OR "sharks" OR "shark's," not including any listing that has the word "replica" in the title.

While Booleans are not absolutely vital to use, it is clear that they can give you superpowers in certain scenarios. Search engine knowledge alone, however, will not

► Searching for Sales Timing and Trends

You can use your searching skills to investigate timing trends that can help you best position your own items. For example, you will want to avoid listing on a day that will result in your auction-style listings ending on a holiday, even if that day is a Sunday. Festive moments are very distracting. Check the holiday calendar and use common sense.

Just for curiosity, I looked up a particular style of popular Samsonite luggage (check out Figure 4–3) and looked at the sales trends across an entire year. Sales for luggage clearly spiked to their highest figures just before the Thanksgiving holiday. I would imagine July would not be the best month to list winter outerwear unless you are selling to customers in Reykjavík, Iceland where summer's high temperature rarely rises above 55 degrees Fahrenheit.

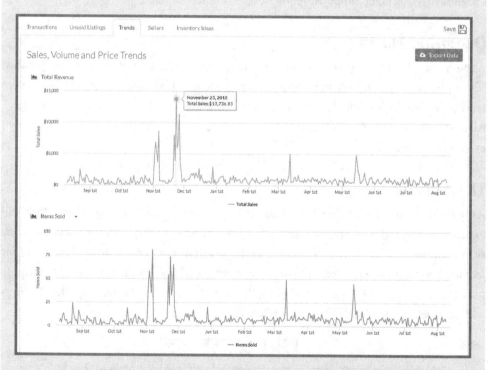

FIGURE 4–3: **Terapeak Research–"Samsonite Winfield Luggage"**

carry you to eBay riches; let's talk briefly about sourcing your products. In Chapter 10, I'll dive deeper into product sourcing, however product and price research go hand-in-hand with three product sourcing concepts: drop-shipping, retail arbitrage, and eBay arbitrage.

Start to think about ways to profit from the results of your eBay research. As you explore what's listed, you can examine the opportunities that are available from drop-ship vendors as well as local retailers—even eBay itself.

Drop-Shipping: The Pros and Cons

Two common subjects that I discuss with my readers and social media followers relate to buying for resale and *drop-shipping*, a supply method in which you don't hold physical inventory, but transfer orders to the wholesaler or supplier, who then ships the products directly to the customer. eBay refers to drop-shipping as *product sourcing*. The manner in which you perform pricing research will be different when you operate a drop-shipping business. Please keep in mind: "There's a sucker born every minute" is an aphorism that simply doesn't hold water. Access to smartphones and computers gives us all superpowers. We can research pricing instantly. We can find out virtually anything anywhere we are.

Drop-shipping sounds awesome: Someone else buys high-demand, high-quality brand-name goods and delivers them directly to your customer. Like rubbing Aladdin's lamp, it's a dream come true. The trouble is that everyone else is trying to do the same thing. And the drop-shipper has already incorporated a tidy profit for their own company in the price tag. Don't forget to factor in eBay's and PayPal's fees. By the time all is said and done, there may be little or nothing left for you.

My advice is to test and explore before spending a lot of time listing someone else's inventory. Be sure it makes financial sense, and do your homework. Before investing time (and eBay fees) into listing items for drop-shipping, be certain that your drop-ship partner hasn't oversaturated eBay by working with too many sellers. When this occurs, it typically results in a race to the bottom.

Don't confuse the very challenging business of drop-shipping with the very lucrative world of consignment. I am skeptical about the former and very fond of the latter. In no way am I saying that drop-shipping profits are as rare as a unicorn. I'm asking you to be careful about tall tales and wild claims. Drop-shipping opportunities are so well-advertised, you'll need to apply your expert eBay research skills to determine if a particular offer is worth pursuing. Few are, in my view.

warning

eBay permits drop-shipping so long as the product is shipped from a wholesale supplier. You are always responsible for the safe, timely delivery of the items you sell on eBay even if you drop-ship them. Listing an item on eBay and then buying the item from another retailer or website that ships directly to your customer is not allowed on eBay.

Before you become seduced by the YouTube dude standing in front of his red Ferrari offering to allow you to enter his "circle of special friends" by granting you access to his special "system," please run the other direction when you're asked for a credit card number. Hard work beats systems. Knowledge also beats systems. Knowledge is abundant, and there is no system in the world that will motivate you to work hard and do your homework, which isn't going to cost you anything. While you're busy studying someone's expensive system, your competition is busy taking photos, writing descriptions, packing and shipping, and counting dollars. I tried drop-shipping, and it didn't turn a profit for me. Consider consignment instead. eBay buyers aren't just buying on eBay. We all shop at different places, at different times. I'm skeptical about there being a huge amount of buyer loyalty out there. Customers want it faster, cheaper, in perfect condition, and with free shipping. There are always opportunities to make money.

Arbitrage

As you research products and their prices on eBay, start to think of ways to profit from retail and eBay arbitrage. *Retail arbitrage* is a technique used by eBay sellers who buy high-demand sale and clearance merchandise from local retail stores or their online sites (where purchases can be delivered to the local store) and then sell those products on eBay for a profit—after accounting for eBay fees plus packing and shipping costs. Retail arbitrage isn't brain surgery. Anyone can engage in successful arbitrage with a bit of practice. Visit local retailers with your phone at-the-ready to conduct price research. Look for deals on the websites of retailers that offer free shipping to their local store. I love Atkins bars and buy them from Walmart online. Today, you can buy a box of Atkins Endulge brownies at Walmart for $5.48, and a box of the same brownies sold on eBay with free shipping for $15.59.

I ran the term "Endulge™ brownies" through a 12-month search on Terapeak, a price research tool offered at no cost to eBay Store subscribers. Here are some statistics I found:

- ▶ 56 sellers
- ▶ $4,697.34 in total sales
- ▶ 493 boxes sold
- ▶ $9.53 average selling price
- ▶ 88.99 percent of the sales offered free shipping

Perhaps there's a new business opportunity for me trading in Atkins products!

Many eBay sellers make serious listing mistakes. The magnitude of these selling errors is so huge that skilled researchers buy products on eBay to resell back on eBay. This is referred to as *eBay arbitrage*. This is another way to leverage your skill as an eBay researcher and fill your pockets with cash! In my experience, only a very small number of people bother to try their hand at eBay arbitrage. It's a simple process, but not necessarily easy. If it were easy, everyone would be making money doing it. Arbitrage requires skill. You'll have to study and practice to get great at it. Finding seller mistakes can be highly profitable. Here are some ways to source deals on eBay:

- ▶ Become an expert in a handful of product categories so that you're quick to recognize a deal when you see it.
- ▶ Look for commonly misspelled keywords. If a buyer can't find it, the item won't sell (so many sellers don't bother to use spell check).
- ▶ Look for abbreviations. Many sellers shorten or abbreviate because they run out of space in the title.
- ▶ Look for missing important keywords in titles. (Can you believe sellers forget to mention even simple things like what it is they're selling?)
- ▶ Look for listings with horrible images (most buyers gloss over them).

Once you've found a deal and it looks like you've scored a home run, make your move and buy it! Be sure the total price including shipping is still going to turn a profit.

I'll discuss how to list your eBay items in the next chapter; however, I'd like to bring focus on the research that you've been conducting and my recommendations moving forward. Pinpointing product value takes experience, time, and patience. The success of your research will grow as you become better at using the search techniques that I've discussed here.

Unless you like to gamble with your money (and maybe you do), don't start auction-style listings at a penny or 99¢. Those days are over. With so much inventory on eBay, it's possible you may only receive a single bid on an item. Hot products will spark bidding. Even still, skip the reserve and start your bidding at a reasonable price based on your research. Along that line of thinking, it is unwise to consider auctions with very low starting prices as meaningful to your research. As you spend time exploring eBay, start to notice products on eBay and in local retail stores that you can use to profit from arbitrage.

In the next chapter, I'll address the limitations of selling on eBay, selecting the appropriate listing format and placement, understanding and avoiding common issues, staying in compliance with eBay's marketplace rules, and ensuring your listings are well-presented for maximum impact.

Preparing Your Products Before Listing

L et's continue our eBay journey with an in-depth discussion about selling items on eBay. Indeed, this entire book is about starting your very own business on eBay; however, I'd like to really get granular in the discussion of how to list items. I will accomplish this in two chapters: this chapter, which is the 360-degree look at what you need to know before you sell an item, and the next chapter, which is about the actual item listing process on the eBay site.

As we learned in the previous chapter, selling on eBay requires a certain degree of planning and research. If you want to make boatloads of money while having a good time, it would be best to be fully prepared before jumping in. Once you create a beautiful frame for your eBay business, you can create a gorgeous masterpiece of online commerce.

What kinds of items are you allowed (or not allowed) to sell on eBay? Where are you going to obtain your merchandise? These are just a couple of the very big questions that we will be tackling in this chapter.

Knowing Your Limits: Restrictions on eBay Product Listings

You can sell virtually anything on eBay. However, there are prohibited and restricted items. Common sense and your instincts may tell you, for example, that marijuana is not allowed on eBay. Pot leaf motif lighters are just fine. Bong pipes are OK, too. I don't touch the potent green stuff myself, but please read the fine print on what is and is not allowed.

Some merchandise is banned entirely, while other products may be sold with a license. With an appropriate state permit and eBay approval, wine sellers can ship their finest vintage to eBay buyers. The U.S. Postal Service doesn't allow the shipment of intoxicating liquors containing 0.5 percent or more alcohol by content, so a private carrier such as FedEx or UPS will be required. Selling perfume on eBay is perfectly kosher; however, you cannot ship flammable goods through the USPS. You may not sell used cosmetics, makeup sponges, or fragrances and lotions that aren't in their original containers. The person who stole the tusks from that poor walrus or pachyderm cannot profit from goods made from them on eBay. In fact, before you list any animal products from endangered species, you'll need to brush up on the eBay animal and wildlife products policy. You can find a full list of prohibited and restricted items in the "policies" section of the eBay website.

While most *Playboy* issues and racy romance novels are OK to list on the public eBay site, almost everything that is of an adult nature or is sexually explicit must be listed in eBay's Adult-Only section where age verification is required to view those listings. Scan the QR code in Figure 5–1 on page 71 to review eBay's complete list of prohibited and restricted items.

Sourcing Items to Sell

I'll explain lots of product sourcing ideas in Chapter 10; however, start thinking about where you'll find the items you'll be selling. Before your first item goes up, have you determined

FIGURE 5–1: **Prohibited and Restricted Items**

what that item will be? Please do not list the Rolex watch you picked up from the eager street vendor in Tijuana for $20. It wasn't real then, and it's not real now. Not only will you get into hot water with eBay, even if your listing isn't ended by *VeRO* (a system that eBay uses to protect the rights of product manufacturers; more on this later), but the buyer is certain to return it and make you pay roundtrip shipping. If you happened to pick up some fabulous Huichol hand-beaded collectibles on that same visit to Mexico, you're likely to fetch a fine price for them on eBay—and they *are* permitted on the site. I've sold quite a bit of the beautiful art made by the indigenous people of that country.

There are oodles of things you can sell on eBay for a profit. The goods that have done well for me fall into these categories:

- ▶ antiques and collectibles
- ▶ cameras
- ▶ designer apparel and accessories
- ▶ electronics
- ▶ event tickets
- ▶ excess inventory
- ▶ housewares
- ▶ laptops
- ▶ musical instruments
- ▶ phones
- ▶ sports equipment
- ▶ vehicles and vehicle parts
- ▶ video recorders

Earlier I chided the "systems" available that purport to unlock the secrets to eBay riches. I'm not saying it is impossible to buy a boatload of stuff from Asia and resell it on eBay for millions of dollars. What I am saying is that since I started on eBay in 1999, I have never been able to figure it out. I have also never *met* a person who made big money that way either.

Since you are following my advice to pursue an eBay business that you're passionate about, you can follow some fairly obvious leads to source items to buy or consign for resale on eBay. I recommend you start with used goods. eBayers are looking for deals, and the best deals you can give them will be on secondhand merchandise.

Try all of these sourcing opportunities:

- ▶ antique shops
- ▶ around your home
- ▶ auction houses
- ▶ auto mechanics
- ▶ colleagues and co-workers
- ▶ discarded items
- ▶ dollar stores
- ▶ estate sales
- ▶ fairs and tradeshows
- ▶ family
- ▶ flea markets
- ▶ friends
- ▶ government agencies
- ▶ housekeepers
- ▶ online community sites (NextDoor, Craigslist, etc.)
- ▶ pawn shops
- ▶ recycling centers
- ▶ remodeling contractors
- ▶ small local shops
- ▶ street vendors (but not Rolex watches from street vendors)
- ▶ thrift stores

In no way is this a complete list. If you find a fabulous sourcing opportunity in your hometown, keep it on the "down low" as long as possible so you can milk that cow for a long time. That said, your best method for sourcing goods may very well be a big mouth—shameless self-promotion is alive and well. Talking things up works. For example, I told my housekeeper about my eBay enterprise, and she brought dozens of unopened top-brand vintage perfumes that were gifted to her by an elderly client for me to sell on eBay. She offered to re-gift them to me and I said, "No." I split the proceeds with her 50/50, and her cut ended up being *thousands of dollars*. She later called me to come pick up a 40-year-old Peugeot that was also given to her—a gift from a surviving relative of a neighbor who recently passed away. We partnered on the sale of that eBay item as well.

Opportunities are everywhere. Just start paying attention, and you'll see dollar signs where you once only saw stuff.

Choosing the Perfect Listing Type

Seasoned shop owners understand the tremendous profit to be made when you select the right location for what you're selling.

An eBay listing is just like having a physical store. Single listings won't have monthly "rent" other than the insertion fees you pay. eBay Stores, on the other hand, have monthly fees in addition to insertion fees that are assessed once your free allocation is depleted.

Here are some generalizations and assumptions about choosing your listing type:

▶ Auction-style listings allow competition and must be used when an item could be worth a mint and you're not willing to risk leaving money on the table.

▶ Fixed-price format permits you to instantly sell goods at a set price, and you should use this format when there is a very high probability you know the value of your items.

▶ Duplicate listings are two or more listings for items that aren't substantially different—eBay restricts some duplicate items and allows others.

▶ Classified ads are OK; however, there are loads of places that you can list items for sale without cost, such as Nextdoor and Craigslist.

▶ Selling collectible cars on eBay Motors should be done auction-style, and late-model vehicles should be listed with the fixed–price format.

▶ The sooner you need money, the shorter your listing duration should be since some buyers sort by listings that are ending soonest. As a tip, most of my auction-style listings run for seven days—providing ample exposure to potential buyers.

▶ Bidders generally dislike reserve prices on auctions, so I advise you to stay away from using them.

▶ Adding international site visibility makes sense if you are OK with shipping cross-border and are willing to pay the extra fee. There's a little more paperwork for overseas shipments.

▶ Listing in two categories costs more. However, there is an audience out there who browses categories for deals, and this will attract two times more browsing buyers—

a great idea for collectibles and scarce items but less beneficial for commodities that everyone is selling.

▶ Scheduling your listing start times is free to do if you don't have an eBay store and only $.10 per listing if you do. Many seasoned eBayers swear that the perfect time-frame to end an eBay listing is between 3:00 P.M. and 7:00 P.M. PST, when virtually all Americans are likely to be awake (this timing would be less important if your best bids come from overseas buyers).

Tailor your listing like a beautiful dress, and it will certainly bring you profits. Virtually everything you could conceivably sell will be listed differently; once you master this process, you have mastered the art of eBay salesmanship. Making these minor tweaks will be equivalent to a brick-and-mortar store owner selecting an ideal store location, because it deals with how buyer will find your goods.

Giving proper love to each listing is important, as we can see. Now let's talk about some of the challenges and concerns that you will inevitably run into on your journey.

Handling Common Challenges

My eBay business is truly massive; it's epic in scale and yet smaller than so many other eBay sellers. If I had a brick-and-mortar retail shop, it would be about 5,000 square feet of display space. It's truly that large. This poses many unique challenges.

Missing or Damaged Goods

I'll dispense with the obvious such as missing or damaged goods. It rarely happens, but it is an eventuality. For missing or damaged products, the buyer is offered both a refund plus a token cash payment of $5 to $25 depending on the price of that item. This calms the screaming and suspicious buyers down. I also offer a discount on their next item, depending on the product category. I communicate that a "special price" will be extended when they return to make another purchase. They do come back sometimes, but rarely.

Employee Quality Assurance

The law of diminishing returns kicks in as your business enlarges. In this challenge, simply adding more employees will not guarantee more productivity. Adding untrained workers to your company usually results in problems such as people getting in each other's way or staff waiting for management advice or approval. Only well-trained workers generate excellent results and becoming great at training other people requires skill and experience.

I'm still learning myself! If the work is handled by you, or a partner and you, then you can expect stellar productivity assuming you love what you're doing. Adding employees means more social time, breaks you would never take as an owner, etc. When employees decide to vacation at the busiest time of the year, you'll find yourself short-staffed and unable to manage the workload. You may also need seasonal employees to help you. Turn to the hardest working friends and family first. If you can't stand each other, then post a help wanted ad. I use both Indeed and Craigslist to find help.

Oversaturated Markets

When you buy enough new stuff on eBay, you'll notice there's a flood of the same merchandise. I attribute this to all the "get rich quick" programs out there that insist you can own a Ferrari and a McMansion by purchasing goods made in China and reselling them on eBay. It's also because the same factories are shipping directly from China with cheap postage on an already-cheap item from across the globe.

If you have a zillion of the same item, don't flood eBay with it. Of course, there are exceptions. If you are the official, exclusive distributor for a factory, then going wide and deep with inventory would make good sense.

Don't list an auction with multiples of the same product in the auction. Wait for a sale to occur, then relist and sell the next one. Is this a hard-and-fast rule? Of course not. If you sell individual batteries for DSLR cameras, you can list multiples in an auction so long as the starting price is profitable. Always factor in eBay and PayPal fees. Remember to scan the handy QR codes in Chapter 1 to see the most current fees for both companies.

Returns

If you have never sold on eBay and you've never owned a business, brace yourself for the reality of retail—returns! If you never hire employees or have customers visit your place of business, the great news is that you'll also never have to worry about shoplifting or *shrinkage*. Shrinkage occurs when items are lost due to damage, loss, or theft. According to the National Retail Federation, the estimated shrink rate for retail stores was a massive $50.6 billion in 2019. The amount of merchandise returned to retailers as a percentage of total sales averages 10 percent. By comparison, my eBay return rate is a mere 1.95 percent. Returns are not shrinkage because you can resell an item returned in good condition. An eBay return rate that's too low is a sign of a restrictive returns policy. Allowing returns means more sales, higher prices, and confident buyers. Dishonest customers exist. All retailers must cope with liars and thieves and eBayers do, too. Thank goodness it's a very small issue as compared to the bigger profits to be made. Brick-and-mortar retailers have five times as many returns as I do, and the great news is that fraud is rare. eBay has sophisticated software to weed out bad buyers—and those who regularly abuse returns are blocked forever. I'll share some wisdom with you about returns in the next sections.

Phony Buyer Returns

What do you do about the old switcheroo? If you're not familiar with that word, it's the rare practice of eBayers returning a different item than the one you sent them. Granted, this is a super rare event. Possible reasons your buyer returned the wrong item may include:

- ▶ They are buying so much stuff that they're losing track of their purchases—a real possibility.
- ▶ You or your staff inadvertently sent the wrong product out.
- ▶ They are dishonest.

Before you send out the atomics, remain calm and give the buyer the benefit of the doubt. Take pictures of the box and incorrect item. If the buyer is not an honest person, this practice will catch up with them, and eBay will ban them forever. In the meantime, you've got to handle your business and protect your money. If and when eBay formally steps in, be sure to have a rational explanation as well as photos to back up your position. You can call eBay preemptively to make them aware of the potential for a dispute. For your ready-reference, that number is (866) 540-3229.

Milked Return Policies

When you're just getting started in business, you can easily dream of zero customer returns. However, that dreaded day will come when you receive an email alert informing you the buyer wants to send their item back. Even if you have a no-returns policy, eBay will approve a buyer return under certain circumstances, such as when the item doesn't match the description or arrives damaged or faulty. As the seller, it's your duty to ensure the parcel even if the buyer doesn't want to. When a customer changes their mind, sometimes they'll make up a story, such as throwing out the bold statement, "It doesn't seem authentic." eBay will let them send it back. Often buyers select an inaccurate reason for returns, and if eBay determines that the eBayer is misusing returns or abusing the eBay Money Back Guarantee, eBay will consider an account suspension.

Occasionally, a buyer will use the product and then return it. Clever people figure out a way to return something even if your seller return policy says you don't accept returns. My overall return rate is very low (under 2 percent). Return rates in specific categories are higher, such as antiques and apparel. Clothing comes back more frequently because it doesn't fit. New products have lower return rates than used ones. Overall, I suggest you let customers return things. Be calm and friendly when handling returns, and eliminate the "inquisition" of endless questions. Returns should be pain-free. If someone clearly abuses returns, you can block them from buying again. In Chapter 1, I provided a QR code that takes you to the eBay site map where you will find the tools to block undesirable bidders. eBay allows you to offer 30 or 60 day returns, and I permit returns within 30 days.

Mindfully documenting returns can ensure what you receive back is your actual merchandise and not a product that is counterfeit, a different item altogether, or something from another retailer. Busy holiday shopping seasons can be exhausting for a large eBay retailer. Don't let down your guard, or something might slip past you (or your staff if you employ people).

Putting Your Listing in the Right Place

Experienced eBay sellers know that virtually all buyers locate what they want to purchase by typing keywords into the eBay search box. Some buyers browse categories and look for items to purchase that grab their interest. eBay also enforces the correct use of the category system. Some merchandise, such as jewelry items, can belong in more than one category, which is why eBay allows listing in up to two different categories, but you have to pay twice for the additional exposure.

The eBay selling form requires that you pick at least one category for your listing. A simple and effective method for identifying the right category is to review sold items. Search the item's keywords and then tick off the checkbox for sold items on the left-hand side of the search results, and then sort by highest price. Click on a successfully sold listing that is close to what you're selling, and then you'll see the category at the top of the listing page. Even though most buyers are *searching* for what they want, add the "right" category based on my research tip.

Here's a real-world example: Let's say you're listing a vintage Monopoly board game. It could go in more than one category: Toys & Hobbies > Vintage & Antique Toys > Other Vintage & Antique Toys and also Toys & Hobbies > Games > Board & Traditional Games > Vintage Manufacture. Categories have levels. "Toys & Hobbies" is the top-level category and the ">" symbol separates that from the sub-categories. Some people call the sub-categories "leaf" categories. After searching keywords and filtering by sold listings, then sorting by highest price, you discover that the highest prices are being achieved in the sub-category Vintage Manufacture, so that's where you should list your Monopoly game.

Protecting Listings from VeRO Infringement

The Verified Rights Owner (VeRO) program that I mentioned earlier offers enormous protection for eBayers as well as intellectual property owners who sell (and do not sell) on eBay. Way back when there were covered wagons, eBay pioneers would post listings with titles like this, "L@@K! Awesome Nike Blue Cotton Medium T-Shirt (Not Adidas/ Puma/Reebok)." The exclamation "L@@K" is popular, old school, useless, and a waste of precious and limited title space. Plus, adding unrelated brand names is prohibited by eBay. Buyers and brand owners retorted, and eBay put the kibosh on this practice, which is now forbidden under eBay's search manipulation policy.

The brand names, categories, item specifics and details, and pictures in your listing must faithfully represent what you're selling. If you are trying to slip something in that's not compliant, another eBayer will report the listing, or eBay will find the listing and end it. eBay's policy states, "Manipulating eBay's search and browse experience by adding popular keywords in your listings that don't have any relation to your items, or using other tactics that could mislead buyers, is not allowed." The involuntary ending of a listing will put a black mark on your record, and too many of those marks will most certainly result in a suspension, possibly a permanent one. If that occurs, you will never be allowed to sell on eBay again.

eBay's VeRO program enforces the rights of brand and copyright owners. It also manages potential infringement of the rights of those owners. The VeRO team reviews listings to ensure they are legally complaint. Respecting property owners' rights is at the core of what makes eBay a safe trading platform. Here's what you need to do to stay in the good graces of the VeRO team:

▶ Create your own listing content

▶ Use the eBay Product Catalog to create your listing when it's appropriate

▶ Make sure the statements in your listing are accurate

▶ Use brand names appropriately

▶ Review the VeRO participant profiles created by intellectual property rights owners

The high-level overview of what VeRO polices includes:

▶ Trademark claims involving user ID, eBay Store name, and item or listing infringement, such as counterfeit goods or the improper use of a trademark

▶ Copyright claims for unlawful copy of text, images, and counterfeit products or, in the case of opened software (not new and sealed), violations of enforceable license agreements

▶ Patent infringement claims

▶ Design rights infringement (applicable only in Europe, Asia, Australia, and New Zealand)

▶ Violations of a celebrity's right of publicity

I'd be very surprised if you never get "VeRO-ed." If you list enough items, the possibility of that occurring is pretty good. For example, in 2016 I purchased a six-pack of KeySmart KeyCatch, a modern marvel of elegant and simple engineering. The KeyCatch replaces the bottom screw on any light switch cover and holds your car keys magnetically. I stopped misplacing mine, that's for sure. I didn't need six of them, so I installed two and listed the other four on eBay. KeySmart is very protective of their brand and immediately filed a VeRO complaint, thinking the product was infringing. As is my right, I filed a counter-claim and notified VeRO the product was not only genuine, but that I had a receipt for it. VeRO restored my listing and interestingly, KeySmart management bought the four KeyCatch magnets. I presume they wanted to make sure they were indeed real. I also received an apology from them.

If anyone steals your pictures, graphics, or copyrighted materials, including your listing text, you can report them for the infringement, and you *should*. You simply download VeRO's Notice of Claimed Infringement and fill out the form and email it to vero@ebay.com. Everything you put on the form is under oath and under penalty of perjury, so take it very seriously, or you may face civil or possibly criminal action if you're not truthful. Use Figure 5–2's QR code for easy access.

FIGURE 5–2: **VeRO's Notice of Claimed Infringement Form**

eBay Product Images

Before we venture into preparing and managing listings, let's talk about product images.

Working Smarter Using Stock Images

There are millions of known consumer products, and databases that keep track of stock product images. Why reinvent the wheel? For items within eBay's catalog, you don't even need a camera to provide photos. All you need to know is the UPC, ISBN, or part number. In many cases, the catalog information can be pulled up with keywords. eBay's catalog will instantly add product information, such as brand, model number, dimensions, color, capacity, compatibilities, and even professional photos. Sellers of books, DVDs, Blu-ray discs, computer games, and many other categories need never take their own pictures. If you routinely sell merchandise that's in the eBay catalog, I'd recommend installing and using the eBay mobile app, which allows you to launch, edit, and manage listings quickly using the UPC barcode. I do not recommend the mobile app for more complex businesses involving items that have no UPC code and are used or collectible.

Superb Product Photography

When you're not using the eBay catalog or when what you're selling is in the catalog but looks less than factory perfect, you'll need to take photos of the actual product you're selling. When capturing photos, consider a resolution size that is at least 1600 pixels on the shortest edge. If you have a phone that allows for the square aspect ratio popular on social media sites, that's even better. In that case, your photos will be 1600x1600 pixels. Use a JPG (or JPEG) file format. eBay's picture policy requires photos that are at least 500 pixels for the longest side, but this is far too low for today's high-resolution screens.

You are allotted 12 complimentary photos for nearly every category except eBay Motors vehicle listings. Vehicle listings may have up to 24 pictures because vehicles are complex and big-ticket items. Even real estate listings are limited to 12 images. Don't just throw the item on the floor and snap a quick picture. A photo of high heels on your washing machine isn't sexy. A necklace lying on top of your dirty jeans is going to scare the eBayer and have them heading over to the next seller's listings. Show your product in the best way possible. Get every angle needed. That said, don't go crazy. A vintage video game cartridge in mint condition simply doesn't require 12 photos. In fact, I don't feel 12 photos are usually required for most product listings. You'll know when you've mastered the art of posting just the right number of images when no one asks for additional images and your items are flying out the door in nicely packed boxes. Look to other successful eBayers for ideas on which photos you'll need.

Here are some suggestions:

▶ When the product is vintage, collectible, or antique, take lots of pictures because collectors are discriminating, and you'll stand out from the crowd if you do.

▶ If you're selling a vehicle, max out the 24-photo allocation.

▶ For known products in mint or new condition, you simply don't need a bunch of photos.

▶ When in doubt, err on the side of more photos rather than fewer—with the understanding that you will eventually only capture the "right" number as you become more experienced.

Figure 5–3 on page 82 shows my images from an actual eBay listing—Arthur Wellesley, First Duke of Wellington and two-time British Prime Minister, immortalized in bronze. His Grace left this earth in 1834; however, his likeness lives on. This bronze is a true antique. There are a lot of markings, and all of them needed to be shown to the buyers. I was careful not to remove the very old auction sticker, which adds interest, provenance, and value. Pretty cool item, huh? eBay is the spot for interesting stuff. You'll notice that the primary photo has thumbnail images in a ribbon underneath it—scrolling through and clicking these thumbnails displays the clicked image. You'll also notice from the thumbnails that I've captured many views of the bust for clarity and to help bidders make a decision. This bronze sold for $2,495!

I've had cameras since I was a pre-teen, and owning a camera didn't make me any more of a photographer than having a toolbox made me an auto mechanic. Developing an eye for photography wasn't so much an art as it was a process. In my opinion, I'm not the most creative individual, and I always thrive when I can accomplish tasks that involve predictable actions. I much prefer a repeatable way of doing things. When I started my eBay business in June of 1999, I used a Mavica for photography. The Sony Mavica was the first still video camera invented and stored about 50 photos on a removable 1.4MB floppy disk. It still amuses me to recall how long it took to save the photo once I captured it. The disk would chug along until all of the Bytes were written to the magnetic floppy.

These days, I can store so many high-resolution photos on a tiny SD card that I could shoot a warehouse full of stuff before having to change cards. It's amazing! Today's cameras take much better photographs than ever before. The image sensors these days are much more like the human eye and require far less light and user expertise than in years past. Even a smart phone camera is a powerful image-capturing tool. If you own a quality smartphone, then you're all set. A phone takes really good pictures provided you

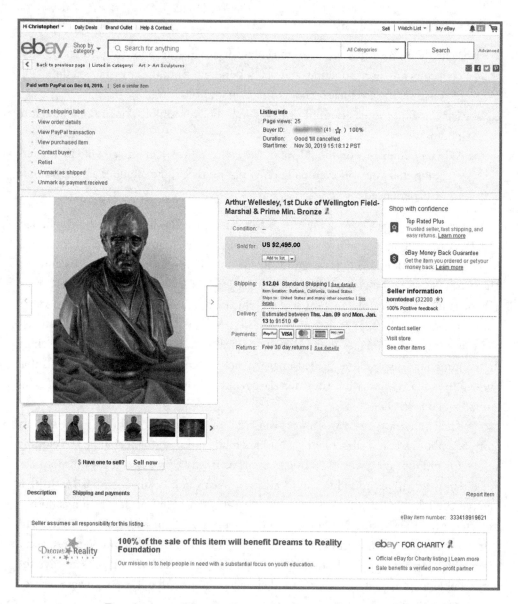

FIGURE 5–3: **eBay Listing Photos for an Arthur Wellesley Bronze Bust**

have good lighting and excellent staging. I'm using a consumer-level Nikon DSLR and strobe photography for most of my listings. Way back in 1999, I spent over $3,000 on lighting equipment, and you know what? I didn't need it. If I knew then what I know now, I would have made do with what I had. Great lighting can be had for dollars, not thousands of dollars. Great images can also be captured without lighting equipment by using indirect light. I sometimes set up a folding table, put a nice velvet tablecloth on it, and just shoot during a really overcast day. Direct sunlight is bad because it creates uneven and unprofessional lighting due to the sun's powerful glare. When shooting indoors, there are loads of solutions available designed for online sellers. Turnkey products include lights and backgrounds for extremely affordable prices.

Here are some pro photography tips:

- ▶ Work with what you've got. If you don't have a lot of money, make do.
- ▶ Use a plain background, and don't put items in the picture unless they are actually part of what's being offered. Flowers and fruit are OK, but random props might confuse the buyer as to what you're actually including in the offering. Exceptions will include products that require props, displays or mannequins such as jewelry or clothing.
- ▶ If using natural light, be sure the area is well-lit. You can use large pieces of white cardboard to bounce available light to provide soft and diffused lighting. Lots of indirect light is good.
- ▶ If you don't have steady hands, it's OK to use a tripod. They're very cheap and having one handy won't hurt. If there's a ton of available light, you won't need one because the shutter will open and close so fast, the image won't suffer any blur. If the light is low, the shutter speed slows down, requiring a tripod.
- ▶ Use a resolution that makes sense. Massive resolution is overkill, so pick a setting that will provide nice, large images, but won't take forever to upload. Optimize your technique to avoid having to crop and resize pictures.
- ▶ Keep things in focus.
- ▶ Photos cannot have marketing text or artwork added to them. Logos or messages are not permitted. A watermark for ownership or attribution is not allowed.
- ▶ Stock photography is only allowed when selling new items and is not permitted for used, damaged, or defective merchandise.
- ▶ Fill the frame—don't have an itty bitty product sitting in an ocean of props and/or backdrop.
- ▶ Show measurement or scale using a coin or ruler. In addition to providing a scale shot, include the product measurements in the description. Show size for rings using a ring sizer, and clearly state the size, provide length for bracelets, pins, earrings, necklaces, etc. To cover global audiences, provide the measurements in both inches and centimeters.
- ▶ Capture the details, and don't hide the warts. Hiding flaws means costly returns.
- ▶ Turn off the built-in flash, as it can leave hot spots and reflections.

▶ Keep everything meticulously clean—avoiding lint, fingerprints, dust, and dirt. Wear lint-free gloves and have microfiber cloths handy to quickly remove fingerprints. A mini shop vacuum is perfect for the photography area.

▶ Provide clear photographs of the maker's marks; gold or silver purity marks (sterling, 14k, etc.); or make, model, serial number, etc.

▶ It's OK to crop the photo or adjust the brightness, but do not use software to doctor your pictures to make them look better than the actual product will appear in person.

Merchandise moves faster when the presentation is gorgeous. Tossing a pair of jeans on a table isn't very alluring. A necklace in a pile isn't attractive. Some items require props for the best presentation. This is very different than adding a bowl of fruit in a shot of a coffee table. "Are you selling the bowl and fruit with that winsome table?" Some things require support or propping up to display them in the correct perspective or to give them appeal. Sometimes I stuff a bit of tissue into shoes, handbags, or the arms of shirts to give them a more pleasing look. In time, you'll master the process of capturing fantastic images.

eBay provides practical photography tips, and I've provided a QR code (Figure 5–4) that will take you directly to them.

In Chapter 6, we'll talk in detail about how to prepare your eBay listings.

FIGURE 5–4: **eBay's Photo Tips**

It's Best to Be Fully Dressed

For many years, a photograph has been circulating of a shiny chrome teapot (the holy grail of teapots) with the reflection of the eBay seller caught flashing his flesh. I mean, really, how is this not on purpose? A quick Google search will reveal the vintage image that's been the mother of memes for years. Perhaps he thought that nudity would raise the bid prices.

Droves of eBayers pushed the limits of good taste with copycat pictures hocking antiques using bare-skinned antics. Another eBayer based in the U.K. accidentally took a nude selfie while posting her eBay listing for an ASOS skater outfit—she staged the outfit on a hanger hooked onto her closet door and a bit of mirror revealed that she had only her brassiere on and nothing else. The racy image induced over £100,000 in bidding before the eBayer pulled the listing.

Don't chase these sellers down the rabbit hole. eBay subsequently established policies that forbid these antics. Be sure that you're wearing neutral clothing with no logos when working with shiny items—but most importantly, wear clothes! Reflective items and colored clothing are like oil and water. The last thing you want is a slew of questions about that "red mark" on your resale flat screen. A white or light gray shirt seems right for most situations. To minimize reflections, you can cut a hole in a large white or black cardboard sheet and shoot through the hole. For shiny silver items, I find white works well. Black tends to work for colorful glass items. Experiment to find the best solution.

Setting Up Your eBay Listings

I n this chapter, we'll enhance what you just learned in Chapter 5 and get into the actual listing and management of items on eBay. You'll want to be sure you have thought about the following before you get into the work of creating actual listings:

▶ What photos you'll need. You can have up to 12 for most items and up to 24 photos for eBay Motors vehicle listings.

▶ Well-considered keywords for your listing title that will attract the most buyers possible.

▶ Tracking your inventory with the optional custom label feature. (The custom label field allows you to enter information you want to track, such as your own SKU number. It's only visible to you.)

▶ The ideal eBay category and sub-category if desired (remember there is an additional insertion fee for the secondary category).

▶ The item condition—be truthful but not overly negative.

▶ Item specifics, which vary by category. These are details about the item you're selling, such as style, size, color, and brand. Item specifics appear at the top of your listing description.

▶ The item description.

▶ The ideal selling format for what you're selling (auction vs. fixed price, etc.).

▶ The item starting price for an auction-style listing, or the fixed price you'd be happy to receive.

▶ Your returns policy.

▶ Packing and shipping methods and whether you'll be shipping internationally or to U.S. customers only.

I'll shine a light on each of these topics in more detail, and for the most part, these subject areas cover every data point you'll be handling when you list an item on eBay. If you are simply overwhelmed with enthusiasm and want to play around with eBay's listing form, you can access it by clicking the "Sell" link on the top of most eBay pages, and from there, click "Create listing" to begin listing an item. I've structured this chapter to follow the sequence of fields you will fill out when you list an item so that you can later use the book as a guide when listing.

Listing Title

Writing compelling eBay titles and descriptions is critical to the success of your eBay business. It involves practice and study so that you attract quality, relevant buyers. Because the eBay title uses keywords instead of sentences, your selection of words for your titles needs to be spot-on. The system has a search engine, and buyers find the merchandise that matches their keywords. I'll be covering how to write powerful titles and descriptions that deliver results. In this section, we'll focus on titles, and later on, I'll discuss descriptions.

Put yourself in the shoes of the buyer and think of the keywords they might use to find your listing.

Titles are limited to 80 characters, while descriptions can be as long as is required, so don't become cranky if you can't fit everything you want to say in your title.

Selection of keywords for titles can be broken down into three parts: the bones, the meat, and the feathers.

OK, I'm using just a little bit of fowl humor in this chapter. The bones of an eBay title provide the absolutely essential keywords, such as the brand name, artist, or designer and a basic description of the item.

The following would be three examples of bare-bones titles:

▶ Samsung Blu-ray Player (22 characters)
▶ LeRoy Neiman Serigraph (22 characters)
▶ Chanel Messenger Bag (20 characters)

Adding meat provides item-specific information such as size, color, condition, model number, and other important searchable keywords.

Let me expand my three examples by adding some meat to their bones:

1. New Samsung BD-F7500/ZA Smart 3D Blu-ray Player with UHD 4K Upscaling (69 characters)
2. LeRoy Neiman Prima Ballerina Open Edition Serigraph (51 characters)
3. New in Box Autumn 2014 Chanel Le Boy Black Caviar Messenger Bag (63 characters)

The addition of item specifics significantly increases the possibility that a buyer will discover these items when searching eBay. You may recall from Chapter 4 that item specifics are additional information about the item that you can add when you list it. Each eBay category has unique item specifics. They elevate the titles because when a search is conducted on eBay, the displayed search results include the data within the item specifics fields. For example, if you sell a man's suit, there is an item specific for many aspects of the suit, including material, size, color, country of tailoring, measurements, and more. The correct use of item specifics means you can avoid including that information in your title while still having the benefit of discoverability. For example, there's no need to add the color of the suit in the title because you will add it within the item specifics.

Each of the example titles still has room left over. When research and imagination have identified every potentially relevant keyword for your listing title, you can add some feathers. Feathers are fluffy and attractive and add appeal. Plus, they help birds soar to great heights, but in the context of your eBay title, they are an exciting addition to your listing. This being said, the meat and bones must always come first and take priority. I added some feathers to our titles, and here they are:

- ▶ Awesome New Samsung BD-F7500/ZA Smart 3D Blu-ray Player with UHD 4K Upscaling (77 characters)
- ▶ Gorgeous & Vivid LeRoy Neiman Prima Ballerina Open Edition Serigraph (68 characters)
- ▶ Scarce & Sexy New in Box Autumn 2014 Chanel Le Boy Black Caviar Messenger Bag (77 characters)

Here are some tips you can follow when creating your own product listing titles:

- ▶ Be sure your title describes the product even if it repeats the category name.
- ▶ Titles should not contain plurals, except in situations where the product comes in pairs, such as gloves, skis, shoes, and so on. Plurals and synonyms are no longer required because eBay's search is smart and handles this seamlessly.
- ▶ Avoid using punctuation, which takes up space and is not recommended. Don't use special, foreign, or gimmicky characters.
- ▶ Ensure that you're spelling correctly.
- ▶ Avoid using ALL CAPS, which is not elegant and is like YELLING. You may use all-caps text if appropriate, e.g., acronyms of countries, like USA, and brand names, such as IBM.
- ▶ Acronyms are to be avoided are abbreviations and contractions.
- ▶ Keyword spamming is not allowed, so your title must describe the actual product and not refer to competitive brands or include promotional text or irrelevant search terms that are intended only to increase "hits."
- ▶ The title may not contain URLs, emails, or phone numbers. You may mention a URL only if you're selling a domain.
- ▶ Avoid foreign language words unless they are common and well understood or form the actual product name.
- ▶ Never use profane or obscene language.

You'll discover many sellers using common acronyms. When an abbreviation is ubiquitous, it's OK to use if it is absolutely clear and understood. Many of the acronyms of eBay yesteryear have become obsolete because of eBay's use of item specifics, which serve the same purpose. Item specifics can be filtered upon after a buyer enters keywords into an eBay search box. MIB is Mint in Box, and NIB is New in Box. NWT describes new with tags. I'd steer clear of using these too much (after all, not every eBay buyer will know the lingo). If you can fully spell something out, you should. Some exceptions exist in certain categories. For example, in cut glass where niche collectors are likely to search an acronym and save that search to discover very specific items. For example, ABP is commonly used to identify listings for American Brilliant Period cut glass. It's debatable if a master's degree in acronym usage will really convert more sales. Common sense works well for me.

Expanding on my earlier comment about keyword spamming compels me to mention some exceptions to the use of brand names. While you may never add the word Tiffany to a listing offering a Chanel necklace, if you're selling a generic brand smartphone cable, you may identify all brands that are compatible with it. This eBay rule is quite liberal. If you assembled Coke cans into a cool model airplane, you could certainly mention the Coke brand in your title and description. When listing something that's fully compatible and functional with a brand-name product, be sure to add the keywords "Compatible With," "Fits," or "For."

Here are three examples:

1. New Toner Compatible With HP LaserJet 1018 Printer MFC
2. New Multi-Media AM/FM Radio CD & DVD Player Fits BMW 5 Series Cars
3. New Pur Brand F4PC6C1 Filter For Maytag UKF8001 and 4396395 Refrigerator

While colorful adjectives describing your product are great, give attention to the essential keywords before adding them into your title. I used to recommend against the use of adjectives in titles, but after title limits were expanded from 55 to 80 characters, I changed my mind and practices.

Product Category

One of the delights of the Harry Potter books is the enchanted hat that once belonged to Godric Gryffindor and sorts students into houses at Hogwarts. Sorting your products into the correct eBay category doesn't require magic, just a bit of thought and experience. In Chapter 5, I shared my thoughts on category selection, but I have a few more remarks about this process here.

Any time you begin a listing, the form asks if you'd like to use a UPC, ISBN, ePID, part number, or product name and (after entering identifiable information) the catalog can search and find what it believes are products that may match yours. If yours is exactly the same as what's presented at this step, then selecting from the eBay catalog will also relieve you of having to select a category. You can browse the category structure if you're brave—the number is thousands and thousands. Recently used categories are also presented. If you don't use the eBay catalog, as you enter your listing title, eBay will deploy artificial intelligence to suggest possible categories. Quite often they are correct, but many times they are not. Being extra careful about category selection will improve sales.

Product Variations

Save yourself time and money by using the "variations" option available in select eBay categories. By using variations, you are given the ability to sell different items that are very similar or closely related in one combined listing. This is particularly useful and relevant if you sell new goods with different styles, sizes, colors, etc. The obvious product would be clothing because you have many different sizes in the same style and color. Perhaps you sell a fragrance in three sizes or a fishing hat in ten different colors. Variations are available only on fixed-price listings, and I should point out that the listing type can be changed at any time while adding a new listing on eBay.

Making a single listing with variations saves typing. When an eBayer discovers your cool hand-carved wood keychain, they'll be able to buy it in oak, cherry, maple, ebony, birch, or basswood—all from the very same listing. It's convenient and saves the buyer from having to look at a bunch of other listings. When they'd like to buy a bunch of cool stocking stuffers, everything they need is in your one listing. Each member of the family receives something different. Listings with variations allow you to track inventory for the items so that you're not caught short.

Subject to change, here's the list of eBay categories that currently support variations:

- ► Art
- ► Baby
- ► Business & Industrial
- ► Cameras & Photo
- ► Cell Phones & Accessories
- ► Clothing, Shoes, & Accessories
- ► Collectibles
- ► Computers/Tablets & Networking
- ► Consumer Electronics
- ► Crafts
- ► Dolls & Bears
- ► DVDs & Movies
- ► Entertainment Memorabilia
- ► Everything Else

▶ Gift Cards & Coupons

▶ Health & Beauty

▶ Home & Garden

▶ Jewelry & Watches

▶ Music

▶ Musical Instruments & Gear

▶ Pet Supplies

▶ Sporting Goods

▶ Sports Mem, Cards, & Fan Shop

▶ Toys & Hobbies

▶ Travel

▶ Video Games & Consoles

Within variations, you can specify size, color, style, and material. eBay allows each listing to have five variation details and up to 60 values for each of those details. Save big money on insertion fees. The price for each variation can be different, but the payment and shipping options must be the same across all variations. Each separate variation supports 12 complimentary photos. Be sure to verify your stock when listing and relisting. If the items you offer on eBay are also offered in your retail store or online elsewhere, either consider a multichannel selling tool (not covered in this book for many reasons), or be really organized and use Excel or a ledger for tracking inventory levels. This can be a daunting task.

Product Condition

New is new. If what you are selling is new, there's no need to spell out the condition. The Books category has five condition levels, which are: brand new, like new, very good, good, and acceptable. Grading old vinyl records is more art than science. I stopped offering opinions about record sleeves after being scolded more than a few times by diehard collectors who apparently know their stuff. Tires can be new, retreaded, used, and damaged—all are acceptable eBay condition descriptions.

When listing, you'll be asked to include the condition in your product listing. Anything but *new* warrants an explanation, and there's an additional box for that. Some categories require you to mention condition, and some do not. Antiques generally do not require you to select a condition because they are, by default, never new. You can sell "new old stock" aka unused vintage or antique items; however, eBay does not require you to clarify the condition on these items.

There's a balance between being honest and being painful. If the photos do a wonderful job of showing the condition, you can provide a brief and honestly-worded account of the condition as an enhancement. If the toaster oven doesn't heat up, you'll need to mention it because photos don't explain a crucial detail like that. The point is to set reasonable expectations about the item's condition. Under-promise and over-deliver. That's much better than having to deal with a claim and unfavorable feedback. How you word things makes a difference. Rather than saying, "The vase has issues and is scratched up all over the base and is not in perfect condition," you can say, "Wonderful condition considering it's over 100 years old. There is notable wear to the base of the vase from years of use. However, you'll never notice this because it's only on the bottom." Think like a salesperson and talk up the positive aspect of what you're selling. The QR code in Figure 6–1 will help you define item condition by category.

FIGURE 6–1: **Item Condition by Category**

Item Specifics

The item specifics are a series of fields you'll be asked to fill in for your listing. In many categories, these are mandatory fields such as brand names for clothing or electronics. You simply cannot proceed with the listing until you accurately answer the required item specifics questions. There are optional item specifics you can elect to enter that improve your probability of being discovered during an eBay search. The item specifics you enter are displayed at the top of your item description, and they clarify what you're selling and improve buyer confidence. Fill in as many item specifics as you can answer. Some products warrant loads of item-specific information, such as car parts. Other items, however, need fewer, such as jewelry. Figures 6–2 and 6–3, each on page 95, are a couple of examples of the quantity of item specifics warranted based on the item in question.

Item specifics

Condition:	New	Interchange Part Number::	HL3Z*3600*AA
Type:	Steering Wheel	Year:	2017 2018
Features:	Cruise Control, Radio Control	Bundle Listing:	No
Manufacturer Part Number:	HL3Z-3600-AA	Interchange Part Number:	HL3Z*3600*AA
Placement on Vehicle:	Front	Model:	F-150 Raptor
Other Part Number:	HL3Z3600AA	Notes:	Leather Red Accent Non-heated Non Adaptive Cruise
Brand:	Ford	Primary Color:	Red Accents
Fitment Type:	Direct Replacement	Make:	Ford
Warranty:	2 Year	UPC:	Does not apply

FIGURE 6–2: **Sample Item Specifics for a Replacement Ford F150 Steering Wheel**

Item specifics

Metal:	Sterling Silver	Material:	Silver
Metal Purity:	925 Sterling Silver	Brand:	Handmade
Main Stone:	Diamond	Country/Region of Manufacture:	United States

FIGURE 6–3: **Sample Item Specifics for a Sterling Silver and Diamond Pendant**

To maximize the benefits of using item specifics, remember two key points. First, refine and clarify your listing by telling buyers more about your items within the item specifics. This understanding increases and improves discoverability during searches. Then, provide all the item-specific information you can answer and be sure to use eBay's recommended items specifics.

Product Description

The description is a stage where you need to deliver your best performance. It's romance or substance and typically a little of both. Writing eBay descriptions can be artsy or technical but should rarely become long and clunky. You're telling a very short story with the emphasis on *short*. Can there be exceptions? Of course there can! A scientist searching for used laboratory testing equipment might expect (and would probably appreciate) a thorough explanation of the device's condition and function—something that might require a high word count. While eBay includes titles in searches, the product description is only added to the search if the eBay member asks that the description be included. This additional search capability requires the buyer to tick off the additional box, "Include description," which only appears after the initial search. It is so tiny, you'll miss it if you blink. Seasoned buyers are expert at searching descriptions, so include helpful keywords here that you weren't able to fit in your item's title.

Tailor your descriptions to what you sell. To help jumpstart the process of creating a product description, I've summarized products into these key categories:

▶ Aspirational

▶ Luxury

▶ Collectible

▶ Commodity

▶ Necessity

▶ Your Voice

From the street bazaar to Rodeo Drive, merchants must communicate with their customers in a unique way, depending on the circumstances. Oftentimes, the type of merchandise being sold determines the style of communication.

Aspirational

An aspirational product speaks to an audience that wishes to own it but the supply is scarce, and the potential number of individuals who can afford it is small. These are products that appear inside the pages of fashion magazines and are represented by gorgeous models. Aspirational products are jewelry, fragrances, apparel, accessories, eyewear, or footwear. I'd also consider a Ferrari an aspirational product, and you certainly can find them on eBay.

Here is an example of an aspirational product, and its proper description:

Title: *Hermes Birkin 40cm Clemence Vert Leather Palladium Hardware "O" Stamp Bag Purse*

Description: *You're anything but the typical. You're graceful, in charge, and living life . . . beautifully. You deserve to carry a handbag that tells the world who, what, and where you are . . . in your life. This Hermes is not only authentic, but it's in mint condition.*

- *11-½" high x 9" deep x 16" wide*

- *Genuine leather in sweet tones of green with muted gray*

- *Silver-tone hardware—lock and key*

- *The original dust bag is intact*

- *Unconditional money-back guarantee within 30 days of receipt*

This approach caters to a consumer who aspires to—but probably never actually achieves—the fashion, beauty, and physical ideals this purse represents. Aspirational fantasies drive these buyers to purchase these products. An aspirational brand and its products bring premium prices. A product that's truly aspirational in nature should not require Best Offer or endless haggling to place it into the customer's hands.

Luxury

A luxury (or upmarket) product may be aspirational, but the marketing strategy speaks more to the ego than emotion. The approach may feel similar, but think about products like expensive watches, designer baby strollers, crystal-studded phone cases, and products that are functional but designed for a wealthier audience.

Sharp sellers position aspirational and luxury goods with a lexicon that evokes a strong response and engages shoppers with their messaging.

Here is an example of a luxury item along with a description that befits it:

Title: *New Patek Philippe Man's Watch Model 3940P Platinum Perpetual Calendar*

Description: *It's flawless, handsome, and rugged in solid platinum with a genuine crocodile leather band. It's brand new and in the original box. A statement of your success and functional as a dress or casual timepiece. Luxury all the way.*

- *Mechanical: Automatic*
- *Display: Analog*
- *Model Number: 3940P-011*
- *Gender: Man's*
- *Features date, day, and moon phase*
- *Water-resistant to 25M*
- *33mm across the face*
- *9" long including the band*
- *Accompanied by the original store receipt for a doubt-free transaction*
- *Returns permitted within 30 days if unopened in the original package; no returns permitted if opened and used*

All warranties provided by the manufacturer must be claimed through them. For confirmation of authenticity, the serial number is 84751402.

At first glance, the luxury goods category feels aspiration, but it is quite different. The luxury goods industry is steadily growing—catering to wealthy (but not wealthy elite) audiences. Luxury goods are available widely and at mass retailers, while aspirational brands are generally sold in high-end boutiques and appointment-only stores.

Collectible

Collectible buyers are interesting. They are endlessly knowledgeable. They can be very price sensitive. Many are bargain hunters, but even the biggest miser of a stamp collector will pony up their last cent to acquire a mint condition 1930 Graf Zeppelin U.S. postage stamp. They are not swayed by flowery language, and you will find that crafting a listing for collectible item buyers provides a stark contrast to listings designed for aspirational and luxury products. Focus on the item specifics and condition.

Here is an example of a collectible item and its fitting description:

Title: *Antique ABP American Brilliant Period Stoppered Cut Glass Cruet*

Description: *This fine cruet is a true period piece, not a reproduction. It is made from a heavy blank. Rings with life when gently finger-tapped. Excellent condition. I don't speak of terms like "near mint" with true antique ABP glass, but the condition is remarkable, and I see no evidence of repairs or restoration of any kind.*

- *Net weight: 15.72 oz*
- *Height with stopper 7" exactly, without it measures 5-¼"*
- *The base is 2-¾" in diameter*
- *The neck has an outer diameter of 1-½"*
- *There is a 1mm x 2mm nick on the base, and I have provided a photo with a ruler for confirmation*
- *No heat checks, cracks, or chips of any other kind were observed*
- *30-day total satisfaction money-back guarantee with free return shipping*

Collectors seek out and acquire items they believe will help them form a greater understanding and deeper appreciation for those collectibles. Their craving is greatest when they perceive that their acquisition will create an increased synergistic value when combined with other similar items (e.g., being able to complete set of trading cards, collector plates, figurines, and so forth). Collectors are not easily "sold," have high standards, and admire sellers with high integrity.

Commodity

Commodity items have a relatively clear and predictable price and are offered by many sellers. Fierce competition also means lower margins. You'll have to differentiate yourself to be seen among the vast ocean of sellers. While a commodity does not have to be a necessity, the buyer is price shopping and comparing carefully. That eBayer is looking for a killer deal on the latest generation Xbox for a teenager's birthday present. She knows what she wants and how much she'll pay. A wordy description is a turn-off. Seconds count because she's in a hurry and barely reading the description. Seller feedback, item condition, and returns policy matter more than a romantic explanation of the features and benefits. You're selling brands and explaining what's in the box. Measurements are far less important than a sealed package.

Here is an example of a commodity item and its respective description:

Title: *New Basics Polaroid Z340 Instant Digital Color Camera with ZINK*

Description: *Polaroid's Z340 is an instant color digital camera that outputs photos immediately with ZINK (Zero Ink) technology. Pictures are captured and printed immediately without a computer or ink cartridge. The internal software adds delightful borders that personalize your printed memories. It even offers editing software for corrections in real-time.*

- *Polaroid part number: 0815361015675*
- *SD card slot*
- *Prints 3" x 4" photographs*
- *14 megapixels for sharpness*
- *2.7" high-resolution LCD viewer*
- *Product dimensions: 4.9" x 3" x 5.5"*
- *Requires four AA batteries, which are included*
- *Factory U.S. warranty offered directly from Polaroid*
- *I am an authorized dealer and will provide you with a purchase receipt for peace-of-mind returns allowed within 30 days if the seal is not broken.*

Commodity buyers seek no-nonsense sellers and competitive terms. It is very challenging to compete in the sale of basic, undifferentiated, commodity items. While service and support is always crucial, the commodity customer makes purchase decisions based on price. Market leaders are generally the best on cost in this field—the most efficient, low-price sellers win the day here.

Necessity

Necessity buyers are practically twins with commodity customers. The difference is that they're filling a need. While all of the other types of customers are probably good with waiting until they win an auction, necessity buyers prefer fixed-price listings that can be had today. They have no time or patience for extra words or auctions. Tell them how large or small, the color, and the condition. Keep it direct and simple: The make and model number. They know all the brands, and while they are open to buying what they need in a compatible product, brand names rule and generally are the keywords being searched. They need that printer ink this second, the truck tire now, and that showerhead yesterday.

Here is an example of a necessity item and a description that would appeal to its buyers:

Title: *New 15-Count Gillette Mach3 Base Cartridges*

Description: *If you're new to the Mach3, it is Gillette's tried-and-true triple-blade technology for a super-close shave and no bumps or redness.*

- *Three high-definition blades for glide and comfort*
- *Flexible comfort guard with five-micro fins*
- *Lubricating indicator strip tells you when it's time for a replacement*
- *I ship to the U.S. only*
- *All product is fresh, sealed, and completely genuine*
- *There are 15 razor cartridges in this listing, all sold together for one price*
- *Free 1.5 oz Gillette series sensitive shaving gel*
- *No returns on personal care products*

Have you ever paid too much for a product (such as batteries) because you simply had to have it immediately? A necessity buyer is looking for speedy shipping and a reputable seller. There's no margin for error. Everything must align perfectly with what they require.

Your Voice

As with all writing, practice makes perfect, and over time, you'll discover your writing "voice." It's in there, just let it out. Start typing. There's no right way to do what you love.

Here are some of my recommendations when describing your items:

- ▶ Place the most important details first and cover them right away
- ▶ Talk about condition again—particularly crucial if the eBay category you're using does not require a condition to be mentioned
- ▶ Provide dimensions in inches—feel free to also include metric (just for fun, type "convert one inch to centimeters" directly into a Google search box and see what comes up)

- ▶ Provide sizes for rings, clothing, shoes, and anything with a size aspect
- ▶ Include the brand name again in the description for clarity
- ▶ Provide the make and model when appropriate
- ▶ Identify materials (e.g., is it genuine leather or faux leather?)
- ▶ Explain the color even if it's clear from your photos
- ▶ Mention any flaws
- ▶ Cover provenance and age
- ▶ Point out the features
- ▶ State the country of manufacture when known
- ▶ Talk about what will be included and what won't (a lost power cord may not hurt you that badly since they are usually cheap to buy on eBay, so mention it)
- ▶ Talk about international shipping
- ▶ Leave out irrelevant information
- ▶ Be completely truthful but never negative
- ▶ Discuss returns options if you allow them
- ▶ Don't include links or email addresses—unless the link merely points to a product manual or a non-commercial web page with specifications about the item
- ▶ Give yourself limits—while eBay may not limit the length of your description, you certainly should keep things brief, relevant, and to-the-point
- ▶ Provide a backstory for collectible items where possible, but not fiction, and mention certificates of authenticity because they might just seal the deal

tip

While a Pulitzer may not be in your immediate future, write comfortably and be faithful to your own voice. Put yourself in the buyer's shoes and consider what you'd deem important when making the same purchase. Put that in your listing, and packages will be flying out the door in no time.

Listing Format and Pricing

At this point in your eBay listing journey, you'll be faced with a couple of key decisions. As you may recall, the topics in this chapter flow in a particular sequence to mirror the data fields you'll be faced with when adding your listing. Now is the time to select your format and set your item pricing. You recall we discussed selling formats in-depth within Chapter 1. Let's examine some scenarios and decide which format to use: the "when" and "why" of eBay selling formats. I'll mention my preferred selling format and suggested fixed- or starting-price strategy for each of the listing examples I provided earlier in this chapter.

Hermes Birkin 40cm Clemence Vert Leather Palladium Hardware "O" Stamp Bag Purse

This purse has a value that's well-known; however, there is still an opportunity for the price to climb. Inventory is limited, and the brand is elite. My recommendations are:

► Format: auction-style.
► Starting price: very close to the fair market value, protecting your investment while leaving an opportunity for the price to increase.
► Duration: either seven or ten days.
► Shipping: make it free since the shipping is trivial as compared to the value of the item, and it will be discoverable when buyers look for free shipping listings
► If your listing is not successful, try relisting it one more time using the same starting price.
► If two auction-style listings don't result in a sale, try converting to a fixed-price listing with the Make Offer feature enabled to allow buyers to haggle with you on the price.

New Patek Philippe Men's Watch Model 3940P Platinum Perpetual Calendar

► Format: auction-style.
► Starting price: very close to the fair market value.
► Duration: either seven or ten days.
► Shipping: make it free.
► If your listing is not successful, try relisting it one more time using the same starting price.
► If two auction-style listings don't result in a sale, try converting to a fixed-price listing with the make offer feature enabled to allow buyers to haggle with you on the price.

Antique ABP American Brilliant Period Stoppered Cut Glass Cruet

► Format: auction-style.
► Starting price: very close to the fair market value. However, for antique glass, fair market value is merely an opinion, and the starting price depends on condition, the pattern of the piece, the current buyer tastes in the marketplace, and many unknown factors—be careful and conservative. After all, there should be no hurry selling it. Start high, and work your way down if needed.

- Duration: either seven or ten days.
- Shipping: charge actual shipping. Antique buyers are a different breed and realize you have to jack up prices to offer free shipping anyway.
- If your listing is not successful, try relisting it one more time using the same starting price.
- If two auction-style listings don't result in a sale, try converting to a fixed-price listing with the make offer features enabled to allow buyers to haggle with you on the price.

Antique items are hard to value and can sit for months or years before the right buyer comes along. Don't let your valuable antique walk off for a song. Be patient, and the right buyer will come along and pay a fair price.

New Basics Polaroid Z340 Instant Digital Color Camera with ZINK

- Format: fixed price with the make offer feature enabled, and it's OK to list multiples within the same listing.
- Price: fair market value and not the lowest price from your research.
- Duration: Good 'til Canceled.
- Shipping: start off charging shipping, and if it doesn't move out in a month or so, change it to free shipping.
- Continue to check market pricing every month and adjust the fixed price to match your research.

When selling new and widely available goods, be mindful of price. Being overly comfortable about your decisions can result in losing money on your investment if you are purchasing wholesale to resell on eBay. Prices on commodity goods can fall very quickly. Margins on these items are small, but if you sell quickly, any profit is better than a loss. Mark your calendar to remind yourself to review for marking down prices.

New 15-Count Gillette Mach3 Base Cartridges

- Format: fixed price, no need to enable make offer. If the buyer needs it, they need it. It's OK to add multiple items to the listing.
- Price: fair market value and not the lowest price from your research.
- Duration: Good 'til Canceled.
- Shipping: start off charging shipping, and if it doesn't move out in a month or so, change it to free shipping.

▶ Continue to check market pricing every month and adjust the fixed price to match your research.

Other eBay Formats

Let's address some other eBay listing formats, particularly eBay Motors vehicles listings and classified ads. eBay Motors parts listings are constructed in the same way as the rest of eBay and should be priced in a similar way as I recommended earlier. However, selling vehicles is different. eBay Motors vehicle listings cover cars, trucks, motorcycles, powersports vehicles, boats, planes, and other vehicles and trailers. Here are some pricing tips:

▶ Start all collectible, rare, and vintage vehicles and parts as auction-style, and set the starting price squarely at fair market value. This allows a rise but inoculates you from disappointing low-bid results.

▶ List late-model vehicles and parts at fair market price using fixed-price listings with the make offer feature enabled to allow a little haggling.

▶ Turn off the make offer feature on brand new vehicles and parts. If no sale occurs, you can add that in later, allowing new vehicles to benefit from market buzz and the newness factor to sell it for you.

If you discover a 1962 Ferrari 250 GTO in your uncle's barn, you'd best hightail it to Sotheby's and let them handle the sale. The last one they sold fetched $48.4 million. eBay is an otherwise fantastic venue for valuable vehicles—not so much for junkers and derelict low-value wrecks.

Remember in Chapter 5, I essentially discouraged you from using eBay classified ads? I discouraged you for the simple reason that there are ways to post classified ads in your local area for free, such as Nextdoor, Craigslist, and so many others. When you use eBay Classifieds, the deal is done off-eBay, and you'll be responsible for your own safe trading, handling money, and avoiding scams and charlatans. An employee at my company had her funds stolen by a grifter in a fake rental ad scam. For off-eBay deals, work with cash or irrevocable money transfers such as PayPal personal transfer. When paying with PayPal using the item or service payment option, the buyer can

> **tip**
>
> I recommend launching "new-to-eBay" merchandise at least twice in the auction-style format before either moving it to the fixed price format or dropping the starting price. Remember that eBay has *nearly two hundred million active buyers.* Like any retail shop, you sometimes have to wait until the right customer walks by (or browses virtually by in this case).

later dispute and reverse the charge, which is not possible with the "sending to a friend" feature. As far as pricing your classified ad, you can always drop your price if needed. However, it is much more difficult when you raise prices. People use eBay's watch feature to monitor eBay listings, and eBay alerts them to price changes on the items they're watching.

I've spent a lot of time on formats and pricing because it's important. This is *your* money, and I do not want you to lose any of your money. I want you to make *more* money.

Listing Duration

Unfortunately, I don't have any magic beans that will assist you with growing your eBay garden. eBay is so global now there's little we can predict about market fluctuations, and no book can provide indelible advice about listing duration and the best time to end your eBay listing. The size of the eBay audience has exploded. This is good for you and me, to say the least; however, the old rules are dead. There are buyers in every time zone. If you offer cross-border shipping, and you *should*, then the listing end date and time is less relevant today than in years past. Time zones aren't the only things that make listing duration somewhat of a nonissue.

There is also the role of the savvy shopper who knows how to get their bid in automatically at the last minute to assure a win. The smart eBayer uses non-eBay tools to *snipe* and win auctions at the last second. These fabulous robotic bidding tools automatically place bids for you at the very last possible moment before the auction ends, as little as a few seconds before the bids are over. This gives other bidders literally no time to react to your bid. The sniping program I've been using since 2001 is AuctionStealer.

For the moment, stick to seven-day auction-style listings and Good 'til Cancelled fixed-price listings. Play with durations when you get bored and need something to do. I so rarely use shorter durations than seven-day listings. The ten-day auction-style format would make sense for the sale of something spectacular; however, I rarely use the duration.

The "Make Offer" Feature

I remain endlessly amused by the nature of people's relationship with money. If I see a good price for something I want, I buy it. I never argue or haggle. If I consider the price too high, I pass on it. There are many people who haggle and argue even the most reasonable price for something they want. I find that sort of negotiating unfair to the merchant. It is one of the reasons eBay's Make Offer feature is so wonderful. An eBay seller can engage in a meaningful negotiation with a potential buyer while silently turning down any offers that don't rise to a level high enough for you to be bothered to receive notification of the lowball offer.

The Best Offer checkbox will be visible on the eBay listing form. It's pretty easy to miss, and you should become very familiar with it. Enabling the best offer option places a Make Offer button on your listing. That's all well and good, but you don't want your time wasted with ridiculous offers. The best offer feature is configurable so you can set a lower limit, which allows eBay to silently reject the offer. How convenient. It's a white knight against indecent proposals. No more annoying emails with 1 cent offers on your Tiffany and Company Schlumberger peridot and ruby brooch. This feature also permits you to set the upper limit price at which eBay will automatically *accept* the eBayer's offer.

Listing Scheduling

Listing scheduling is free if you don't subscribe to an eBay store and is a nifty feature on the eBay listing form that enables you to schedule the precise start (and end) date and time of your eBay listing. That's super handy. When you prepare and launch a scheduled listing, it is sent into an inactive pending state until the start time passes, at which time the listing launches. A scheduled eBay launch is not quite as exciting as watching a SpaceX lift off the platform, but the feature is certainly helpful in a number of ways. While eBay is really global, most of your customers will be in the U.S., and scheduling your listing on high-traffic days is smart. Try ending your listings on various dates and times to see what works for you. While not a hard-and-fast rule, I generally end auction-style listings between the hours of noon and bedtime EST on Sundays.

If you simply can't wait until Sunday, you could also stagger the ending time of your auctions so that customers can bid on multiple items. Bidders love to snipe bids, so staggering your end times by a few minutes gives them time to bid on multiple items ending the same day.

Your scheduled listings are visible only to you until the start time passes. You aren't charged an insertion fee if you cancel the scheduled listing before it goes live. Before you drive yourself crazy sweating bullets over the decision to schedule or not to schedule your listing, let me say a few final words: I am all about the data. I spent time looking at the closing price of popular consumer products on eBay. In earnest, I could not find any evidence to suggest that final auction prices were better when an item ended on any particular day. In fact, I simply scratched my head after conducting the research and have nothing valuable to share from the exercise except that there seems to be no good answer or pattern to follow. Experiment and do what works best for you.

Sunday has been widely held to be the best day to end an auction. Arguments include this being the day of the week someone is going to be at home in front of their computer.

Avoid ending your listings on holidays and review my other views on scheduled listings in Chapter 1 when you sit down to make listings.

Private Listings

You'll occasionally come across an eBay listing where the bidders' identities are hidden, and this is known as a private listing. Private listings have been around a long time and allow sellers a free way to prevent prying eyes from peeking at the identities of their customers. In the Wild West days of eBay, you could see the complete user ID of any eBay bidder on a listing. Not anymore. You can see a partially-concealed eBay ID, which when clicked allows you to view the bidder's feedback and 30-day bid history. Select sellers prefer not to allow even that much data in the hands of competitors and tick the checkbox to make their eBay listing private. I discussed private listings in Chapter 1 and alluded to the fact that you could simply make all your eBay listings private. I see no issue with that. Since bids are hidden, the private listing feature makes it impossible for the public to link a specific eBay listing to a specific eBayer. Here are a few things to know about private listings:

▶ The option should be used when sensitive goods are involved, such as products in the adult or medical categories.

▶ Use the feature for gift-giving season or if you're selling goods that are likely to be given as gifts (gifts need to be a surprise, right?).

▶ You can use it when selling to other eBayers or online merchants who would be much happier if their curious customers didn't know how much they paid for something they're reselling.

▶ While eBay IDs are not displayed, the feedback comments members leave for each other on private listings is public—be careful what you say when leaving feedback so that you're not revealing what was purchased.

It's not unusual for a spouse or family member to peruse a loved one's eBay account to see what they're buying. A private listing would maintain the secret! Sellers of wholesale and sensitive merchandise should always add privacy to their listings to encourage more business from customers who value that privacy.

eBay for Charity

At this point on the eBay listing form, you'll happen upon a feature that permits you to become an instant hero. Tax-exempt organizations that are formally recognized by the Internal Revenue Service may register with *PayPal Giving Fund*, which places them on the eBay for Charity registry. You may assign 10 percent to 100 percent of your successful eBay sale to the eBay-approved nonprofit of your choice. This is a wonderful benefit to the organizations that receive these funds, and it's a simple way to help your favorite organizations fundraise. Don't see your local civic group on the list? Your Girl Scout troop is missing? Encourage them to register so that you can donate at will and give them the financial leg up they need.

Any eBayer can donate through eBay for Charity; however, if your eBay account is used solely for fundraising on behalf of an eBay for Charity-listed organization, you can associate your eBay user ID with that specific nonprofit. All sales associated with a *direct selling* eBay for Charity account will be considered direct sales of the nonprofit, bypassing the need for those funds to be routed through PayPal Giving Fund for disbursement. Community sellers can give as little as 10 percent (1 percent for eBay Motors vehicle listings). You can't list eBay for Charity items in the Adult Only or Real Estate categories.

There's more great news when using eBay for Charity. Sellers are charged the same insertion and final value fees for eBay for Charity listings; however, you'll receive a fee credit for the insertion fee and final value fee that is prorated to the percentage you agreed to donate. Donate 50 percent and receive a 50 percent credit back on the combined insertion fee and final value fee. You'll still pay for upgrades and PayPal fees.

Payment Methods

You'll have to let eBay know what forms of payment you accept for your item. You'll want to register for a PayPal account and allow eBayers to make purchases using PayPal. It's as simple as checking the PayPal box and entering your PayPal registered email address. PayPal allows customers to purchase from you using a PayPal balance or any major credit card. Buyers don't have to register for PayPal to pay you through PayPal, though. They can simply enter their card information and check out. If they have a PayPal account, eBay will remember their PayPal details to facilitate rapid checkout.

You aren't required to accept PayPal on eBay. You can inform buyers that they will need to complete their payment offline. You'll have a space to explain your payment requirements. Unless you sell vehicles or other items for pickup only, or perhaps high-end merchandise like antiques, you'll need to offer PayPal as your method of payment. That's what customers are used to, and that's what they prefer on eBay. If you stubbornly insist on trying to go against convention, hand this book to a friend and give up on eBay selling. It won't work for you. Heinrich in Hamburg isn't going to fly in to pick up his winnings, and Heinrich is going to insist on payment with PayPal, or he'll pass on your sweet deal.

Few payment methods will elevate buyer confidence as well as PayPal. Always put yourself in the shoes of your customer when selecting payment methods for your listing. Convenience, proof of payment, traceability, security, and chargeback protection are all important to eBayers. Scan the QR code in Figure 6–4 to view *eBay's Accepted Payments Policy.*

FIGURE 6–4: **eBay's Accepted Payments Policy**

Sales Tax

When you're selling on eBay, you are solely responsible for compliance with tax laws. Based on tax laws in effect, sales taxes are calculated, collected, and paid directly by eBay to many states. Some states have not mandated this practice yet, and if you're in one of these jurisdictions, you'll need to check what's required. If you are expected to charge and collect sales tax, this is the point at which you'd let eBay know the percentage to charge the buyer. You are then responsible for forwarding these sales taxes to the government within the time frame they require.

I started my company in 1988, way before eBay was born. I learned long ago that virtually every government agency is *very helpful* in explaining to you how you can pay them. Your best source of advice regarding taxes is the tax agency themselves. Give them a call or visit their nearest office for help staying in compliance. Large companies can afford to hire big-time tax attorneys. If you're just getting started, ring up the tax expert nearest you about staying compliant.

Shipping Methods

USPS offers tracking service on virtually everything, and parcels usually arrive in good shape. While loss or damage is rare, any insurance claim is paid quickly. FedEx offers low-cost and reliable ground service at prices even lower than UPS. eBay customers appreciate low-cost, fast shipping.

eBay has partnered with USPS and FedEx to offer an excellent variety of choices for shipping. You can always ship with whoever you want and there are other carriers, such as DHL and UPS. Timely upload of tracking information is a requirement for staying in good graces with eBay. The tracking must show delivery within the time frame specified on the eBay listing, which eBay calculates based on the method of shipping you select.

You can offer up to four domestic and four international shipping options. Be warned—if you don't offer cross-border trading, you will be leaving money on the table for most shippable items.

In 2019, 71 percent of my eBay sales were from U.S. customers and 29 percent were international. The percentage of international business has been rising over the years. Are you convinced?

Here are my basic recommendations for domestic shipping options (we'll dig more deeply into the intricacies of shipping in Chapter 9):

▶ Offer local pick-up only when the item is so heavy and shipping is cost-prohibitive that no one would want it shipped.

▶ Ship items one pound and under using USPS First Class Package—it's low-cost, has tracking, and allows insurance (one to three business days for delivery).

▶ Send items four pounds or less that are dimensionally small using USPS Priority Mail (one to three business days), and if an item is light and bulky, you'll need to check which carrier offers better rates for that item.

▶ Use FedEx Ground or FedEx Home Delivery for items more than 4 pounds (one to five business days).

▶ Send very heavy items by truck—check with https://www.freightquote.com/ to compare rates from multiple carriers as well as their promised delivery speed.

▶ Anything with a very high value should be sent fully insured.

▶ Low-value items do not require insurance—use your own judgment by asking yourself if you can afford to refund the money and eat the loss.

If you need to provide international shipping, take note of these tips:

▶ Offer worldwide shipping with the understanding that some countries have more reliable postal systems than others (P.S. buy insurance).

▶ For all low-value, cross-border shipments four pounds or less, use First Class Package International Service (delivery speed varies greatly by country).

▶ For shipments more than four pounds, use Priority Mail International (six to ten days).

▶ Buy insurance for cross-border shipments unless you self-insure and can accept a percentage of lost or stolen parcels.

▶ Ship Priority Mail Express International if delivery must occur faster.

▶ For very heavy shipments, consult FedEx or UPS for assistance before offering to sell it on eBay.

Virtually all of the parcels leaving my company are handled by USPS. An occasional big box has to be sent via FedEx Ground or FedEx Home Delivery because it's cheaper that way. By weight, most carriers are competitive on rates. *Dimensional weight*, aka *volumetric weight* or *DIM weight*, is a pricing technique for commercial freight transport (including courier and postal services), which uses an estimated weight that is calculated from the length, width, and height of a package. When adding your listing, you'll need to consider the box size before proceeding, or you may feel the sting of an additional bill from eBay when the carrier calculates and charges for dimensional weight.

> **tip** ⓘ
>
> First Class Package service is limited to mail up to 13 ounces except when buying your shipping label from a USPS preferred partner such as eBay, in which case you can send items weighing up to 15.9 ounces. This is a great benefit of using eBay shipping.

eBay's Global Shipping Program

While shipping cross-border has become quite simplified, many eBayers still retain fears relating to the additional paperwork and potential complications that arise from shipping internationally. Remember that nearly one in three of my boxes are going to another country. If you have reservations about shipping internationally on your own time and dime (see my tips above), eBay has you covered. The *Global Shipping Program* provides a concierge service. You ship the box to a U.S. address, and eBay takes the remainder of the responsibility from that point forward. They manage the international shipping and customs process entirely for you. To have eBay manage this for you, simply enable the Global Shipping Program checkbox at the time you list.

Here are some program benefits:

▶ All eBay Money Back Guarantee issues will be closed in your favor if an item is lost, broken, or stolen during shipment.

▶ You'll never suffer a seller performance hit for lost, broken, or stolen items.

▶ When you offer free domestic shipping to the eBay Global Shipping Program facility, you automatically receive 5 stars for shipping costs on the detailed seller rating.

▶ Your detailed seller rating will be 5 stars for shipping time if you send the item the same business day or one business day later, add the tracking number within one day of payment, and the package arrives at eBay's facility within four business days.

▶ You'll receive real-time email updates at every point along the way, from the time eBay receives the merchandise until the day it's delivered to the customer.

I think eBay's Global Shipping Program is great. I think dry cleaners are great, too. Valet parking is also wonderful. There's definitely an audience for concierge-level services. I rarely use dry cleaners; I almost never valet park my car, and I never use the eBay Global Shipping Program. Why? Because everything they can do, I can do. The paperwork needed for a cross-border shipment is very minimal, and I can fill it out on eBay's shipping label form in a few seconds. The most compelling reason not to use the Global Shipping Program is the cost. There are two costs: additional fees eBay charges to the buyer because the seller used the Global Shipping Program—the buyer, not the seller, pays the fees; then, there are lost sales on low-dollar-value items because a potential buyer looks at the estimated cost of shipping plus eBay's Global Shipping Program fees and decides not to complete the purchase (I'm not guessing—they message me and say so).

If you choose to use eBay's Global Shipping Program, be aware of the costs and implications. Depending on your type of business, this could make or break you. Figure 6–5 is another QR code that you can scan for more information on the program.

FIGURE 6–5: **eBay's Global Shipping Program**

Product Weight and Dimensions

In Chapter 3, you'll recall the toolbox essentials you'll need to keep your eBay enterprise alive. In my list, I included: packing supplies, a postal-compliant shipping scale, and a $1 tailor's tape measure. Without actually boxing up your item, place the box you'll use to send it plus the item on the scale. Be sure to tare the scale (set it to zero) at the start of every workday. You're seeking the estimate of packed weight. Bubble wrap, tissue, a label, and tape will add a teensy-weensy bit of additional mass, but not enough to make much of a difference. Jot down the weight.

Grab the tailor's tape and measure the length, depth, and height of the box. There's no need to assemble it, you can simply measure it flat ensuring you're placing the tape on the correct edges for each measurement. Now enter the weight and dimensions into the eBay listing form. This data will be used to quote actual shipping costs to potential customers. The shipping methods can be changed by revising your listing; however, the weight and dimensions should never change. After the sale, eBay allows you to pay for and print a shipping label using the USPS or FedEx option(s) you selected earlier. If you ship with UPS, DHL, or any other carrier, eBay can quote the rate, but you'll need to print the label some other way and manually enter the tracking information into the eBay system to stay compliant.

Shipping Exclusions

You'll now come across a listing form option that allows you to exclude the regions or countries you won't ship to. When you run into just one too many lost or delayed parcels to a particular country, you can boycott sending to that location. You can even ban an entire continent. Wow, this is some serious international intrigue! If all your shipments are sent via FedEx, you can ban post office boxes. This tool is highly flexible and can be configured per-listing. You generally want as many potential buyers as possible; however, some products simply cannot be shipped to certain countries. Maybe civil unrest is disrupting shipments; military mail is taking longer than you'd like, or freight to Alaska is cost-prohibitive on your free-shipping listings. There is an endless number of possibilities, and here you can adapt to the needs of your business as situations change.

Item Location

The item location field is usually a one-and-done sort of thing. You enter your zip code, and away you go. It changes when you move. You'll love the sameness of this field. But what happens when Aunt Marie in Massapequa learns how to iMessage pictures to you, and in her excitement, she realizes that you're an eBay guru, and she wants to spend more e-time with you? Now you're listing her Fenton glass collection on eBay, and because Aunt Marie is a stickler for packing carefully, you're simply thrilled when she offers to ship everything herself. The only thing is, you're all the way in Houston. Be sure for her listings you enter *her* zip code and city in the item location fields. This ensures accurate shipping cost calculation and shipping lead time. A misstep here, and you'll find yourself flagged for an eBay defect when the shipment arrives past the estimated delivery date. Worse yet, you'll lose money on shipping because what you collected falls short of what you paid the carrier. When product sourcing and drop-shipping, enter the distribution center city and postal code for your wholesale supplier into the location field when listing the item.

Promoted Listings

I was joking about shattered Ming vases in Chapter 3, and now I'd like to share the sobering reality with you about Ming vases: They are rare. Real ones are *very* rare. When you sell your Ming, it'll be a gorgeous unicorn in the forest; breathing will stop, and every living thing will start to stare. It's hard to get lost on eBay with super rare objects. That listing will be viewed, shared, and re-shared. Bidders will watch the listing, and that Ming vase will be a celebrity.

If you aren't fortunate enough to be selling rarities, you may want to dig into your profit margin to buy VIP placement on eBay. Any eBayer in good standing can use the eBay *Promoted Listings* option to pay for improved discoverability. You're only billed the additional cost of a promoted listing if the buyer clicks on the listing and purchases it within 30 days. You set a percentage of the item selling price for the placement fee. eBay recommends a percentage based on machine learning and artificial intelligence so that you're paying just the right amount—not too much and not too little. You even get analytics to let you know how the listing is performing. If you have a high margin or lots of inventory for the same item in a multiple-item listing, you'll want to take advantage of this feature. I use it and love it.

Volume Discounts, aka Bulk Pricing

If you have a warehouse full of what you're selling, why not offer a little volume pricing? The last customizable aspect of your listing is volume discounts. You can offer three levels of discounts and extend a 1 percent to 80 percent price reduction for those discounts based on multiple items added to the cart by your customer during the same transaction.

If what you sell is readily replenished, offer your most generous discount. The more you sell, the better your buyer power will become with your wholesale supplier. If you're selling 100 rare old beer trays you found in Oma Marie's barn, you'll want to skip the volume discounts.

At this point in the listing form, you'll be able to view the eBay insertion fees and list the item, preview the listing (recommended for eBay newbies), then save the listing as a draft or cancel.

Congratulations! You've just walked through the process of preparing and launching an eBay listing. If this all seems daunting, hang in there. The great news is that many of the fields on this form remember your previously entered values so that you don't have to keep re-keying the information. As you list more, you'll become more confident in what you're doing and more proficient in adding new items. You are on your way to becoming an eBay mogul!

I'd like to encourage you to re-read Chapters 5 and 6. They are meaty chapters and contain considerable knowledge that will reap you substantial profits when the principles are applied. Hopefully, you're really excited about the prospect of making a ton of money selling on eBay, and you're already scheming up a list of things to photograph today. I hope so. In the next chapter, I'll cover the management of your eBay listings.

Managing Your eBay Listings

Every garden needs tending in order for it to grow, and your eBay "garden" is no exception. Listings may need a bit of tweaking; unsold items should be relisted, and potential customers will message you and ask questions. Prompt reactions are needed to not only catalyze sales, but to avoid unhappy buyers. Don't worry you won't become a slave to your eBay venture because your business is mobile and goes anywhere you are. Manage your eBay listings from your desktop at work, a laptop in your den, or while cruising to the Bahamas on the family vacation.

In this chapter, we will discuss proper management of your eBay empire. Let's start by exploring all you can access with the Account tab.

The Account Tab

From the top right of the homepage, click on *My eBay* and then click the *Account* tab. You'll be able to see your account summary, including the latest and unbilled fees as well as which payment method you've set up to pay your seller fees. That's only the tip of the iceberg, and there's quite a bit more that the Account tab can do for you. Here are some of the things you can accomplish from here:

- ▶ View 18 months of eBay seller fee invoices
- ▶ View and update your account information
- ▶ Change your eBay ID
- ▶ Change your password
- ▶ Change your email address
- ▶ Add two-step account verification for higher security
- ▶ Link social media accounts for social sign-in
- ▶ Add and remove your addresses
- ▶ Add and remove payment options from your eBay "wallet"
- ▶ Fine-tune selling (and buying) communication preferences
- ▶ Configure site preferences
- ▶ Set up business policies
- ▶ Link to your seller dashboard
- ▶ Leave feedback for other eBayers
- ▶ Connect to your PayPal account
- ▶ Configure your eBay for Charity preferences
- ▶ Manage subscriptions to eBay and third-party services
- ▶ Adjust advertising preferences to control what marketing messages you'll accept from eBay and their partners
- ▶ Add and remove authorized account users for people trusted to help you with your eBay business

Take a self-tour of these links and make the adjustments that suit your preferences.

The eBay Mobile App

Are we really phone junkies? I read that people now spend hours of their lives each day looking at phones. Life sure looks different today than when I listed my first eBay item in 1999. I hadn't even sent my first text message yet, and when I finally "got there," I had to use a thing called T9 (aka text on nine keys). Smartphones hadn't been invented yet.

My motive for using any business productivity tool is to *make money*. If a tool saves me time, it also saves me money, which still accomplishes the goal of making more money. Having fun is important to me; however, making a profit means more than simply bean-counting. My time is very valuable, and I never like to waste in on useless activity. We have all spent way too much time on a task and later regretted it.

The eBay mobile app can and should be an element of your business management. There is far less you can do with the eBay mobile app than you can accomplish using the complete eBay experience of working on a desktop or laptop. While there are limits, the mobile tools available are still very useful, such as being able to quickly check the status of your listings, accept or counter an offer, and even print and email shipping labels.

I stock most of the shipping boxes needed to fill orders. Occasionally an item is bigger than the boxes in stock or has an odd shape that won't work with my current options. I have developed a routine that includes using the eBay mobile app. Gina at the Box City in North Hollywood is an incredible packer. She expertly boxes even the most expensive bronze or delicate glass vase for safe delivery. Rather than haul the packed box back to my place, I fire up the mobile app and enter the box dimensions and weight Gina provides me. The mobile app prepares a PDF label that I email to Gina so she can print and tape that label to the box. She even provides a receipt with the tracking number on it, should an insurance claim be required. This is one of the many ways this useful tool advances and elevates my eBay sales. Figures 7–1 and 7–2, both on page 120, will take you to the iOS and Android installation pages for the eBay mobile app, respectively.

The eBay Seller Hub

Your centralized "war room" on eBay is called the *Seller Hub*. This is the virtual hang-out spot where you'll handle your business and grow your sales. The Seller Hub provides the launching place to discover:

▶ Your listings and orders
▶ Orders reports
▶ Promoted listings

FIGURE 7–1: **eBay's Mobile App on the App Store for iOS Devices**

FIGURE 7–2: **eBay's Mobile App on Google Play for Android Devices**

- ▶ Promotions Manager
- ▶ Global Shipping Program
- ▶ Stores management feature
- ▶ Competitive listing guidance

Take a moment to find the Seller Hub. Use a desktop or laptop and sign into your eBay account. If you're not registered yet, this would be the time to get it done. From the Home screen, hover on (don't click) "My eBay" at the top-right corner of the viewport. When the menu unfolds, click "Selling." You're now looking at the Seller Hub. See Figure 7–3 on page 121 to see a view of

tip

Seller Hub may not be available until after you commence selling activity. You may also have to enable the feature if eBay presents you with a simplified view [things do change all the time].

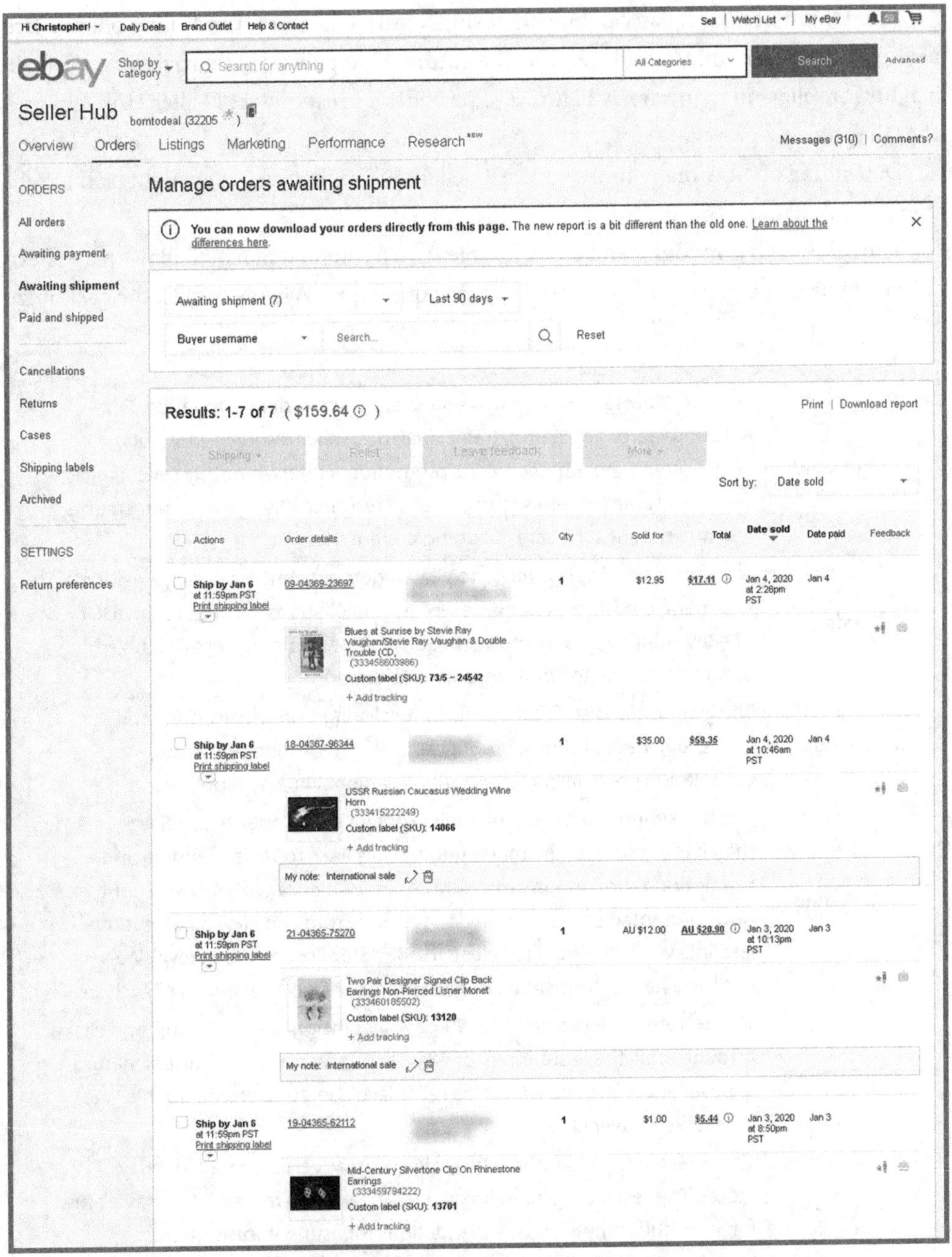

FIGURE 7–3: **View of the Orders Tab on the eBay Seller Hub**

the Orders tab on the Seller Hub. This is where your sales appear when they're ready for shipping.

From this dashboard, you can quickly springboard to the resources section eBay sellers need and the seller links you'll need in the future. The Seller Hub provides actionable insights for sellers in many areas. Figure 7–4 provides a breakdown of Seller Hub tabs and what they do.

Depending on how many times you visit Seller Hub each week, now might be the right time to bookmark the page.

The Seller Hub is modular and customizable. You'll find that many of eBay's pages have a discreet link that allows you to tailor the page to your liking. When you click the customize

Overview	The overview tab displays tasks, sales statistics, order information, links to listings across all stages, traffic analytics, seller resource shortcuts, eBay account "health" scorecard, promotional offers, monthly seller limits, feedback summary, links to useful eBay resources, selling announcements, and an account summary including current fees.
Orders	The orders tab displays filters to view orders awaiting payment, awaiting shipment, paid and shipped, as well as cancellations, returns, cases, a list of eBay shipping labels you've purchased (for reprinting, etc.), archived orders, and a link to adjust return preferences.
Listings	The listings tab displays filters for active listings, unsold listings, listing drafts, scheduled listings, product submissions, listing templates, automation optional preferences, and optional business policies.
Marketing	The marketing tab is more of a sales tool for eBay to sell their eBay Stores than it is a resource. The marketing tab has links to store branding and promotions and for non-store subscribers (which is probably you right now) promoted listings. If you don't have a store and click on all but the last link, you'll be asked to select an eBay Store subscription level. Wait until you have a consistent supply of items before opening an eBay Store.
Performance	The performance tab provides 90-day sales insights, listing traffic and click-through analytics, a summary of eBay selling fees, and the current status of your seller performance (such as seller level, defects, late shipments, and unresolved buyer cases).
Research	The research tab is another eBay sales team advertising tool for eBay Stores. The research tab has links to Terapeak price research (only available for Store subscribers), recommendations for listing improvements, sourcing guidance, and restocking advice.

FIGURE 7–4: **Seller Hub Tabs and Their Purpose**

option, you can move the information panes around or remove them entirely. You can add back removed panes at any time. If you don't want to see something, just hide it. On most days, Seller Hub will be where you see reminders to answer buyer questions, ship orders, and leave feedback.

The Watchlist and Making Offers to Watchers

Head over to the Seller Hub, and click on the listings tab. Assuming you have not yet customized this page, you'll find a cool search tool that allows you to quickly look for your listings. If you have a few, it's not *that* helpful. If you have a boatload of items, you'll appreciate the flexible search capabilities. There's an endless number of ways to filter and find listings.

You'll be able to see how many times your item was viewed and how many eBayers are watching it. Using the pull-down filters at the top of the page, click to show only those listings with watchers. Every eBay listing has a button that lets a potential buyer or bidder add the listing to their watchlist. The watchlist is accessible by hovering over My eBay and then clicking the watchlist link.

Here's where the magic begins. Next to each qualified listing, you'll see a pull-down menu under the Actions column. There are quite a few options in this menu, but the one that I love the most is the link that permits you to send offers to watchers. You can send private offers to all of the watchers on your fixed price listings. eBay won't disclose who is watching but will email your offer to all watchers simultaneously. Your offer has to be at least 5 percent less than your current fixed price. You can include a note with the offer, and you should send something personalized to explain why you're extending the special price. The offer is valid for 48 hours and can only be sent once. You can send future offers only to new watchers, but not to anyone you've sent an offer to already.

eBay Messages

Direct member-to-member messages are allowed on eBay. You can start a conversation with another eBayer either from the Contact seller link on any eBay listing or from the Member Profile, which is found by clicking the user ID.

You'll find your eBay Messages area by hovering over the My eBay link and then clicking Messages. From here you can read communication from potential and actual buyers of your listings as well as official eBay messages. Messages from other members and eBay are conveniently prioritized into separate folders.

Fraudsters harvest email addresses online and then spam the world with fake emails posing as real companies, such as eBay. These *spoof* or *phishing* emails ask for sensitive personal information such as passwords, or bank or credit card details. Protect your password and financial data with great care. Official eBay communication will include your real name or eBay ID. Skip the email and go directly to Messages to make sure that it's really eBay and not a charlatan trying to hoodwink you. Clicking links in emails exposes you to fraud, viruses, and phishing attacks. Promptly report suspicious emails by sending the shady email as an attachment to spoof@ebay.com.

eBay also places rules on communication. Messages between members are private; however, eBay may review what was said in the event of a dispute or if one of the parties to that communication reaches out for help. eBay occasionally reads messages if there is a concern about fraud, abuse, spam, or other policy violations. eBay does not allow members to:

▶ Make offers to buy and sell outside of eBay
▶ Send spam
▶ Threaten others or use profanity or hate speech
▶ Exchange email addresses, phone numbers and other contact information, or web addresses and links

It's very common to have a potential customer ask you to contact them off eBay. You cannot seek eBay's help if you trade off the site and if problems pop up with the other eBayer. I discuss the eBay Classified ad format throughout the book (which allows off-site communication); however, I'm not a user of the product. I recommend against trading off eBay for reasons of security and liability.

Best Practices for Communicating with eBay Buyers

Let's cover the essential and important topic of customer service. Communicating with your customers will become a routine. You must master this routine. eBay is far-reaching, and you'll be receiving messages from people from across the globe in different time zones. While there's no need to sleep with your phone under your pillow waiting for an eBay message alert bell, provide total clarity on the frequency with which you check member communication in your Messages. You'll need to give awesome customer service. Respond to messages with alacrity.

If you're a solopreneur, you'll wear at least three hats with your buyers: customer service agent, product sales support specialist, and technical support specialist.

Approach every interaction with cheer. Busy buyers won't always read your lengthy item description and will contact you with a quick question. Don't be testy if the answer is in your listing. Every message is a selling opportunity. Have a positive attitude. Never say, "I've already answered that question in the listing." Buyers will get turned off in a jiffy. Here are a few suggestions and reminders:

▶ Respond quickly.
▶ Be fun and keep things light.
▶ Share gratitude.
▶ Be helpful with product questions and return requests.
▶ Don't argue or fight over things like returns.
▶ Help buyers with damage claims—it's ultimately *on you* to do so.
▶ Be thoughtful in responses.
▶ Have essential details, such as tracking numbers, handy.
▶ If you have the time, follow-up with buyers to ask if they were happy with their purchase.
▶ You can always contact your buyer from the order details page.
▶ Go the extra mile—it pays dividends.

Establish written policies for eBay communication when working with a team and when you aren't the only person communicating with your buyers. Provide stunning customer support—the very same service you expect when you are the buyer in a transaction. Dealings with buyers won't always be peaches and cream, however. Be fluid and prepared. Strict policies are headwinds against success. Don't ditch your best practices, but know that there is no one-size-fits-all approach to helping people. Be kind and clear, even when you can't or won't do what the buyer wants. People want conversations, not correspondence.

Words matter. Find a positive way to say what needs to be said. "I can't refund your money because the insurance has to reimburse you" becomes, "The insurance will reimburse you for the issue, and I'd like to help you file a claim."

You can always try the CARP method, which was developed by Robert Bacal to help customer service workers calm angry or abusive customers:

▶ **C**ontrol the situation
▶ **A**cknowledge the issue with empathy and active listening
▶ **R**efocus the customer from being in an emotional state to dealing with the actual issue at hand
▶ **P**roblem solve and come up with helpful solutions so the customer is happy

Do everything in your power to respond or resolve the first time around. I discourage you from checking your eBay messages every five minutes. That's manic and inefficient. It also means you're not attending to all the other aspects of your business. Responding to eBay questions within a few hours (or less) represents excellent response time. Don't head out for a vacation to a remote log cabin in the mountains with no internet, during which time a bunch of auctions is going to end.

When a Listing Doesn't Sell

Remember the huge warehouse at the end of the movie *Raiders of the Lost Ark*? The items on eBay would certainly fill that government warehouse many times over. There are so many items on the eBay site. You must optimize your listings so that buyers can find you. *Structured data* works to improve discoverability. I covered item specifics in-depth earlier. Have you made your first listing yet? In your haste, did you simply fill in the required fields and leave the optional boxes blank? No wonder your item has so few views. Many eBay categories use product-based shopping that pulls from known items within eBay's database for a consistent buying experience. Most consumer products have either a *Global Trade Item Number* (GTIN)—such as a *Universal Product Code* (UPC) or *International Standard Book Number* (ISBN)—and *Manufacturer Part Number* (MPN). Listing with these data points increases your SEO. Fill in as many of the item specifics as you can.

Within the Seller Hub listings tab, you can sort your active and unsold listings by view count. A low view count is a clue, and you should follow the clues to a solution. Is yours a low-demand item? Are other sellers having success with the same product? Do you need to adjust your keywords? Should you add more item-specific data? Most buyers will filter the eBay search results using the menu options on the left-hand side. The Seller Hub lets you know which listings are missing item specifics so that you can focus on improving them to jump-start your sales.

The Second Chance Offer

Here's a neat trick: Say your auction ends with heated bidding, and a boatload of eBayers participated in the action. Your little secret is that you have many more of the same product in stock. You can make a *Second Chance Offer* to the underbidders for up to 60 days after the auction ends. This feature is free; however, if the offer is accepted you pay the final value fee.

You can leverage Second Chance Offers for additional profits when the reserve wasn't met, when you have multiples of the item, or when the high bidder backs out. To extend a Second Chance Offer, head over to the Seller Hub and click on the Orders tab. Apply the filter of your choice to bring up the appropriate listings. You'll see the Second Chance Offer link next to all qualified listings. When you click that link, the bidder list will pop up, and you can send offers to desired bidders. The Second Chance Offer price must be the same as their original bid price.

Here are some other things to keep in mind when you're making Second Chance Offers:

▶ Whenever a high bidder backs out, you are required to cancel their transaction before you make offers.

▶ If you have more than one of the items available, you can make as many offers as you have stock.

▶ eBayers can block offers within My eBay under the Account tab by changing their Member-to-Member message notifications. But why in the world would they want to miss out on all the fun deals?

You may leave feedback for Second Chance Offer buyers and for any bidder who doesn't pay for a transaction.

Remorse—for Buyer and Seller

Regret can occur on either side of an eBay transaction, and I'll guide you on dealing with different scenarios. Handling buyer remorse is sensitive and needs a skillful hand. Here are a few thoughts on how to protect yourself against the most demanding, slow, wishy-washy, unethical, or difficult customers:

▶ Block buyers who have account issues or are chronic deadbeats using eBay's buyer requirements feature. Adjust these settings by going to My eBay > Account > Site Preferences > Buyer requirements (and while you're at it, take a self-tour of Selling Preferences and make desired tweaks along the way).

▶ Send invoices to winning bidders promptly so that they will pay promptly and be less likely to have spent their money on something else.

▶ Reach out quickly when your message has been ignored and payment is still tardy—once per day is OK, but keep it professional, for example, "I hope you're doing well; I sent a message about payment yesterday and didn't hear from you, so I wanted to make sure you received it."

▶ Always be polite, but firm in your messages, for example, "I understand you must be busy, do you still want the Seiko watch or have you changed your mind?" No matter how much money is involved, never lose your temper with a customer—if you have a returns policy they can send an item back anyway, and if you press them to pay when they've lost their interest in the merchandise, you'll end up getting it back with an excuse attached to it.

► Open an unpaid item case if payment or a promised payment date is not received— this option is found under the Actions column under Seller Hub > Orders > Awaiting payment, or you can click "Resolve a problem" from the item listing page and follow the prompts to report the unpaid item.

► Block all buyers who are difficult to work with, don't pay, or break eBay rules. Go to the eBay Site Map > Sell > Sell activities > Block bidder/buyer list, and from there, enter their eBay ID, and they will be banned from ordering from you again.

► Ask eBay for a final value fee credit, cut your losses and relist the item.

► Cancel the sale and make a Second Chance Offer when there are multiple bidders (more on cancellations shortly).

Let's shift to a discussion about seller's remorse. Cancellation without a request from the buyer is one of the eBay cardinal sins. Your risk of selling for too low of a price should be avoided by carving out sufficient time to properly research the item and list it for an appropriate and acceptable-to-you price. If you're selling antiques and simply have no clue what you've got, hold off until you can find answers. In Chapter 4, I provided a QR code you can scan to pull up the eBay Community page where you can post an image and receive opinions on what you've got and the value. Sometimes you simply can't secure answers. Selling blind is foolish, and if you do it enough times, you very well may sell a $20,000 Ming vase for $20.

If you list and sell an item, you are duty-bound to complete the deal. If you cancel the sale, you'll receive a transaction defect (not a "public" thing, but an internal bad mark eBay tracks), and too many of those will result in you being banned from selling. When running auctions, if the listing is still active and you've got enough time before the listing ends, you can cancel the bids and end the listing, making corrections during the relisting process. I'll explain canceling bids in the next section. If this is your "first rodeo" and you cancel a sale, it won't really hurt you too much. If you list enough items, you're bound to miss a decimal place. That $500.00 starting bid was incorrectly entered as $50, and the listing sold with one bid. It happens. The decision to proceed or not is up to you. Message the buyer and explain what happened. Offer them some compensation. I've paid as much as $20 to *not ship* an item. I don't do it often, but it happens. I once consigned a rare *Star Trek* collectible figurine, and just as I was about to ship it out, my staff told me that the client ran in, grabbed it from our shelf, and ran out. I have secure storage now. You're running a business and mistakes happen. Pause and reflect on what to do. Never make any decision in haste. The answer will come to you.

P.S. if you drop the item and it turns into a pile of broken shards, take a photo and share it with the buyer, extend an apology, give a refund, and use PayPal to send a token additional payment for the buyer's trouble.

When a Listing Gets an Offer

When you have robust margins, add the Best Offer option, which will display a Make Offer button on your listing. In Chapter 6, I explained how you can set your "floor" price to avoid annoying low offers. You don't want a $5 offer to come through on a $100 item. The lower-limit setting rejects those proposals silently. When an offer comes in and you don't find it attractive, the knee-jerk reaction is to quickly counteroffer. While you can do this, the power of time is on your side. Consider what you are selling. The rare collectible warrants more thought and therefore patience in the negotiation. Wait a while before making a counter offer. That could be hours, or in the case of something really rare, you could get back to the customer in a day. Include a brief note with your counter offer supporting your price decision. For commodity items that are widely available, you can expect fewer bites on counteroffers and less success with this waiting tactic.

Best offers are valid for 48 hours, so respond to them quickly. Buyers can make five offers on the same item within a 30-day period (10 for most vehicles categories). An offer applies to the item price and shipping costs and other item terms remain the same. Read any notes included with the offer such as, "This price must include shipping".

Here's a lesser-known feature that's very exciting for sellers. When an eBayer asks a question about a fixed price format listing, you'll see the "Send an offer" button in the top-right corner when you click the reply button on the message. Now you can propose a special price and include a message to the buyer. Accepted offers become a binding agreement between the buyer and you. There are many spirited discussions online that extoll the virtues of hard-nosed negotiation. I take a softer approach. I focus on the price I want, and if the offer is too low, I include a kind note explaining why. Many times the deal proceeds with the eBayer accepting my counteroffer. You'll run into plenty of people who chase you to the bottom price. Let it go, and wait for someone nicer and more generous.

When a Listing Does Sell

In all your excitement, you've listed a whole bunch of items, and no surprise, they're selling. By default, eBay will alert you with an email when an item sells, and PayPal will send notifications when the payment arrives. Don't spend your earnings just yet. If you have a returns policy, your customer still has between 30 to 60 days to return the item. Fingers crossed that it never happens. Also, you'll need to settle up with eBay and pay their bill when it comes due. The good news is that Seller Hub will tally and display your fees in real-time.

For items sold but not yet paid, you can head back over to Seller Hub and click the orders tab. There's a filter for orders awaiting payment. If payment hasn't arrived within a day after the eBayer committed to buying it, you'll want to reach out with a gentle reminder, which is as simple as, "Hello Satish, do you still want the Nikon?" This generally is enough of a reminder to lubricate the wheels and get them turning. The buyer's full name and address are on the order details page. Personalize the message even if you use a copy-and-paste form note. I had a customer send a cranky reply when I failed to sign my name at the bottom of the message. People can be that way sometimes.

I'll talk about packing and shipping later, which will include a discussion about printing shipping labels. For now, you can familiarize yourself with the filters under the orders tab, which includes items awaiting shipment, items paid, and items shipped. When your order volume grows, you can use the convenient search and filter options within the page to isolate individual orders.

Best Practices for Revising an Active Listing

Changing your mind, fixing an error, or adding photos can all be done for free. You can typically change your listings with a few restrictions. There are no fees unless you raise your asking price or add special features. Most of the time, you can edit the title, edit the description, change or add photos, and purchase upgrades. For listings with at least 12 hours remaining that have no bids, you can change the price. You cannot change the listing from fixed price to auction-style or vice versa, and listing duration cannot be changed, either.

What you're able to revise on an auction-style listing is limited once it has received bids, however. For example, you can't change the description or remove photos on listings with bids. There's a sound reason for this: The previous bidders made their decision to place the bid based on the information and photos they saw at the time they viewed your listing. When additional details need to be added to the description, but the bids prevent revising it, eBay allows you to amend the description without changing what was already there. Familiarize yourself with the complete listing revision policy by scanning the QR code in Figure 7–5 on page 131.

FIGURE 7–5: **Revise a Listing Policy Page**

Regulations for Repeating a Listing

You might be curious what eBay charges if you'd like to repeat a listing. In regard to that, I have some great news. eBay's fixed-price listings stay active until you end them. Auction-style listings can be relisted if they end without a sale, because you ended the listing early, you canceled the order, or the buyer simply shirked their duty to pay you. The insertion fee applies to relisted items, or the relist will count towards zero insertion fee listings. Every eBay account receives a minimum of 50 zero insertion fee listings monthly, and eBay Store subscribers are provided with even more.

You'll receive insertion fee credits for relisted items if you relist your item because it didn't sell the first time around or a transaction has fallen through. eBay will credit your account for the insertion fee if your listing meets all of the following circumstances:

- ▶ The relisted item sells
- ▶ It isn't a classified ad
- ▶ The listing and relisting have the same format
- ▶ Your relisting was launched using one of eBay's relist tools, and you didn't simply copy-and-paste into a new listing form
- ▶ No more than 90 days have elapsed since your original listing ended
- ▶ This is your first relisting
- ▶ The starting price has not been increased when you relisted
- ▶ You didn't add a reserve

eBay allows you to pay monthly fees in exchange for specific selling advantages, called an eBay Store. There are five levels for eBay stores, which are Starter, Basic, Premium,

Anchor, and Enterprise, listed in order of price from cheapest to most pricey. Active Basic, Premium, Anchor, or Enterprise Store subscribers receive insertion fee credits on all paid auction-style listings that sell, excluding zero insertion fee listings, Motors vehicles, Real Estate, and select Business & Industrial categories. Listing upgrades aren't credited. If eBay removes your listing for any administrative reason, you'll receive fee credits. Best of all, relisting takes only a couple of clicks, and the ended listing is back to life again.

Canceling Bids and Blocking Bidders

You're crushing it and your first edition *Moby Dick* book auction is receiving insane bidding action when a rare book dealer informs you it's worth $16,000, not the current bid of $1,600. You don't want to risk losing your shirt. Cancel the bids quickly so you can then end the listing and run it again with a more appropriate starting price (or reserve).

There's no reason to have sleepless nights over the situation. Canceling bids and then ending a listing allows you to relieve yourself of any future pain of having to sweet-talk your way out of a deal when the high bidder wins the really expensive *Moby Dick*. eBay has strict rules about this sort of thing. After all, they don't want sellers flippantly putting the smackdown on eager bidders and tipping the apple cart for buyers with cash in hand ready to score deals at auction.

You'll be required to provide an explanation with a reason for why you canceled the bid or bids. That reason becomes public for all who visit the bid history on your listing page. Here are the legitimate reasons eBay allows for removing a bid:

▶ The buyer asked you to do it and you consent to the cancellation
▶ The item is no longer available
▶ You made an error in the listing
▶ You are concerned that the buyer may be fraudulent

To cancel a bid, click Help & Contact from most eBay pages and complete the following steps:

1. Type "canceling bids" into the box that says, "Search eBay Help . . ."
2. eBay displays suggested pages: Click on the link for the page entitled "Canceling bids and managing bidders"
3. Click the link: Canceling bids placed on your listing
4. Type the item number, the eBay ID of the bidder, and the reason for the bid cancellation
5. Click the "Cancel bid" button

There's no going back once you cancel the bid because canceled bids cannot be restored. If you'd like to remove bids from multiple eBayers, then you'll repeat these steps for each bidder. Please note that bid cancellation does not end the auction. If you no longer wish to sell the item or the listing contains errors that require you to revise it, you'll need to end the listing (I'll explain how to accomplish this later in the chapter).

If you'd like to restrict certain buyers from bidding on your listings, configure the buyer requirements. This is accomplished by doing the following:

1. Click "My eBay" at the top-right-hand corner of most eBay pages
2. Click "Account"
3. If visible, click "Switch to classic view"
4. Click "Site Preferences"
5. Click "Edit" under the "Buyer requirements" section
6. Make your desired edits
7. Click the "Submit" button

If an unwanted bidder is feisty and just won't take a hint, then stop them dead in their tracks by blocking their user ID from placing any more bids or purchasing your fixed-price listings. Block buyers in a jiffy by doing the following:

1. Go to the eBay "Site Map" link available on most eBay pages
2. Navigate to the "Sell activities" section under the heading "SELL"
3. Click the "Block bidder/buyer list" link
4. Click "Add an eBay user to my Blocked Bidder/Buyer List"
5. Enter the user IDs that you'd like to block (separate multiple user IDs with a comma)
6. Click the "Submit" button

Remember that there are tons of bidders on eBay. Blocking one eBayer will not diminish the demand for your excellent goods. Now, let's talk about ending listings early in the case of a minor error or disaster.

Ending Your Listing Early

Sometimes the realities of life are headwinds and your eBay business faces challenges. Illness, personal issues, and unexpected situations can all cause problems for your eBay activities. While ending auctions early is a multi-step process, you can end fixed-price listings at any time for any reason. You never have to explain yourself; eBay simply doesn't require it. When you cancel an auction, there's a real risk of disappointing potential bidders who are watching and plan to bid at the very last moment. Savvy auction participants know to place bids moments before the auction ends to stifle bidding competition (a method called sniping, which you read about in Chapter 6). eBay allows you to end your auction early if the item is lost, broken, or no longer available, or if you made a mistake, such as listing the wrong starting price in an auction.

There are rules and being able to end your auction depends on a few conditions, which are:

▶ Your listing has no bids (or you canceled the bids before ending the listing)

▶ If there are bids, you are willing to sell the item to the highest bidder

▶ If there are at least 12 hours left in the listing, it has bids and you want to cancel all bids and end the listing

You can't end an auction if there are fewer than 12 hours left, you've received bids, and you don't want the high bidder to win. You also can't end the listing if there are less than 12 hours left, you have bids, and the reserve price isn't met. If eBay doesn't permit you to cancel bids due to their rules, then message your bidders and explain what's going on and ask if they would retract their bid. If the comforter you're selling was chewed up by your pet pygmy pig, then see if the bidder will agree to cancel the transaction.

Buyers fume when sellers cancel their bids and end auctions early. It's disappointing and can be downright upsetting. eBay won't charge you fees if you end one auction a year. Beyond that, there's a toll for traveling along this road; eBay will charge you the final value fee if you cancel the bids and end a listing early (Real Estate and Classified Ads don't apply). The final value fee assessed will be calculated based on the highest bid received at the time you ended the listing. If you agree to sell to the highest bidder, you pay the customary final value fees. I don't recommend ending a listing early and selling to the highest bidder because you'll be leaving money on the table. You'll never know how much you could have received in bids at the last minute when you do this.

If you get into the habit of ending auctions early, eBay will be watching you (or their smart computers will), and they will review your account for possible limitations or restrictions.

To end a listing, follow these steps:

1. Hover over "My eBay" at the top-right-hand corner of most eBay pages
2. Click "Selling"
3. Click the "Listings" tab
4. Click the pull-down menu next to the listing from the "Actions" column
5. Click "End item"

6. Select the reason for your decision to end the listing on the next page
7. Click "End My Listing" (as shown in Figure 7–6)

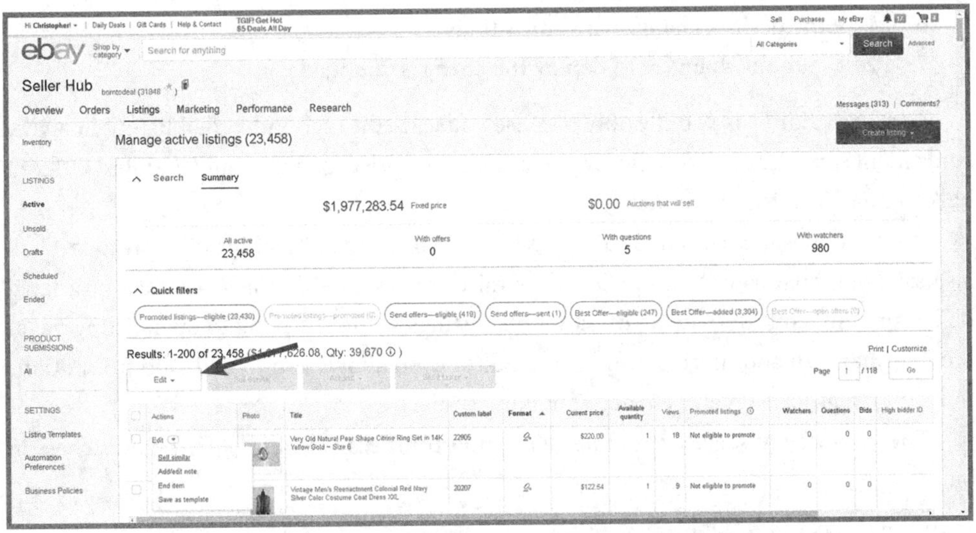

FIGURE 7–6: **Use This Link to End Your Listing**

Bulk Actions

While it's dreamy to imagine a business that runs all by itself, allows you to lounge in the backyard hammock all day, and rakes in wheelbarrows full of cash, eBay isn't that business. In fact, no customer-facing business works that way. I haven't found *that* business opportunity yet. Your listings require management, and your business will grow with hard work and laser focus.

The clever computer programmers at eBay are constantly finding ways to save you more time and help you sell more (after all, eBay works on commission, aka final value fees). The more you sell, the more you make, and the more eBay makes. It's a win-win.

You can use the *Mass Editor* tool to facilitate large-scale edits in your listings. The Mass Editor tool permits you to change multiple listings, even *hundreds* from a single page—quickly and in bulk. Here's how you access Mass Editor:

1. Hover over "My eBay" at the top-right-hand corner of most eBay pages
2. Click "Selling"
3. Click the "Listings" tab
4. Apply the "Active" filter

5. Either tick the checkbox next to the listings you'd like to edit and then click the "Edit" button and click "Edit selected," or click "Edit" without selecting listings and choose which group of listings you'd like to edit (up to 500 at a time)
6. Make the desired changes to your listings
7. Press "Submit changes" to deploy the changes you made

The Mass Editor is very flexible because you can edit each individual listing in a very convenient spreadsheet-like view, or you can edit the price, quantity, and add Best Offer in bulk to up to 500 listings at once.

It's not only super cool to be able to view and amend your listings this way, but it will also save you boatloads of time. Drop (or raise) prices by either a percentage or a fixed dollar amount; edit every detail of individual listings without having to open listing pages one-by-one; even add more photos. Mass Editor even allows you to add paid promotions to your listings for a greater chance at making a sale.

There's a way to score even more sales opportunities by sending offers to watchers in bulk:

1. From the "Active" filter
2. Click on the "Send offers—eligible" button under "Quick filters"
3. These are listings with watchers, select the desired listings (those you'd like to send offers to)
4. Click the "Send offers" button
5. Enter either a fixed amount or percentage to take off, and a message to your future customer
6. Click "Send offers"

eBay will send an email to everyone watching the listings with the special price you extended to them. If you have more than 200 eligible listings, you'll need to send offers to them in batches of 200 because you can only select as many listings as will display on the page, and the maximum pagination for the page is 200 rows. The default message isn't good enough in my view. I send something more personalized and meaningful, "Hello. I see that you're watching this listing. I'm sending you a special price privately for your consideration and hope that you'll take advantage of it. Feel free to let me know if you have any questions. Thank you." You and the buyer can negotiate an offer by exchanging up to five offers and counteroffers for each negotiation.

The plethora of bulk actions you can apply to your listings is expansive, and eBay is adding new features all the time. Here are a few more cool things you can accomplish en masse (starting from the Seller Hub > Listings tab):

▶ Add Best Offer to hundreds of listings at once:
1. From the "Active" filter
2. Click on the "Best Offer—eligible" button under "Quick filters"
3. Select the desired listings
4. Click "Sell it faster"
5. Click "Add Best Offer"
6. Set the optional upper and lower price limits
7. Click the "Add Best Offer" button

▶ Automate the relisting process on a few or all of your listings:
1. From the "Active" filter
2. Select the desired listings
3. Click "Actions"
4. Click "Assign automation rules"
5. Use the "Rule" pull-down menu and select the desired relist automation strategy
6. Enter the values under "Quantity available to list" and "Average unit cost: $"
7. Click the "Assign" button

▶ Convert a bunch of fixed-price listings to the auction-style format:
1. From the "Active" filter
2. Select the desired fixed-price listings
3. Click "Actions"
4. Click "Change to auction-style"
5. Optionally edit your listings
6. Click "Submit all"

▶ Elevate multiple listings with improved paid placement using the Promoted Listings option:
1. From the "Active" filter
2. Select the desired fixed-price listings
3. Click "Sell it faster"
4. Click "Promote"
5. Set the ad rate (try "Apply trending rate" initially, which is the rate paid by other sellers for similar items)
6. Select your campaign (or eBay makes a new one)
7. Click "Promote"

▶ Rapidly relist all your unsold items:
1. From the "Unsold" filter

2. Select the desired listings
3. Click "Relist" or "Relist as fixed price"
4. Optionally edit your listings before relisting them
5. Click "Submit all"

▶ Change the launch time for multiple scheduled listings:
1. From the "Schedule" filter
2. Select the desired listings
3. Click "Action"
4. Click "Reschedule"
5. Set the new start time
6. Click "Reschedule"

I simply love the convenience of the many ways eBay automates seller activities. I appreciate that my time is saved, and I can apply the time savings to accomplish other tasks and get more done.

Working Through Account Limits

Both eBay and PayPal worry about posers and fraudsters who prey on the unsuspecting, so you may notice that as a first-time seller, you are subject to some limits on your account. New sellers can be (and usually are) frustrated by *account limits,* published monthly limits on all eBay accounts that restrict both how many listings you can post as well as the dollar value. These limits are in place to protect buyers and to make sure eBay is a safe place to trade. Don't fret, you can always ask to list more. But before you make such a bold request, sell some stuff. When you've seen a bit of action and the money is rolling in, then convene your courage and let eBay know, "I deserve better." I'm sure they'll agree to raise your limits, provided you're shipping on time; the tracking is uploaded promptly, and customers are raving about your product and service. Don't expect too much. eBay limit increases are gradual. As you prove yourself, keep asking for more. I did this many times. There's a link that says "Request to list more" on the monthly limits pane with the Seller Hub that you can use, but I prefer to call and speak with a real person. Call eBay at (866) 961-9253 to ask for a limit increase. Today, as shown in Figure 7–7 on page 139, eBay lets me list as many as two billion items with a value of $2 billion. I wish I could find that much stuff to sell. I really do.

Promotional Offers

I am in the habit of reading everything. It pays to read (often). The generous folks in eBay's marketing department are handing out free stuff *all the time.* Want free listings? Of course.

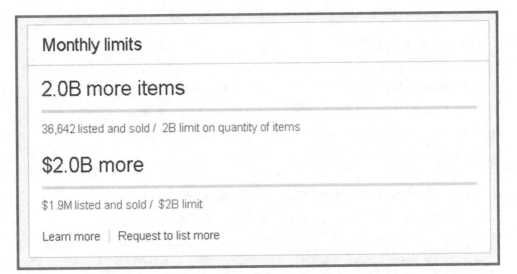

FIGURE 7–7: **Access Your Current Monthly Selling Limit Information from the Overview Tab within the Seller Hub**

Reduced final value fees? C'mon, you've got to be kidding me. To get in on the bounty, head over to the Seller Hub and look up the promotional offers (shown in Figure 7–8 on page 140) that are waiting for you. These are usually time-limited offers that require you to accept them (and why wouldn't you?). There's a cornucopia of free stuff here that will periodically pop up on your account.

Building a Strong Seller Reputation

Way back in the day, eBay was pretty free-wheeling and everyone kind of just did *whatever* they wanted. Yes, there were rules, but eBay was growing really fast, and people often bent the rules. Soon, all that bending meant more rules. As the eBay marketplace grew, the volume of listings became pretty massive. Buyers rely heavily on feedback profiles and detailed seller ratings to make purchasing decisions (I explained the feedback system and DSRs in Chapter 1). Eventually, eBay studied oodles of seller activity and later quantified their view on what *good* and *great* sellers looked like by applying some metrics. Keeping your eBay metrics looking good in eBay's eyes is critical to managing a successful eBay business. Are you shipping on-time? Do you upload tracking numbers quickly? Do you have very few buyer complaints? Is your return rate low? These and other factors are systematically evaluated, and if you come home with a spectacular report card, you'll earn the badge of honor known as the Top Rated Seller. Buyers trust the best of eBay. Being

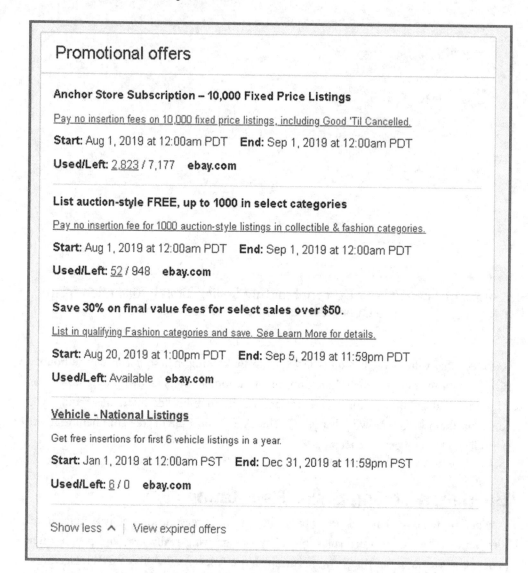

Promotional offers

Anchor Store Subscription – 10,000 Fixed Price Listings

Pay no insertion fees on 10,000 fixed price listings, including Good 'Til Cancelled.

Start: Aug 1, 2019 at 12:00am PDT   **End:** Sep 1, 2019 at 12:00am PDT

Used/Left: 2,823 / 7,177   **ebay.com**

List auction-style FREE, up to 1000 in select categories

Pay no insertion fee for 1000 auction-style listings in collectible & fashion categories.

Start: Aug 1, 2019 at 12:00am PDT   **End:** Sep 1, 2019 at 12:00am PDT

Used/Left: 52 / 948   **ebay.com**

Save 30% on final value fees for select sales over $50.

List in qualifying Fashion categories and save. See Learn More for details.

Start: Aug 20, 2019 at 1:00pm PDT   **End:** Sep 5, 2019 at 11:59pm PDT

Used/Left: Available   **ebay.com**

Vehicle - National Listings

Get free insertions for first 6 vehicle listings in a year.

Start: Jan 1, 2019 at 12:00am PST   **End:** Dec 31, 2019 at 11:59pm PST

Used/Left: 6 / 0   **ebay.com**

Show less ∧ | View expired offers

FIGURE 7–8: **Promotional Offers Appear on the "Promotional Offers" Pane within the Seller Hub**

Top Rated affords you the privilege of receiving big discounts on final value fees plus, and buyers are extremely confident when ordering from you. If you're wondering how you size up, here's how to find out:

1. Click "My eBay" at the top-right-hand corner of most eBay pages
2. Click "Account"
3. Click "Seller Dashboard"

Managing eBay listings involves a lot of moving parts, but rest assured, given time and practice, your high-quality merchandise will not only look fantastic, but your buyers will love your high caliber and beautiful customer service. As you're learning the nuts and bolts, you'll instinctively develop the skills required to delight buyers and raise your eBay business to the next plateau. And the best part is that you won't need to memorize anything. Keep this book within reach to help you overcome any confusion you're coping with.

In the next two chapters, I'll go into considerable detail about the handling of your sales and shipping processes (who doesn't love the money part, right?).

Communicating with Buyers Pre- and Post-Sale

Now that you've sharpened your pencil and your desk is well-organized, you'll need to get into the management of your sales. Whether you ran one auction or a thousand fixed-price listings, the customer experience needs to be the same—extraordinary. Everything starts with the customer.

Expert communication with people requires experience (and hunch, intuition, and gut), and if you're new to running your own business, you'll make many mistakes along the way. Don't be too hard on yourself because we all do. For the most part, people are decent and honest, but the occasional "bad egg" does come along to throw a wrench in your day. Never let occasional bad experiences cause a knee-jerk reaction that places a dark cloud over your business, and don't let it affect the positive interactions you should be having with your other customers.

eBay is not an online garage sale for discards and crappy goods. Your new and loyal customers are on the prowl for quality stuff, committed customer service, and fair prices. Many times, the buyer's first purchase is an audition—a test to see how you'll perform. It's critical to listen closely to what customers want and to provide it carefully and rapidly. Customer obsession and speed in business matter and will result in many happy returns. The worst thing about shopping in a physical store remains the checkout line. Customers hate to wait in line. eBay eliminates the line, and your approach to buyer communication must be pain-free and helpful.

Communicating with Buyers: The Basics

You can customize the way eBay notifies you about selling (and buying) activity. To make these "your own," you can click on My eBay > Account > Communication Preferences and edit the Seller section. As your volume grows, your email inbox will become flooded, and you'll want to turn off all the friendly eBay alerts so that you can manage your orders in a, well . . . more *orderly* fashion. Here's how to quickly find your orders and specifically those that are unpaid sales:

1. Hover over "My eBay" at the top-right-hand corner of most eBay pages
2. Click "Selling"
3. Click the "Orders" tab
4. Click the "Awaiting payment" filter

You can print a hard copy of this page using the Print link or download a comma-separated values file (aka CSV) using the Download Report link.

The orders on the Awaiting Payment filter are unpaid. Volume sellers need to bookmark this page and come here daily to check on the payment status.

tip

Don't want to lose your place? Right-click over the Send Invoice link (or do this for any hyperlink) and select the option to open the link in a new tab or window. That way, when you're done sending the invoice, you can close the tab or window and you're right back to where you started. It's a huge timesaver.

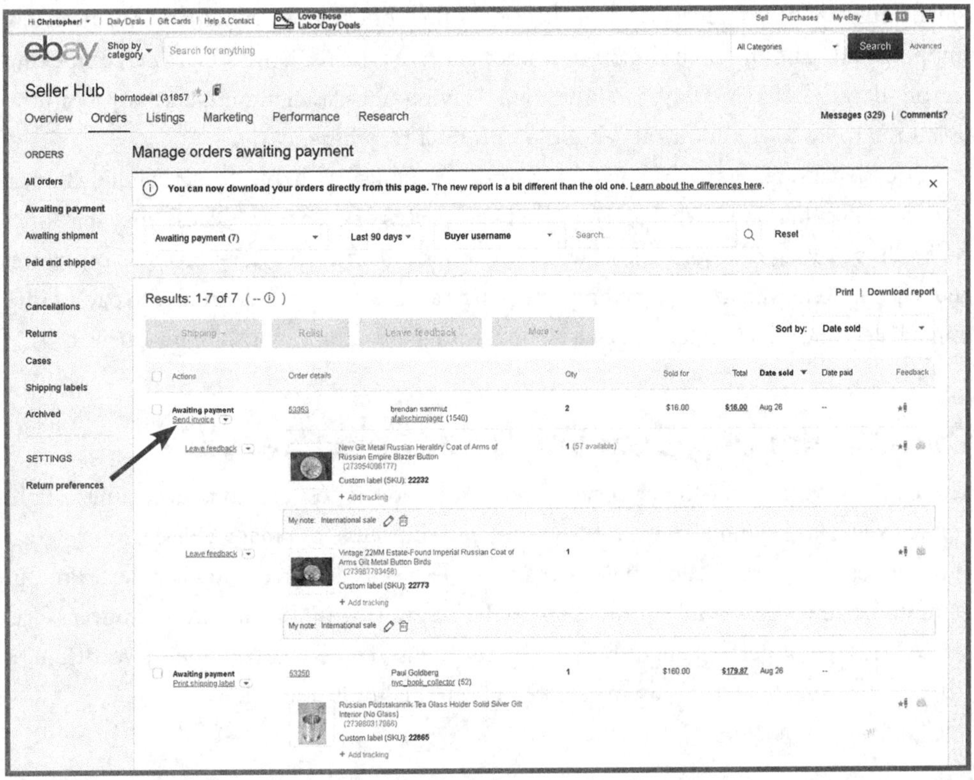

FIGURE 8–1: **Send Invoices to Unpaid Sales from the Orders Tab in Seller Hub Using this Link**

Now's a good time to send a gentle payment reminder to your buyer. Click the Send Invoice link under the Actions column (look to Figure 8–1 for a visual aid). If the same person ordered multiple items and didn't use the cart feature within eBay to place the order, you will need to combine the purchases, figure out the new shipping rate based on the combined weight, and edit the shipping costs. If you forget to combine shipping, the buyer will either retort or pay in disgust and leave you a low DSR for shipping and handling charges. At the time you send the invoice, make any needed adjustments or discounts you've promised.

This would be the right time to do a little product recommendation and offer other items to the buyer before shipping their order. Encourage additional purchases with a friendly message and offer discounts and free shipping (you'll include the item in the same box as their original purchase).

Same-day handling time makes it harder to offer buyers additional goods before shipping because you have to ship the same day. A Top Rated Seller can display a Top

Rated Plus seal prominently on their listings if they offer same-day or one-business-day shipping and handling time and 30-day or longer free returns. Unless there's a compelling reason, don't offer same-day handling time. Having one-day handling allows you a little breathing room to communicate and make product recommendations.

Occasionally, buyers ask you to hold their shipment. Failing to meet your handling time is an order defect that can hurt your Top Rated seller status or even worse, cause eBay to restrict your selling privileges. Communicate with your buyer and offer a few solutions. You can cancel and relist the item with longer handling time, cancel and relist when they are able to pay, or ship immediately and ask them to set up a mail hold with the post office (or shipping carrier).

Communicating Excellent Customer Service

The path to ultimate customer service communication is to have fun. Keep things light and relaxed. Having fun also means to "mind your business." As many eBayers know, great customer service is rare, and fabulous customer service is admired and cherished. Prompt communication begins with you and is one of the best ways to put a smile on your buyer's face.

While a good percentage of buyers pay really fast, some will take their sweet time to pay you. I've got some tricks up my sleeve to keep the funds flowing.

Here are some of my tips:

▶ *Respond fast.* Be connected to your eBay email on your mobile device at all times. A sale means money. This is not a 9-to-5 job. It's your business. Think like an owner and be mindful of speed. The faster you reply, the quicker a sale occurs (or a disaster is averted).

▶ *Keep your promises 100 percent of the time.* Ninety-nine percent isn't good enough. Only make promises you'll be in a position to keep. No matter how good or bad you deem any situation, do not lie to anyone. Trust is priceless. Use a calendar to follow through on anything you've promised. For example, a bidder won but has asked you to check on faster or cheaper means of getting their item to them, and you said you would look into options.

▶ *Be helpful and outgoing.* Don't act aggressive or be sarcastic. Jokes, even harmless ones, may be misinterpreted. eBay is a global marketplace. Many buyers are cross-border, and their messages are often translated by eBay automatically. Keep your communication kind, clear, and friendly.

▶ *Give your business an amazing personality.* You're not a big box company, so don't act like one. Small businesses have an advantage over large ones—in their customer service. Boring businesses fail, and fun firms flourish.

▶ *Keep tabs on your regulars.* Know them and welcome them back. How? In my Gmail, I can always search for an eBayer's ID or email address and instantly pull up their purchase history. I remember customers and lead the conversation with, "Welcome back."

▶ *Business involves risk and occasional losses.* When a situation goes south, you may have to eat the cost. It happens and is part of doing business. Forgot to buy the shipping insurance and the candy arrived crushed? Issue the refund quickly anyway. Waiting on an insurance payment, and it's a trivial amount? Refund the customer now, and wait for the payment later. Why should they wait? It doesn't make sense to them, and they will appreciate knowing you stand behind your business.

▶ *Be a great listener.* When someone pitches a fit in an email, respond with empathy and always offer solutions. Let them vent.

▶ *Avoid the words "can't", "don't," etc.* Always talk about what you can do for your customers.

▶ *Apologize for your mistakes or anytime something doesn't go as planned.* It's that simple.

tip ⓘ

You'll always be able to contact your buyer from the item listing page. However, another quick way to reach out is from the Orders tab within the Seller Hub. Click the pull-down menu from the Actions column, and click Contact buyer.

Customers are going to do business with companies that treat them well. The good word about a great company spreads like wildfire to friends, family, and colleagues. Rotten service is the end for you. Customers are savvy and have set expectations based upon the service they have come to expect from other online sellers, eBay or otherwise.

When I worked for eBay, I was attending an apparel trade show at the Las Vegas Convention Center. While managing a booth for eBay, I interact with actual and potential eBay users. A pleasant man came up and asked me some questions about eBay, and at the end of the conversation, I came to realize that he had the impression he could post up some items on eBay and cash in BIG with little or no effort. I was amused. eBay, like any business, requires hard work, care, and attention in order to yield fruit.

With millions of items for sale on eBay, by the time you respond to yesterday's customer questions today, that eBayer already bought from someone else. Unless you're completely out of touch with the times, you can receive email notifications about eBay questions and quickly respond to them anywhere. An instant response means a greater chance at a sale.

With each passing minute, hour . . . day (really?), you can bet they've already moved on. Timeliness is so crucial when dealing with customers because they've already committed to buying. They've expressed far more than just an interest. They made a commitment to do business with you.

Handling Customers Who Haven't Paid

Well, you asked but were not answered. What's the problem? Payment hasn't arrived and you're getting nervous (or angry?). Chill out and think hard. What could be the reason? A broken computer or lost phone? A sudden illness? Family vacation? Did someone forget to pay the internet bill? No need to get testy; work on being proactive. Within 24 hours of the end of the listing, a gentle reminder is in order. Say, "Hello Javiera, thank you for making this purchase. When can I expect to receive your payment?" If payment remains tardy by the second day, say, "Javiera, I hope all is going well with you, however, I still have not received your payment for this purchase. Could you please respond to me and let me know your intentions? Thank you." If you're wondering how I knew the buyer's name is Javiera, I can see the full name and address of every customer by clicking the Order Details link on the item listing page.

Still being ignored? eBay has a solution. If it's been more than two full days since the listing ended, you can open a case, and eBay will mediate the unpaid item. Deadbeat bidders can be a drag, but you can fight back. If the customer wants to cancel the deal, you should do so willingly and painlessly. After all, the buyer can still return the product and could make up a phony reason for doing so—and you'll pay freight both ways. Deadbeats can be put on notice quickly and easily, and here's how you do it:

1. Hover over "My eBay" at the top-right-hand corner of most eBay pages
2. Click "Selling"
3. Click the "Orders" tab
4. Click the "Awaiting payment" filter
5. Click the pull-down menu under the "Actions" column
6. Click "Open unpaid item case"
7. Depending on the state of the order, different options will appear; follow the instructions given

To check on existing cases or to open a case if the item isn't on your list of orders awaiting payment, from the Seller Hub, click Orders and then click Cases.

"You're Banned from the Club"

eBay is very much like a club, and you have to follow rules in the eBay club. Buying and selling on eBay is a privilege, not a right. You'll have to stay in the good graces of eBay to use the site. If you opened a case because a buyer didn't pay for the item, you can wait a little while longer (I'd say no longer than a week) and then ask eBay to refund your final value fee that was charged when the item sold and the buyer made the commitment to buy. From your active cases, you can close a case, and then eBay will record the unpaid item on the buyer's account. When you relist the item, you will receive a credit for the insertion fee on the listing. People who are chronic deadbeats on eBay will lose their buying privileges, but why wait for eBay to step in? Block everyone who bids or buys and fails to pay you.

When you're asked to accept a method of payment that you don't normally accept, be on high alert. Common online scams involve phony cashier's checks and fake money orders. When we started in 1999, we accepted checks, money orders, and direct credit cards, but PayPal allows buyers to pay with card, an e-check, or PayPal balance, which has made other options unnecessary. We don't trade off-eBay or off-PayPal. Promptly report suspicious emails to spoof@ebay.com.

Handling Buyers with Urgent Questions

I don't know any sellers who love returns; however, I do not mind them. My return rate is very low and always has been. Returns do not increase dramatically when we offer free returns or extend the returns window. A no-returns policy reduces sales, and I've proven time and again that allowing returns and paying return shipping increases sales. Don't offer free returns on bulky or heavy items if the freight is significant. You'll regret it. Offering free returns on light items is cheap and a catalyst for greater profits.

So now you have a winning bidder in an auction with fierce bidding competition who never asked a question prior to bidding, and after winning the bid now tosses a flurry of questions at you. Even worse, they paid and the clock is ticking—you must ship within the handling time stated on your listing. More upsetting is that you've already spent a bunch of time meticulously packing it up. Will this person return the item anyway? Perhaps the underbidder isn't quite as picky and would love it if you sent them a Second Chance offer for their bid amount, which is nearly the same as the high bidder's.

Answer all questions honestly and quickly in the friendliest way you can. If you're getting the clear sense the buyer won't be satisfied, then you can ask, "Do you want to cancel the order? No hard feelings if you do, I'll be happy to take care of it." If the agreement to cancel is mutual, here are the steps to cancel an order:

1. Hover over "My eBay" at the top-right-hand corner of most eBay pages
2. Click "Selling"
3. Click the "Orders" tab
4. Click the "All orders" filter
5. Click the pull-down menu under the "Actions" column
6. Click "Cancel order"
7. Select "Buyer asked to cancel the item(s) in this order"
8. Click "Submit"

Do not select the out of stock option or you will be hit with an order defect that will adversely affect your eBay account. Remember to send the underbidder a Second Chance offer as quickly as possible to increase your chances they'll still be interested in buying from you. Block difficult customers to avoid having to deal with them again in the future.

Handling Buyers Who Want to Renegotiate

I'm always puzzled why buyers message me, "What's the lowest price you'll take for this item?" It's not against eBay policy, but virtually all my fixed-price listings have the Best Offer feature enabled. Why not just press it and enter an offer? That doesn't bother me, but what concerns me greatly is the person who haggles before paying for their winning bid, or even worse, who receives the item and wants to keep it, but demands a discount for some vague or off-the-wall reason such as:

▶ "The condition wasn't as good as your pictures." (I don't retouch my eBay photos.)
▶ "The quality isn't as good as I had expected." (Why not just return it?)
▶ "There aren't any batteries, and I had to buy them, and they were expensive." (I didn't say batteries were included; I said it worked.)
▶ "It didn't come with the case." (It's used, and I didn't show a case in my photos.)
▶ "The color isn't the same as your photos." (Screens vary.)

This sort of renegotiation is common among resellers who are buying to resell in their bricks-and-mortar store or who resell online. Big-time collectors have a tendency to spend more money than they have, and I find they're sometimes asking for a discount. If you accidentally overcharged for shipping, and they call you out on it, then you owe a discount to make the buyer whole and bring the shipping charges in line with what you paid. "Would you like to return it?" I say. Usually, the answer is, "No, I want it, but I think you should give a discount of $X because of the (whatever excuse they are using)." I once sold a mechanical watch, and the buyer didn't know how to set it and said it was broken, and I was stuck with return shipping. The watch came back, and it was in perfect working order. I might have avoided a return if I had included written instructions on winding and setting it. Live and learn.

Whatever the reason you experience trouble in paradise, it will happen. Any business that you run for long enough will have snags along the way. Perhaps a curious spouse became irate after discovering the purchase. Use your good judgment. If there were a bunch of underbidders, then encourage the buyer to return the product. If the value of the item is really low ($5 to $10?), avoid negative feedback and just refund their purchase price. Did the buyer threaten you with negative feedback? As long as the message was sent to you *on eBay,* you'll most likely be able to get feedback removed if you were subject to what eBay calls *feedback extortion.* A buyer cannot threaten to use feedback or DSRs in an effort to extort you into providing goods or services that weren't included in the original item's description or purchase price; or a return, refund, or replacement item not covered by the original listing or the eBay Money Back Guarantee. Call eBay the moment you've been subject to feedback extortion and report it before you engage the buyer in further communication. The number for support is (866) 540-3229.

While on the subject of dos and don'ts, you can't require a buyer to leave positive feedback, specific detailed seller ratings, or revise existing feedback in exchange for a number of things, including, but not limited to:

▶ Receiving the purchased item
▶ Issuing a full or partial refund
▶ Monetary compensation
▶ Additional items

Don't forget to block those hard-to-please buyers so they don't come back to haunt you.

Buyer and Seller Feedback

The debate continues to rage around feedback timing. Should you leave buyer feedback the moment you're paid or when the buyer leaves you feedback? Bringing consensus to the endless debate is not only difficult, but it also seems to raise all kinds of emotional responses. You need only read posts within the eBay Community discussion boards to realize the feedback conundrum that persists with certain sellers. It's not that complicated and should never be made a big deal. I'll explain a little more in detail.

When you purchase or sell on eBay, you are allowed to leave feedback relating to the actual experience. Feedback cannot be used to comment on something unrelated to the transaction, or it is subject to eBay administrative removal at the request of the person receiving it. Feedback is the heart of the eBay system and how buyers and sellers "get to know" each other in a meaningful way. Feedback lets trading partners know what kind of eBayer you have been in the past (which is an indicator of future behavior).

There was a time not long ago that sellers could leave buyers negative feedback, but too many sellers retaliated against buyers when the buyer left them a bad comment. Today sellers can only leave a positive rating for buyers (but sometimes, sellers still use the comment space to "rate" the buyer in a negative way). Some sellers use the positive-only buyer feedback limitation for emotional cleansing, venting about a bad experience with the buyer there. See Figure 8–2 on page 153 for an example of my feedback profile.

eBay encourages sellers to leave feedback as soon as payment is received (or has cleared). Sellers can never revise their feedback, but buyers can change their negative or neutral feedback to a positive at your request. When WWIII breaks out and you've been dinged

▶ Exploring Selling Manager Pro

Selling Manager Pro is a subscription eBay service that allows you to manage products, track inventory, store listing templates, generate sales reports, and here's the big one . . . fully automate feedback for buyers. It's $15.99 per month (totally free with a Premium or higher eBay Store). Learn more about Selling Manager Pro tools in this way:

1. Click Help & Contact at the top of most eBay pages

2. Type "Selling Manager" into the search box

3. Select a subscription, if desired

To automate feedback (once you're subscribed to Selling Manager Pro), follow these steps:

1. Hover over "My eBay" at the top-right-hand corner of most eBay pages

2. Click "Selling"

3. Navigate to the Feedback pane

4. Click "Manage automated feedback"

5. From this page you can edit stored comments and configure automated positive feedback for buyers

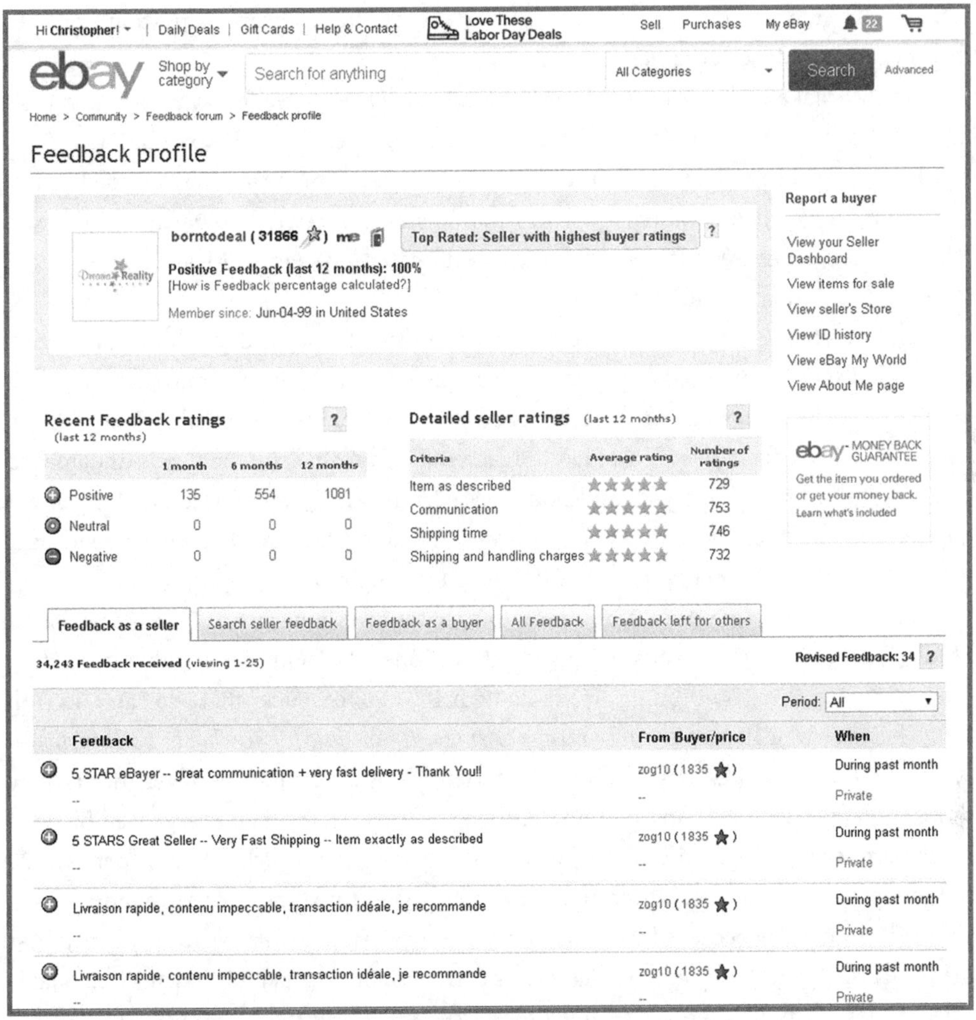

FIGURE 8–2: **A Screenshot of My eBay Feedback Profile**

with negative feedback but later entered into a peace accord (e.g., made a refund, fixed the offending issue, etc.), you can ask the customer to mend the injury they inflicted by *your* going to the Site Map (at the bottom of most eBay pages), navigating to the Community section, and under the Feedback section, click Request Feedback Revision. Once you request the revision, the buyer has ten days to act on the request, or the feedback becomes permanent (unless the buyer violates an eBay rule that allows for feedback removal). In the same Feedback section of the site map, there are also links that allow you to make your entire feedback profile private, follow up on feedback you left, and reply to feedback received. If a stubborn buyer won't budge, you can get in the last word by posting a reply to their negative feedback comment.

When I make eBay purchases, I really don't expect seller feedback, but some buyers take great offense if you don't leave a nice comment for them once they've paid. Go ahead and leave positive feedback the minute you receive payment. Some hard-headed sellers insist that the buyer leave them feedback *first*. I've even received foolhardy emails from sellers asking me to leave feedback so their "automated" system will leave one for me. I never do it. I think it's kind of rude.

As a personal rule, I never ask an eBay buyer for feedback, and I don't think you should, either. That's not to say you should become Silent Bob. It is 100 percent appropriate to reach out with a friendly message after tracking shows the parcel was delivered, "Hello Tecoya, I see the package has arrived. I wanted to reach out and make sure the box is undamaged and everything arrived in good condition. Please let me know if you need anything else. I hope you enjoy your new Gorham dinner plates." It can quickly backfire when a seller asks for feedback because you never know what the buyer might say.

eBay does a fine job of emailing every purchaser reminding them to leave feedback. Feedback is voluntary. With eBay's ironclad eBay Money Back Guarantee policy protecting every purchase, there is nothing you can do with 100,000 feedbacks that you can't do with 100. There's a well-known saying among eBayers, *if you ask for feedback, you might get feedback you don't want.* Imagine if waiters started asking diners for tips. Overpriced coffee shops dispensed with tip cups, and now they swipe my card for the $6 large iced blended mocha and swivel the iPad around for me to finger sign and pick a tip: 18 percent, 20 percent, a custom amount, or "no tip." I'm supposed to tip 20 percent for handing me a cup? I stopped going because the drinks were already way too expensive for my liking, and the pressure of that iPad panhandling me for extra money was just too much (McDonalds coffee tastes pretty darn good at a third the price). eBay feedback is a bit like that. What if your customer was too lazy to return the undersized shirt (oops, did you measure it correctly?), or just didn't want to be mean and mention the hairline crack on the antique teacup (time for you to get new glasses)? Pressing for feedback is poking a stick at a sleeping lion. You may regret it.

Packing and shipping deserve their own chapter and that's up next.

Packing, Shipping, and Delivering to Buyers

I have been packing and shipping professionally since at least 1988, and I have come up with best practices for everyday item shipping that considers both speed and cost. I outlined my basic recommended shipping methods in Chapter 6 when covering how to enable shipping options on the eBay listing form (sometimes called the *Sell*

Your Item form or SYI form). Here's a quick recap for your ready-reference before we take a deeper dive into all things *shipping*:

- ► Offer local pickup only for heavy or bulky products.
- ► Ship items under one pound by USPS First Class Package.
- ► Ship items that weigh between one and four pounds by USPS Priority Mail.
- ► Items over four pounds should be shipped FedEx Ground or FedEx Home.
- ► Cross-border shipments up to four pounds should be sent First-Class Package International Service.
- ► Cross-border shipments of more than four pounds should be shipped Priority Mail International or Priority Mail Express International.
- ► Contact FreightQuote for items that are too large to be accepted in any of the above situations.
- ► Add insurance to high-value items.
- ► Self-insure low-value items.

In this chapter, I'll walk you through more details on how to make smart shipping decisions that will get your products safely in the hands of your customers.

Choose Your Shipping Method

You can use any shipping carrier you'd like just as long as you upload the tracking information using the link displayed on the item listing page. If you ship using eBay's integrated shipping tool, this is handled both automatically and elegantly. To be protected against buyer claims of non-receipt, eBay requires that tracking include:

- ► A delivery status of "delivered"
- ► The date of delivery
- ► The recipient's address that matches the one shown on the order details page
- ► Signature confirmation if an item has a total cost of $750 or more

Tracking without a signature is good for items of lesser value (that's $749.99 or less per eBay's rules), but you still need to retain proof of delivery as long as it is still possible for the buyer to open a case. (In most situations, you can shred the shipping and insurance paperwork after 90 days or sooner if you receive positive feedback.) Tracking can be problematic on international shipments since some overseas postal networks simply don't talk nice to American postal tracking computers.

Shipping Precious Cargo

For precious and pricey cargo, you can use the high-touch USPS add-on called Registered Mail, which requires each person handling your parcel to log it into a shipping manifest with personal accountability at every step of the way. While this is a good solution for jewelry, gold bricks, and priceless art, it also costs more and is slower due to the additional paperwork and security involved. While FedEx, DHL, and UPS all offer international shipping, I don't use them for cross-border shipments due to substantially higher rates and fees. Cross-border buyers are price sensitive.

When shipping overseas, you'll be required to fill out a customs declaration form that faithfully (and honestly) describes the package contents and value. It's probably not wise to inform the world when shipping an expensive watch. Rather than calling it a watch, perhaps you'd use the word "souvenir." Terms such as "used clothing," "grooming item," or "health and wellness product" all sound less tempting than expensive brand names. Cross-border customers will periodically ask you to underreport the item value so they can save money on import fees and taxes. No matter how persuasive their request may be, you are ultimately responsible for delivery of the product in good condition. Lost, stolen, or crushed packages that are not fully insured will end up as a chargeback when the buyer opens a case, and you'll be the one stuck holding the bag. Import taxes and duties are based on the type of product. An antique item may be exempt from duty, or an item going back to the country of manufacture may be exempt. Identify the country of origin on the customs paperwork. For example, you should clearly identify a Sevres teapot going to France rather than simply a "teapot."

Making the Most of Media Mail

If you're educating the masses, the kind folks at the USPS have such a deal for you. It's called Media Mail Service. This is a dirt-cheap mailing service that's much less expensive than regular parcel rates. There are some substantial limitations. Media Mail rates are available only on the following goods:

- ▶ Books (at least eight pages)
- ▶ Sound recordings and video recordings, such as Blu-rays, DVDs, and CDs
- ▶ Play scripts and manuscripts for books, periodicals, and music
- ▶ Printed music
- ▶ Computer-readable media containing prerecorded information and guides or scripts prepared solely for use with such media

▶ Going International

Beginning in February 2020, eBay started offering a new shipping service called eBay International Standard Delivery. Sellers can enable this option when listing items and save an average of 9 percent when shipping to cross-border customers. It's less expensive than eBay's Global Shipping Program (which I don't use) and is super easy for sellers. Sellers can use this option when printing shipping labels even if it wasn't added to the listing at the time the item was listed. This option is a Delivered Duties Unpaid (DDU) shipping solution—buyers won't pay duties and tax at checkout on eBay, but may have to pay the carrier for duties and tax on delivery. I recommend this shipping method because eBay provides $100 in shipping protection automatically and extends seller and shipping protections for these shipments.

▶ 16-millimeter or narrower width films
▶ Printed objective test materials and their accessories
▶ Printed educational reference charts
▶ Loose-leaf pages and their binders consisting of medical information for distribution to doctors, hospitals, medical schools, and medical students

When you list a qualified product on eBay, add Media Mail as the main shipping option (with the below exception). Add a faster shipping method as your second option, such as Priority Mail. Media Mail is a tad bit slower, but it has tracking and insurance available.

If what you're shipping is 4 ounces or less, it's faster and just as cheap to send it First Class Mail. For these featherweight items, such as Blu-rays, DVDs, and CDs, use First Class Mail for faster delivery.

Media Mail is a very special discount service, and there's a catch—it may not contain advertising. Magazines and comic books are two examples of products that don't qualify for this deal. Don't try to fudge because these packages will be X-ray inspected or, in rare cases, opened for inspection, and if you're caught bending the rules, the package will either be delivered with postage due or returned. It happens both ways depending on the whim of the USPS employee. Oh boy, that would not be a happy customer.

Insuring Your Shipments

An actuary is a business professional who deals with the measurement and management of risk and uncertainty. I'd like you to think like an actuary. Why part with hundreds (or thousands) of dollars in profits to pay for shipping insurance when shipping is very reliable? eBay allows you to add reasonable shipping and handling costs to your listings. The policy allows the handling cost fee to cover the cost of packaging materials and insurance costs. Merchants blindly buy insurance "just because," and in most cases, it's not required.

Less than one in 500 shipments are lost or damaged. I add a very small handling fee that covers all refunds for these issues. Priority Mail has $50 in automatic coverage. UPS and FedEx cover $100 in losses on every parcel. Great news for Top Rated sellers who ship at least 300 boxes a month—Priority Mail is insured for $100 when you print labels from your eBay account.

We all eventually suffer a broken Baccarat or a mashed Fender Stratocaster. It happens. Protect yourself from unnecessary heartache. Damaged and lost parcels is a reality of business. Even the best pack job can fall victim to mishandling by the shipping carrier. My goal is to help you get it there with the *smallest* chance of an incident. Packing is a process that requires knowledge and experience. Safe delivery means happy customers and a fistful of dollars. Here are some critical key points:

▶ Wrap items separately, especially if they scratch easily. Friction within the parcel during shipment may cause unforeseen damage.

▶ Use enough packing and cushioning materials. Not too much, however. Big boxes cost more to send. All carriers have size limits, and some charge what's called *dimensional weight* (aka volumetric weight or DIM weight), which means you get billed for the size of the box (as explained in Chapter 6).

▶ Double-box the fragile stuff. A relic will become wrecked if you don't keep it well-spaced inside the carton. The nested box should be padded with packing peanuts or bubble wrap.

▶ Use strong boxes. Recycled, used cartons are fine for the less fragile things, but for a porcelain princess statue, you'll need a new carton to keep her safe along the journey. The flaps of the boxes you are using should be intact. Never reuse boxes that have creases or have lost their rigidity.

▶ Cover or cross off all previous labels on recycled cartons.

▶ Buy quality shipping tape. Flimsy film tapes will come undone in the warmest summer or wettest winter. Don't risk it over a few pennies saved. The clear packing tape I use is super thick (3.2 mil).

▶ Sellers of valuable items include a packing slip or duplicate shipping label inside their boxes. When the outside label is torn or damaged—or worse, falls off—the package can be delivered safely to its proper owner by simply opening it to locate the paperwork inside.

When you follow all of these tips, you will have greater peace of mind, and hopefully less damaged items as well. As a general rule, simply remember to give proper care to your merchandise. Imagine yourself in the shoes of the buyer, and then prepare your package in the same fashion you would expect if you had purchased it yourself.

Now that we've talked about the procedural aspect of shipping, let's discuss shipping from the perspective of your buyers.

Offering Free Shipping

Buyers always consider the *total cost* of an online purchase. When you list an item, eBay won't be telling you the shipping fee to ferry it to Fiji. The selling form will ask you for the box dimensions and the shipping weight. You'll be adding at least one shipping service to your listing. Buyers enter their zip code or country, and eBay displays the shipping cost based on the methods of shipping you enabled at the time you listed. Their location is "sticky," which means that they only need to enter it once, and every time they browse items, they will see the shipping fees on the search results pages as well as the item listing page. Test this out yourself. Conduct an eBay search, and then look at some item pages. Check the shipping information. Change the location to another country and see what happens. It's important to experience this just as your customer would.

Buyers are *addicted* to free shipping. Some even shop exclusively within the Fast 'N Free listings. Interestingly, a buyer will select an item with free shipping over one that has a shipping charge even if the *total cost* is the same. Curious! eBay charges their final value fees on both the item value and the shipping and handling costs. Seem unfair? eBay shipping labels are discounted (thanks to negotiated rates with the carriers), and that makes up for it.

Offering free shipping isn't as simple as it sounds. If you elect free shipping on your Sharp Blu-ray player to Sri Lanka, you'll find the freight frightening. Sellers of stamps may be tempted to ship by dropping a bit of philately into an envelope and slapping a regular stamp on it—a cheap way to attract the free shipping shoppers, but don't mail a mint 1933 Century of Progress Graf Zeppelin 50 cent stamp this way. A package that valuable without stiff cardboard protection and tracking is like driving a car without a seatbelt, with malfunctioning airbags, and a missing windshield.

Free shipping will earn you an automatic five-star DSR for shipping cost and will boost your fixed price listings in the search results. More buyers will take an interest too. Conduct a lab to test out the actual profits when offering a free shipping item. Consider the total cost to you of the item, packing materials, and freight. Add it all up. See how much you're earning and adjust a little here and there along the way to ensure you're taking home the profits needed to support your online adventure.

Sourcing Your Shipping Supplies

Being stingy isn't an evil thing. When you walk into a packing store, you'll pay a lot for a shipping carton. You can go online and obtain free Priority Mail and Express Mail shipping boxes and envelopes of various sizes from the USPS—including free shipping of these supplies to your home or office. Yes . . . free shipping supplies. These can be used for both domestic and international shipments. Don't try and use them for any other class of mail, or the package will be coming back to you. When your business grows, always check around for wholesale deals on boxes.

Here's another little known trick: Check out the USPS flat-rate mailing program. You can score substantial savings on shipments of up to 70 pounds. What you ship must fit in the flat rate envelope or box, and there is no weighing required. While it may be easier to use flat rate packaging, it's not always the best choice for your customers. Shipping across town using weight-based shipping is very affordable and will probably cost more using a flat rate. Delivery distance plays a significant role in the cost of shipping. A flat rate box going from Florida to Alaska filled with 60 pounds of pennies will set you back only a fraction of what you'd pay if you shipped by the pound. In fact, I calculated that it costs 6½ times more to ship without flat rate. FedEx and UPS offer free packing materials too. You'll find most of these complimentary shipping materials are for expedited services, not the lower-cost ground freight.

When you work for another company, worrying about the cost of everything the company purchases is probably someone else's job duty. You own your own business and you will have to analyze every purchase to ensure you're getting the best possible price. Do you enjoy saving just to see if you can? Being frugal can be lots of fun.

In our society, temptations to dive into more debt are everywhere. Pay cash whenever possible, and finance only when it makes good business sense (e.g., if the financing company includes free service with the contract). Here are some tips for you to stay fit and trim financially when you are making decisions about shipping methods and supplies:

▶ Before making any purchase, ask the question, "How much will this investment return for me in actual dollars?" or, "Is this purchase absolutely necessary for the successful operation of my company?" Do I need a fancy electronic scale, or will this *paid for* old faithful remain accurate?

▶ Never finance anything unless you're sure that it will generate additional profits. Otherwise, pay in cash or wait until you can afford to do so. I recall leasing an expensive UPS shipping system only to later discover UPS offered cheap rentals directly.

▶ Compare three different vendors' prices for every item you purchase. When contacting vendors for prices, be sure to let them know that you're price shopping and that your company's policy is to buy from the cheapest vendor (given, of course, that the product is the same from vendor to vendor). This applies to supplies and equipment. Bubble wrap purchased on eBay may still come out way cheaper than buying from a local packing supplies distributor. I buy all my bubble wrap on eBay. I purchase my cartons locally.

tip

eBay Store subscribers receive a supply of free eBay-branded shipping supplies (boxes, tape, etc.) based on their store level.

▶ Shop on the internet and pay reasonable shipping costs to save time, allowing more focus on what makes you money—selling, not shopping. Padded mailers are readily available on eBay at superior prices, including the cost of shipping—and are delivered conveniently to your door.

▶ Pay in cash if you can receive a substantial discount.

▶ Buy any items you use frequently in volume to get the best discount possible.

Being frugal does not necessarily mean settling for a generic brand or inferior product. It means finding the best possible wholesale or discounted price for the brands and products you use every day.

At my company, one of our most frequent purchases is shipping boxes. One major office supply superstore, that shall remain nameless, sells 12x12x12-inch cardboard boxes in packs of 25 for $34.68, which comes out to $1.39 per box. Another vendor sells the same box for $0.51 each. I can get free delivery from the first vendor with no minimum purchase, but the second company with a lower price requires a minimum order of $300 for free delivery. Because of my volume, I can always get free delivery and am saving more than 63 percent on this box. I stock up on many low-cost supplies from this discount vendor and order much less frequently—perhaps once a month or less—to meet their delivery minimum and ultimately to get the best prices.

Using Recycled Shipping Supplies

Recycling saves you money and helps the Earth. Clean, reusable shipping cartons can and should be given a second life. If I'm double-boxing an item, these repurposed cartons save me a considerable amount of money.

On 1,000 shipments, each with a reused carton at 50 cents each, I save $500 that I put directly into my pocket (well, bank account, actually). It's good to reuse bubble wrap, foam peanuts, clean packing paper and anything that looks professional and ensures safe delivery. A document shredder provides an endless supply of free void fill. Since they're free, I never reuse the complimentary boxes USPS provides.

Sometimes holding yourself in high regard can form a low opinion of you with customers. Things start to fall apart and become tacky when sellers ship with filthy packing peanuts, tape-infested bubble wrap, or boxes that have been through the wringer. Who wants to receive a long-anticipated present that looks like it came from a dystopian future? It's also a big no-no to use flimsy boxes. Reused cereal cartons won't cut it. I'll throw one out there you may not have thought of: I often use construction-quality heavy-duty plastic trash bags to wrap up low-value clothing shipments (never couture clothing). The same thick trash bags are ideal for wrapping and shipping area rugs. They save space, weigh virtually nothing, are waterproof, and resist cuts and tears. They must be contractor-strength to keep the contents safe. And why not? Customers love the cost savings since the average 12x12x12-inch brown box weighs a pound—just for the box itself. The buyer has to pay for that extra pound of shipping weight. Ouch.

Rushing Your Delivery Options

First, we had buyers demanding fast delivery. Then, they wanted free next-day delivery. Then, cheap same-day delivery. We now have retailers offering to deliver goods within hours the same day they're ordered. eBayers love to get things fast. When I sell a diamond ring, I offer free overnight delivery because a proposal might be, well, imminent. When your margin is healthy, offering quick, free delivery is great for business.

eBay requires that you indicate your handling time within the listing. This occurs when you fill out the listing form. You'll be rewarded with an automatic five-star DSR for shipping time when you ship the day you're paid and upload tracking timely. When you use eBay's shipping labels, tracking is uploaded automatically.

eBay displays their Fast 'N Free logo on your listing when these conditions exist:

> **tip** (i)
>
> When someone clicks the "Make Offer" button on your Fast 'N Free listing and enters a lower price, counter-offer back that you'll accept their price if they agree to a slower, less expensive means of delivery (ground vs. expedited shipping).

- ▶ Both the buyer and the item are within the 48 contiguous U.S. states.
- ▶ eBay can estimate the item will be delivered within four business days.
- ▶ For the first (or primary) shipping option, you offer a free shipping service.
- ▶ For the first (or primary) shipping service, you don't offer local pickup or freight.
- ▶ The listing isn't in Classified Ad format.
- ▶ For eBay Motors, the Fast 'N Free logo is used only for listings in the Parts & Accessories category.

tip

Sending items that use batteries and the batteries are included? Make sure they are fresh and working. I'd replace a watch battery. Then the watch would sell months later and by the time it arrived, the battery ran out. For electronics that are constantly using power, take the batteries out for storage so they'll be good when you sell the item.

Your listings qualify for the Fast 'N Free logo when it has free expedited shipping and same-day or one-day handling time.

The American addiction to ridiculously free shipping has set stratospheric expectations; however, do not generalize. While most retailers are focusing on reducing the time it takes customers to receive their goodies, not all items have to get there "yesterday." A smaller company (P.S. that's you.) has less scale and doesn't benefit from the huge discounts the big guys enjoy. Savvy eBayers know that free shipping isn't free at all—you're adding the freight cost into the price you charge. Some customers don't want or need things fast. They are looking for a great deal on what they love (e.g., collectibles buyers).

Recovering Incorrect Shipments

Shipping the incorrect item is a bummer for both you and the customer. You'll be stuck paying to ship three times— the first shipment out, the return, and the shipment out again to send the correct item. Mixing up shipping labels and sending the wrong items to two different customers happens when you're packing multiple shipments at once (remember my advice about never multitasking?). If you have employees, have two members of your staff inspect every item before it is shipped (you can be one of the "inspectors").

Handling Fragile or Delicate Items

When you're handling delicate items such as china, crystal, etc., pack immediately and securely for shipping and to avoid accidental damage during storage. A prepacked Haviland plate won't end up as powder on

tip

If you have a commercial UPS or FedEx account, your discounts are based on shipping volume. If you run a retail store that's not terribly busy, increase your parcel volume by offering packing and shipping services to the public. Then negotiate deeper discounts on freight and shipping supplies. There's always more power in numbers, and everyone will treat you like a VIP when you spend lots of money with them.

the floor if it's accidentally knocked off the shelf. Items with fragile appendages, such as porcelain figurines, are very likely to meet their doom if left unprotected. That beautiful, hand-painted maiden without fingers will not attract as much money or may not interest a buyer at all. I use Ziploc bags for non-breakable items to keep them dust-free. Don't allow employees to eat or drink while handling the merchandise. It's not a matter of if, but simply when, coffee or soda will spill and ruin something expensive or rare.

Protecting Yourself from Buyer Disputes

I'm not going to mislead you here. eBay follows the "customer is always right" mantra of business (usually). If a dishonest buyer falsely claims the product was not as described and opens a case, eBay will reimburse you up to $6.00 per return shipping label if you report the buyer. eBay is the judge and jury in deciding these situations, so have proof, such as video or photos to back up your position. eBay will remove negative and neutral feedback, defects, and open cases in your profile metrics when these dishonest people pop up.

And any item used or damaged by your customer that is then returned also requires some backup proof. eBay allows you to deduct up to 50 percent from the refund to cover the lost value of the item before you open a case, or they'll work directly with the buyer to resolve any issues relating to the return and mend any nasty feedback you've suffered when the buyer wronged you.

If you're in business long enough, someone will scam you (or try to). Dealing with this is part of the cost of doing business. With an internet-only business, you'll be fortunate not to have to cope with shoplifting as retailers do. Return fraud affects all mail-order businesses. eBay will usually help you when this occurs. The most common shipping-related issue is a claim of non-receipt (which is why you must have tracking unless cost is so low you can simply send another one). From eBay's view, if you can prove delivery, you will win every non-receipt case. "Did you ask your neighbor if they received it?" I'll ask when I am messaged about a box that shows delivered but the customer can't find it. Almost always the parcel shows up, and if not, I encourage my buyer to file a police report for porch piracy.

Here's a list of buyer behaviors eBay simply won't stand for:

▶ Demanding something not offered in the original listing
▶ Making false claims, such as falsely stating the product didn't arrive when it did or claiming it wasn't as described in order to return the item when the seller isn't offering free returns
▶ Misusing returns, e.g., sending back a different item, using or damaging then returning the product, or falsely claiming it was not as described

▶ Bidding for any reason other than to buy the product, e.g., bidding up the price to prevent others from bidding and then later retracting bids

▶ Opening up excessive eBay Money Back Guarantee requests or abusing the eBay feedback system to harass a seller

Report naughty buyers by calling eBay at (866) 540-3229. It's a great idea to call eBay prior to engaging in a vigorous virtual shouting match with the customer. Ask for advice and the customer service agent will explain your options and give recommendations on how to move forward.

Preventing Shipping Errors and Mishaps

When it occurred, you didn't give it a second thought. You were so excited to sell your mint 1989 Sony Walkman that you didn't question the buyer asking you to change the shipping address. After all, $1,200 is a lot of cha-chings. You packed so well a Mack truck couldn't scratch her and you agreed to the signature waiver. "I'm traveling and will be out enjoying my vacation, so could you waive the signature since I'm at my vacation home most of the day?" he said.

Then it happens. The dreaded case is opened. Apparently, the account was taken over by a fraudster who just fleeced you. Had you only followed the rules and shipped to the address on the order confirmation page and required signature delivery (on orders $750 and higher), you would have been covered by eBay's fantastic seller protections. A very expensive educational mistake.

Do not make these errors. Ship only to the address on the order. If a customer makes an error on the shipping address and it's a $5 pack of temporary tattoos, then sure, send it out to the new address. Who cares? No biggie. If you can't suffer the loss, then you need to inform the buyer you'll cancel the order and relist it so they can buy it again and enter the correct address. If they balk, they very well could be a charlatan, and you should call eBay for an opinion before proceeding further. PayPal also extends seller protection. If you sold something tangible (not digital or downloadable), and you shipped to the address on the PayPal transaction details page (on orders $750 and higher, PayPal also requires the recipient's signature), you'll be covered in the event of a dispute. I do not recommend using a shipping service that is arranged by the buyer. In the event of a dispute, you must be able to provide valid proof of shipping and delivery.

Every successfully sold item's listing page has a link to print one or more shipping labels. If you make a clerical error, void the label to recover the funds you paid for it. Here's how:

1. Hover over "My eBay" at the top-right-hand corner of most eBay pages
2. Click "Selling"
3. Click the "Orders" tab
4. Click "Shipping labels"
5. Click "More Actions"
6. Click "Void"
7. Use the "Select reason" pull-down menu
8. Click "Send request"

Follow steps 1 through 4, and click "Reprint" if your printer ran out of ink or you need to print the label again.

If you're shipping during the rainy season (a close friend lives in Washington state where he says that's all-year-round), tape over the shipping label to avoid it becoming wet and falling off. If you use an inkjet printer, you'll thank me for this tip as the ink runs when wet. Another bad weather tip: Always wrap the merchandise in a plastic bag before packing. This is not required for glassware or china, but mandatory for a fine silk tie. Imagine the disappointment when a flawless first edition of *Little House on the Prairie* arrives with water stains because the package sat on the porch in the rain. Oh no!

Packing well and shipping swiftly scores you an eBay Top Rated seller status. Be vigilant and avoid scams such as account takeovers, under-insurance demands, and parcel address re-direction. Remember to recycle so long as it's tasteful and not tacky. The USPS offers free co-branded, recycled cardboard boxes, and you can find them using the QR code in Figure 9–1.

In the next chapter, I'll uncover the holy grail of sourcing and share my precious tips for highly profitable "treasure" hunting.

FIGURE 9–1: **USPS Free Co-Branded eBay Priority Mailboxes**

CHAPTER 10

Sourcing Items to Sell on eBay

I started this book by explaining my eBay journey and how it all began with the consignment of a handful of dusty old war medals. That was June of 1999. If you fast-forward to *today*, I am still sourcing goods by consigning them. Consignment is a simple and pain-free sourcing opportunity. A person has something they no longer want (or never wanted, e.g., a gift without a gift receipt), and you offer the convenience of a service where you prepare, photograph, sell, pack, and ship their item, and divvy up the loot. Everyone has something to sell, but not everyone has the time needed to list on eBay. The commission you charge can be very healthy. For most items, I charge 50 percent. Quite a bit of that goes to eBay and PayPal to cover their fees, and from the balance of my commission, I have to cover overhead. Not everyone will fork over half the value of their stuff to have you manage it, but many will gladly do so. So long as the supply of consigned items exceeds your ability to list, you can charge whatever fee the market will bear. To the novice, asking for half seems absurd, but as you dig deeper both online and by speaking with bricks-and-mortar consignment stores, you'll discover that it's status quo.

In the world of consignment, the person or company providing the product is referred to as the consignor, and the retailer (that's you, eBayer) is the consignee. You don't pay for the inventory until it sells. Remember that storing the merchandise costs you something (e.g., rent or mortgage payments), and the cost of doing business must be considered, too.

With consignment relationships, you'll expand your selection into new product categories and offer buyers a broad selection. There's little risk since you don't own the inventory, and if the product doesn't appeal to customers and remains unsold, you can simply give it back.

What about contracts? No money for a lawyer? I cannot dispense legal advice because I don't have a law degree. However, my own attorney has informed me that oral agreements are "just fine." I even looked this up: "All contracts may be oral, except such as are specially required by statute to be in writing." *California Civil Code* § 1622.

If you know the consignor really well, a handshake will get you going. For everyone else, how about a simple agreement in plain English without all the legalese? It's not brain surgery.

And how long should you keep the item on eBay? For my regulars, I ask for a minimum of 30 days and most consignors are happy to *let it ride* until it sells. After all, you're providing free storage.

Although you'll notice that I absolutely love consignment, there are oodles of other ways to source goods to resell on eBay for mega profits. Quite often, the surplus items that both people and companies are trying to get rid of are stuck in storage for a reason—nobody wants them and you don't, either. There's also a bunch of people out there who are lazy and won't put in the modest amount of work required to primp, present, and sell their items on eBay. In this chapter, I'll help you identify the market trends so you don't acquire hard-to-move items. Let's also explore big profits from scratch-and-dent, imperfect, open box, damaged, and discarded goods. I'll be your guide on the path to discovering the perfect products to help you really get cooking on eBay. Let's put our heads together and go hunting for great stuff to sell!

Researching and Testing the Market

Make no mistake about it, business is very competitive. Some might say "business is war," but I tend to think of a successful business environment as a *dolphin tank,* not a *shark tank.* My most successful business friends are collaborators, not instigators, and that's why I love to connect with other businesspeople to query them on important topics. Hours before I typed these words, I telephoned a highly successful fashion icon and retired businesswoman and listened to her tips on identifying fashion trends. She said that with all the money she poured into fancy surveys and reports, her best intel came from walking the aisles at retail stores. This validated what I already knew, which is that there are no magic beans in research, just hard work.

Always have the courage to try something new by putting up a little inventory and testing the market. eBay is *immediate,* and the results are fast. When selling products that you think should appeal to young people, conduct your research by scanning through the social media posts of young people. Look at influencers with massive followers. Check out product reviews, and see how many "hits" the post received.

Look at the big chain stores and their ad campaigns. Benefit from their big advertising spends by looking for products they are promoting heavily, and take advantage of the halo effect. If you sell fashion, subscribe to the latest fashion magazines and peruse the ads.

While I'm convinced that discount stores and the "dollar" stores are ripe sources of goods to sell on eBay, look no further than the clearance shelves of big chain stores to identify slow-moving and unsuccessful products. You'll learn a lot about the latest, hottest products by asking people in your immediate orbit.

> **warning**
>
> Only buy what you're willing to lose. Never bet the entire farm on an inventory purchase. You can score big profits on the "right" purchasing decision, but if you make a mistake, the loss shouldn't put you out of business.

Identifying Market Trends on eBay

Way back in Chapter 4, I explained how to pan for eBay gold and the importance of using the sold items filter on eBay's completed item search when conducting item price research. Looking for the next big trend and hottest product to sell? Look no further than eBay to identify the latest trends to help you make predictions. eBay allows dummy auctions, which are listed in their test category. Be sure to exclude these listings from your consideration during research because they do not represent actual sales. These mock listings are easy to identify because eBay requires the word "test" in the listing title.

Common commodities are a breeze to research. Rare items are more challenging, which also opens up opportunity. The harder it is to find something, the more likely you'll be able to sell it at your asking price. Retail demographics and consumer preferences transform rapidly, and digital channels such as eBay make product pricing and demand transparent.

> **tip**
>
> Use the Research tab within your Seller Hub to search for products by keywords, manufacturer part number, UPC, EPID, EAN, or ISBN. If you have a Basic, Premium, Anchor, or Enterprise Store, Terapeak Research is included in your subscription, free of charge; if you don't have a Store, you can spring for a Terapeak subscription.

Drop-Shipping Products to Sell

There's a ton of skepticism surrounding drop-shipping (which you first read about in Chapter 4). Drop-shipping is a form of product sourcing involving a "middleman," in which the seller markets the actual goods being sold. Once a sale is performed, the seller orders the item for a (usually slightly) lower price and then forwards it to the end-buyer. The seller then keeps whatever profits are left over. Opportunists are advertising drop-ship "systems" and offering the hope of easy money. Drop-shipping is one means for sourcing product to sell on eBay, but you'll need to filter out all the noise and ignore the unrealistic claims you'll find all over the internet. Many (if not most) of the programs that are aggressively advertised make money for someone other than you (the program creator). Run quickly in the other direction if anyone wants to charge you a fee to allow you to drop-ship their merchandise. Wholesalers should only charge you for the product and a reasonable fee for packing, plus the actual cost of shipping.

The big problem with drop-shipping is that it's not easy to find products that will earn enough profit to pay the eBay and PayPal fees and put money in your pocket. Sourcing goods for drop-shipping takes research like any other method of sourcing, and you'll have to review your progress to ensure slow-moving items are taken off eBay to avoid paying insertion fees on dead business opportunities.

If you are a computer genius and can get eBay's computer system to automatically send your orders to your drop-shipping supplier without human intervention, you wouldn't need to make much on each sale. Labor is generally your biggest expense after the cost of the item. Here's a dreamy scenario: If you made one penny on each sale and moved one million orders a month, you'd earn $10,000 a month for doing nothing more than posting the listing. If you aren't a computer guru, then you'll need to manually send every order to the drop-shipper and upload the tracking information into eBay. The reality is, every supplier that will agree to ship directly to your eBay buyer will have their own way of accepting orders, and only a very limited number of them will allow direct access to their computer systems for automated ordering (such as connecting via an *application programming interface*, aka an API).

eBay permits drop-shipping, but you're ultimately responsible for the safe delivery of the item. You'll usually need more than same or one-day handling time enabled on your listing with a few exceptions—if you can persuade your wholesaler to ship fast and return the tracking number back to you in short measure, you might be able to avoid order defects caused by missing your handling time deadline.

You are not allowed to list an item on eBay and then purchase from another retailer or marketplace that ships that item directly to your buyer (e.g., you can't buy from another eBay seller and drop-ship the product without them being "in on the gig"). eBay doesn't allow this type of arbitrage activity, and you'll get a slap on the hand if you're caught doing it (or worse, be banned from selling).

After finding the hot products and steady sellers on eBay, reach out directly to the brand manufacturer of each product and ask if they offer to work with eBay sellers on a drop-ship basis.

Taking a Chance on Less-Than-Perfect Goods

Competing in brand new, low-margin goods is bound to lead to failure. Everyone has tried or is trying to do that. Analysis and intuition are not enough to profit in a low-profit retail space. The only thing to do is source goods that have generous margins, and that means exploring everywhere. Buying for resale is a skills-based job and you have to actually develop the skill for it or you will fail. But failure is a part of success and there will be failures along the way. Failed experiments are not only acceptable, they are necessary, but you must not bet the farm on these experiments. Never undertake experiments in a cavalier way. Study and research carefully before adding inventory. The less-than-perfect and secondhand business has always been a bright space for online resellers. There's someone out there who likes to tinker and fix things or doesn't care about a scratch or dent here and there. Explore this lucrative opportunity and fill your pockets with wads of cash!

Customer Returns

There are oodles of sites that offer entire pallets of consumer products that are customer returns. You can even buy pallets on eBay. The majority of these product aggregators are official liquidators for retail stores, and the pallets are generally uninspected returns. You gamble when buying them. You can find these firms by Googling "customer returns." As with all business opportunities, you'll face competition, and uninspected returns involve some probability of risk since you don't know what's working or why the products were returned in the first place. Pallets of goods involve substantial freight charges, which can cost nearly as much as the merchandise itself, so be sure to factor in the freight as part of your acquisition cost.

Make the rounds at your local independent retailers, and ask to speak with the manager. Ask if they'll sell you customer returns at a discount; or even better, offer to consign the items and sell them for a fee so you have zero investment and no risk. Most big chains have existing relationships and won't change their returns process management, but local, family-owned businesses will appreciate the opportunity to cash in on their dead returned stock.

Floor Models

Retailers take products out of their original packaging and display them as floor models to generate interest and retail excitement. Millions of these floor models are either sold at clearance, or they pile up in stockrooms. This can mean money for you, as a reseller. In order to tap into this wellspring of goods, it would be wise to build relationships with store managers and discover opportunities through networking. Here are some of the potential places to meet brick-and-mortar store managers:

- ▶ Call the store and make an appointment (busy store managers prefer scheduled meetings over walk-ins)
- ▶ Attend events hosted by your local chamber of commerce (membership is generally not required to attend paid mixers)
- ▶ Talk with volunteer business mentors found at places like http://www.score.org, which is the nation's largest network of expert business mentors (and a resource partner of the U.S. Small Business Administration)
- ▶ Attend Rotary Club meetings
- ▶ Drop in on church events to meet other business owners
- ▶ Search on social media and online
- ▶ Visit local business-oriented conferences

▶ Volunteer for local nonprofit organizations

Don't miss out on frequently-overlooked floor models that are otherwise completely perfect profit opportunities on eBay. Furniture and jewelry have big margins and are often marked up double what the retailer paid. Most everything else isn't really marked up that much, but as a new retail season approaches, the floor models have to go and retailers are more than willing to sell them for a song.

Broken Items

A dead smartphone can still fetch a pretty penny on eBay (the buyer knows how to fix it). There are literally millions of broken items (and perfect ones) sitting in dresser drawers, hall closets and garages. Offer hauling or personal organizing services to locals on sites such as Craigslist or Nextdoor. You'll be simply amazed at the amount of profitable merchandise that's collecting dust in people's homes. You can charge for your time and then offer a credit on the bill for any items you offer to buy from your clients. Busy executives, hectic parents, and retired seniors all appreciate help decluttering their residences. Score big profits this way and be a do-gooder at the same time.

Everyone has broken stuff at home. If you're handy and know how to fix things, let everyone in your orbit know that you'll take their broken items off their hands. Battery operated watches come back to life with a couple of inexpensive tools and a ten-cent battery that you bought on (you guessed it) eBay. A laptop becomes usable again when you purchase a readily-available power adapter to replace the one that's missing. If you're willing to restore items, you'll uncover the big profits to be earned with unwanted merchandise.

Shop Retailer Specials and Outlet Stores

Your smartphone makes you a shopping master in seconds. Retailers have proprietary apps you can download that will recognize the store you're standing in. Walmart is an excellent example. You do not need coupons to land lucrative deals at Walmart. Scan the barcode on the shelf or the UPC on the product enough times, and you'll discover Walmart's hidden clearance deals. These are unpublished, in-store clearance specials. Whatever the price is you see on the app, that's what you'll pay at the register, even if the shelf price is higher. After scoring retailer specials, you'll be able to turn a profit by immediately reselling them on eBay.

Outlet stores are a bit like a wolf in sheep's clothing, giving the perception that you'll be on a treasure hunt to find superior deals. The truth is that many outlet stores operate as their own separate "brands" with goods being sold that were only designed to be in an outlet. Many "better, off-price" stores don't carry many of the really high-end products shoppers want.

A mobile deal-sleuthing app can help. While not the only game in town, Shopular is among the most popular. There are shoppers who won't make a decision without it. The eBay mobile app has a tiny camera icon on the right-hand side of the search box and when you press it, you can scan UPC (and QR) codes to instantly check prices. To see eBay's sold item pricing, click Filter and then click the Sold Items toggle. When checking out deals in-store, you'll know if you can turn a profit. Remember to add sales tax into your profit calculation unless you have a resale permit on file at the store.

Buying from Well-Established Dealers and Sources

I love buying from older people. Shop owners who have *been in business forever* typically own the building they're in. They're established and have lots of experience reselling to other retailers. These long-time retailers have no rent and don't need to make as much profit as their competitors who just opened their doors. It's smart to buy from well-established companies because they have the smarts to know the big difference between a retail customer and a wholesale buyer such as you. Most seasoned businesspeople work out their wholesale pricing, knowing you have to make a reasonable profit.

The margins with second-hand goods are usually the best. Trading in secondhand goods is more lucrative when you have specialized knowledge. A generalist like me is less likely to take big risks on items unknown. A person who deals exclusively in candelabras wouldn't hesitate to drop big bucks on a pair of Sheffield Georgian period Rococo candlesticks. I lack the confidence in such decisions and would prefer to consign over buying such an offering.

Here are some places to find merchandise to resell where seasoned sellers tend to trade:

- ▶ *Antique malls.* With shelves full of dusty toys and cabinets lined with obscure curios, thrifting pros know how to shop relics in these precious places.
- ▶ *Consignment stores.* They survive on commission and are motivated to move items and make deals. Plus these stores aren't as picked-over as thrift stores and flea markets.
- ▶ *Pawnshops.* Long-established pawn brokers have loads of inventory and can wheel-and-deal because they make loans for a fraction of the item value and have lots of room to negotiate (they make most of their money on interest from making loans).
- ▶ *Flea markets.* Avoid the vendors who are obviously commercial, and ask merchants if they sell online—many don't and won't because they love cash and being "under the radar."

▶ *Garage sales*. Advertised sales will have more vultures clawing at the good stuff, so go very early (and drive around the neighborhood looking for unadvertised garage sales). I don't mind "professional" garage sale operators because they tend to know how best to price items for the wholesale trade such as eBay sellers.

▶ *Estate sales*. Use caution here because most are operated by professionals who really know what they're doing; however, there are deals to be had.

▶ *Live auctions*. Be careful because other frenzied bidders will pay more than the true value of some items; however, government-seized property auctions can present some juicy opportunities.

There's a huge opportunity trading with well-established dealers and sources and as you develop relationships with these prime suppliers, the opportunities will grow as these businesspeople get to know and trust you.

Making the Most of Found Items and Freebies

Look for opportunity in places everyone else scoffs at. When I worked at eBay, I was responsible for handling budgets amounting to millions of dollars, and I traveled the world setting up exhibits at the most exciting and well-attended trade shows. eBay gave away truckloads of unique, branded merchandise. We would open up case after case of T-shirts, pens, notebooks, pinbacks, and a zillion other tchotchkes. Most big companies give cool stuff away for free at trade shows to anyone who stops by their exhibit space. Go to the website for the convention centers and big hotels in your area and check their calendars. Attend all the free tradeshows you have time to visit, and take a backpack or rolling cart with you. Go at the start of day one to get the most popular stuff and then come back at the end of the last day to see what's left over. The employees for these big firms would rather unload their freebies on you than deal with packing them up and shipping them back to corporate. Plus, they'll look good in the eyes of their managers when they return home empty-handed, having given all those_____(fill in the blank with whatever's appropriate, e.g., "adorable", "awesome", "cute," etc.) promotional items away.

I should take this opportunity to say that I never have too much self-pride stopping me from grabbing potentially valuable items from the parkway in front of people's homes on trash day (a parkway is that bit of grass next to the curb that the city essentially compels you mow by not maintaining it themselves, but you don't legally own it).

While it's convenient to source sellable items locally, you can also take your search global during the course of your business or vacation travels. You know all too well how expensive vacations are. Either you go on them regularly and max out your charge cards, or you're bitter that your friend is rubbing your face with their selfies from Montenegro because they heard about the place in the Bond film *Casino Royale* (the one with Daniel Craig, not David Niven). Cool local handmade goods are how the indigenous peoples of many countries survive. Tourism is the engine for many destination towns, and you can pick up curiosities and sell them on eBay. For many years, my Mexican friend would bring me back a bag full of beautifully beaded Huichol handcrafted masks made by the indigenous people of the Sierra Madre Occidental range. He still makes several trips a year to the region. I made fistfuls of money reselling the masks, and he kept a tidy profit for himself, too.

Think of other opportunities to acquire unique merchandise. Monuments, museums, iconic amusement parks, and most places of interest sell items that are not readily available everywhere. Sell a "piece of the place" to eager buyers across the globe.

> **warning**
>
> Be wary of advertised "going out of business" sales. Many are legit, but some are bogus. Clever shop owners use this scheme to lure in customers, sell through their inventory and close, just to re-open with a different name (and the same owners). Most states regulate these sales and limit their duration. Check prices very carefully. Most of these sales don't permit returns.

Letting Consignor Come to You

There is nothing wrong with having a big mouth. Upon reflection, I realize that *many* great business opportunities unfolded because I'm a vocal person. Announce what you're doing, and in time, the merchandise will be arriving by the truckloads. Print up flyers and post them on local community boards. You can say, "I clean garages and attics. We can make a deal on unwanted items. Top prices paid. Text or call me at (818) 555-6789." No need for those tear-offs with your number. Anyone interested will take a photo of the flyer.

Post want ads on free and low-cost sites. The obvious ones are Craigslist and Nextdoor. Many communities have local sites. Join social media groups, but be sure you're following their posting guidelines. You'll find wholesale deals on other marketplaces that you can buy to resell on eBay. Check prices carefully because retailers love to lure unsuspecting buyers by using the term "wholesale" for products that are priced at retail.

Just after every major gift-giving season, remind family, friends, and colleagues that you will sell their unwanted presents for a commission. Christmas is the largest gift-giving occasion for Americans—even for those who aren't religious. For the Japanese, there's Ochugen in July and Oseibo in December. Hindus and Sikhs have Diwali.

Italians exchange gifts during the Feast of the Epiphany. With so many cultures exchanging presents and the huge diversity ever-present in our communities, you'll find an endless number of items to sell without investing a single dime of your own money. Figure 10–1 shows a plethora of goods that a local church literally set outside for anybody to pick up—and I did.

I responded to an online social media post by the church down the street from my home. The post said, "Tons of Free Stuff—Boxes and boxes of items that need to be gone. We have a rescue mission that is only able to collect 15 boxes, so there are tons left. First come first serve." Within seven minutes of this

> **tip** ⓘ
>
> eBayers can contact each other by clicking the Contact link from the profile page. You can find your profile page by typing https://www.ebay.com/usr/[your-ebay-id] and add a message of up to 250 characters. eBay does not allow contact information (such as a phone number) on your profile, and you cannot promote the sale of items outside of eBay.

FIGURE 10–1: **A Pile of Goods Resting in the Rear Parking Lot of My Local Church**

Marketplace › Musical Instruments

New violin wholesale

El Monte, CA · 5 days ago · 🌐

$50

Italian classic varnish,
Hand made instruments,
Build in four fine tuners,
Professional set up by violin maker in Los
Angeles,
Ready to play,
Come with Brazil wood bow, rosin, violin case,
extra strings,
Size: 4/4,3/4,1/2,
Local pick up in El Monte, Less

Condition   New

Report

Seller Information

Yuan Hu
Joined Facebook in 2009

Send seller a message

Is this available?

Send

Message   Save   Share

FIGURE 10–2: **Facebook Marketplace Wholesale Ad for $50 Violins**

post going "live," I arrived at the church and hauled away hundreds of valuable, collectible vintage CDs, movies, vinyl record albums, and antiquarian books. All for free. Figure 10–2 shows a wholesale opportunity that I found on the Facebook Marketplace.

Building Lasting Relationships

There is something that I cannot emphasize enough, which is that in order to succeed in business you must build meaningful, lasting business relationships, and that certainly applies to how you source your products, too. You'll catch more flies with honey than you will ever snag with vinegar. Be authentic and show mutual respect for consignors and vendors. Nurture strategic relationships rather than making transactional ones. Let go of expectations and focus on exploring supplier relationships. Trust is the secret sauce of building long-lasting alliances. Time and hard work glue it together. A closing thought—if you invest heavily in a relationship that isn't moving forward (e.g., your supplier's prices leave no room for you to profit or your consignor wants you to work for an impossibly low commission), then be frank with your trading partner, cut your losses, and move on without being a jerk about it.

In the next chapter, I'll discuss in more detail what I know you've been thirsty for—eBay Stores.

Running a Branded eBay Store

While you're hanging around on eBay, you'll notice some eBayers have a little blue door icon sitting snugly next to their feedback score in search results and on their profile page—this signals that they have an eBay Store (shown in Figure 11–1 on page 184). Stores are affordable tools for sellers that provide a branded shopping experience, additional free

FIGURE 11–1: **Search Results with the eBay Store "Blue Door" Icon**

listings, free packing supplies, and free business management tools. Free is a great thing, right? In this chapter, I'll introduce you to the benefits and challenges of running your own eBay store.

Why eBay Stores Are Not for the Faint of Heart

An eBay store is for experienced sellers with oodles of inventory. A common reason for Store failure is a lack of items in the store. If you have loads of stuff and plan to kick things into high gear immediately, then today would be a great day to open a Store.

There are five levels of eBay Stores, as mentioned in Chapter 7—Starter, Basic, Premium, Anchor, and Enterprise. I've mentioned them in order from least expensive to highest cost. As you would imagine, a more expensive store has better benefits than a lower-end store. When you're paying a higher monthly fee, you receive more freebies and better discounts on final value fees. Figure 11–2 outlines the fees associated with each tier of eBay store subscription.

Store Subscription Fee per Month		
Store Type	Monthly Renewal	Yearly Renewal
Starter	$7.95	$4.95
Basic	$27.95	$21.95
Premium	$74.95	$59.95
Anchor	$349.95	$299.95
Enterprise	Not currently available	$2,999.95

FIGURE 11–2: **Subscription Fees per Store Type**

Wait until you can consistently maintain 100 listings before launching a store. The Store level that's right for you depends on your listed item volume. While a Starter Store supplies 100 zero insertion fee listings for either auction-style or fixed price formats, all other levels provide a mixed allocation of auction-style and fixed price listings at no additional cost based on the chart in Figure 11–3. The allocations are *use them or lose them*. You have to use them up within the calendar month, and they do not roll over into the next month.

	Zero insertion fee listings allocation per month/insertion fee per listing after allocation	
Store Type	Auction-Style Listings	Fixed Price Listings
Starter	100/$0.30	
Basic	250/$0.25	250/$0.25
Premium	500/$0.15	1,000/$0.10
Anchor	1,000/$0.10	10,000/$0.05
Enterprise	2,500/$0.10	100,000/$0.05
All Store Types	All listings appropriate for and listed in the Musical Instruments & Gear > Guitars & Basses category are not subject to insertion fees	

FIGURE 11–3 : **Zero Insertion Fee Listings Based on Store Level**

Just as you suspected, there's always a catch. The complimentary auction-style listings are only valid in these categories:

- ▶ Antiques
- ▶ Art
- ▶ Clothing, Shoes & Accessories
- ▶ Coins & Paper Money
- ▶ Collectibles
- ▶ Dolls & Bears
- ▶ Entertainment Memorabilia
- ▶ Health & Beauty
- ▶ Jewelry & Watches
- ▶ Pottery & Glass
- ▶ Sports Memorabilia, Fan Shop & Sports Cards
- ▶ Stamps
- ▶ Toys & Hobbies

There are a few subtleties to the Store selling fee structure and you should read the entire article on this subject by scanning the QR code in Figure 11–4.

FIGURE 11–4: **eBay Store Selling Fees Page**

Once your Spidey sense alerts you that you're probably spending way too much of your hard-earned profit on eBay fees, and you've decided to make the leap into owning your very own fancy eBay mall space, follow these steps to launch your subscription:

1. Hover over "My eBay" at the top-right-hand corner of most eBay pages
2. Click "Summary"

3. Click "Account"
4. Under the section "My eBay Views" click "Subscriptions"
5. Click "Choose a Store"
6. Click "Select and review" under the desired Store subscription level
7. Select either a yearly or monthly subscription option (I recommend starting with monthly)
8. Enter your Store name
9. Click "Submit order"

Venture out into calm waters until you gain your sea legs. While it is absolutely fine to upgrade or downgrade your Store subscription level, downgrading or canceling a yearly contract (yes these subscriptions are legitimate, binding agreements) means eBay will charge you an early termination fee. Read the fine print at https://pages.ebay.com/stores/subscriptionterms.html before you leap into your eBay Store nuptial. Start with a monthly agreement to test the waters.

Unlocking Your eBay Store Toolbox

You may be asking yourself, "Now that I have it, where do I find it?" The eBay Store dashboard is well-appointed with all sorts of cool features. While there is absolutely no requirement that you pimp your Store profile, at least whet your appetite by checking out what's possible now or in the future. Follow these steps to navigate to your Store management page:

1. Hover over "My eBay" at the top-right-hand corner of most eBay pages
2. Click "Selling"
3. Scroll down to the "Selling tools" pane
4. Click "Manage Store"

You're now sitting pretty at the Manage My Store page where you'll be able to design, manage and market your store, and promote listings.

Users and Permissions

If at any time you feel you'll need helping hands to support your eBay Store, you can extend Store management permissions to trusted individuals (and revoke the permissions at will). To grant access to members of your team, head over to the Manage My Store page, and click Permissions under the Store Summary subheading. Adding users is as simple as keying in their name and email address and selecting the level of permission you'd like them to possess. While you can allow anyone to list items, you can also limit their authority to set up draft listings. Worried about letting the mice play while the cat's away? There's an activity log (can you say "accountability"?) that informs you what each person has been up to.

Store Categories

You can add, edit, and reorder Store categories as an additional way to organize and present merchandise within your Store. This is a pain reliever for buyers who don't want to scroll through a bunch of your listings to find the genre of products they're interested in buying from you. An eBayer selling collectible trading cards would setup custom Store categories for hockey, football, basketball, and baseball, for instance. A car parts dealer would have Store categories set up for individual vehicle makes to enable a buyer to find just the parts for their car. A jewelry seller would setup Store categories for watches, necklaces, rings, brooches, cufflinks, and so forth.

Here are a few things to know about Store categories:

▶ Make them *your own*—they don't have to mirror eBay's categories in any way.

▶ A Store supports 300 different custom Store categories and sub-categories.

▶ Store categories can have up to three levels, i.e., a top-level Store category and up to two additional levels of subcategories (e.g., Jewelry > Watches > Digital Watches or Clothing > Men's Clothing > Suits).

▶ Assign the Store category at the time you list your item.

▶ If you don't have an assigned Store category, a category called Other will be assigned to the listing by default.

▶ Your Store category name may be up to 29 characters long.

▶ Store categories can be added, renamed, edited, reorganized, and deleted any time.

▶ Store categories will become hidden from your store navigation if you have zero listings assigned to it.

▶ You can change the Store category on a listing.

▶ List your items in up to two distinct Store categories for free.

You should set up store categories when you have a healthy number of items to assign to them. A vintage video game seller who has a handful of Atari games would start with a Store category called Atari Video Games and as the inventory for a specific system grows, a sub-category should be added when there's sufficient variety to warrant it. For example, Atari Video Games > Games for Atari 2600.

When you're running a clearance sale, add an eye-catching category, such as 25 Percent Off or Daily Deals, to incentivize buyers to browse your sale items. Click the link Store

Categories found in the Store Design section of the left-hand-side menu. Assign up to two Store categories when you list or add your newly set up Store categories to existing listings by revising them.

Branding Your eBay Store

While you can spend an eternity customizing your Store, please don't fret. You can always refine and improve things in the future. *Good enough* will get you started. List products and make sales as swiftly as you can while putting forward quality listings. Bigger businesses can afford to unleash an army of brand experts who fuss over the details. Entrepreneurs are in this game to make profits.

tip

Some sellers find custom categories unnecessary (or unwanted extra work) and prefer to display eBay's categories in the left navigation bar of their Store. You can configure this when you manage your Store by selecting eBay Categories under the heading Category Type when you're in the Edit Store page.

Go to Manage My Store and click Edit Store—from here, you can make the cosmetic adjustments to help you realize your vision for Store branding. This is the place where you can edit your Store name and description, then upload branding. eBay supports custom billboards—exactly like social media profiles. Make your own 1200 pixel by 270 pixel billboard or hire someone. Upload your logo. Make sure it's square, or it will look distorted. The logo size is 300 pixels by 300 pixels.

If you've stocked up on key merchandise, you can extol the virtues of these items by featuring them (up to four) on your Store landing page. The remainder of your listings can be sorted and displayed the way you prefer. I prefer showing the big ticket items first and I think a gallery of images puts my best eBay "foot" forward.

You can make changes to your Store in seconds. When you're signed in, you'll see the Manage My Store button in the upper-right-hand side of the Store landing page (see Figure 11–5 on page 190).

Changing your Store name will also change your Store URL and since the URL is based on the name, you can't control it. That means anyone who has the old URL will need to be notified, and anywhere you linked to the old URL will need to be amended.

Setting Your "Out of Office" for a Break

Avoid the stress of being unavailable by informing customers when you're away. As a business owner, I can relate to the high blood pressure that being separated from your

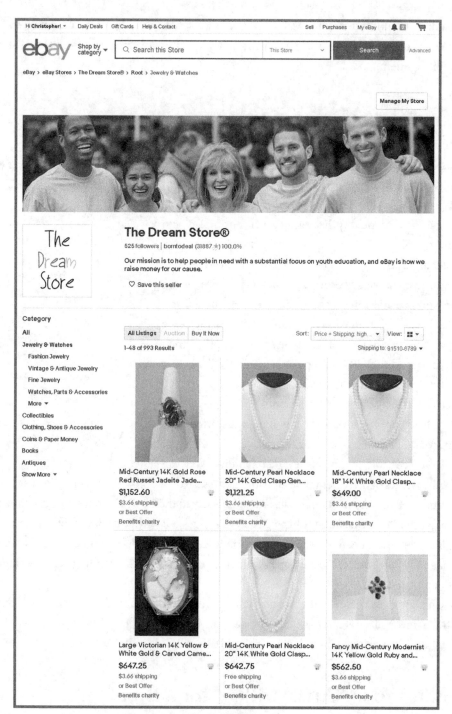

FIGURE 11–5: **The Dream Store®, an eBay Store I Set Up for a Cause Dear to Me**

busy company causes. eBay has solutions, so put away the hypertension pills and keep reading.

Turn on the "out of office" message when you're simply unable to answer emails in real time but are still taking care of order fulfillment "business as usual." The away message area can be instantly toggled on for preplanned absences and emergency moments. Sick days are covered with a friendly custom message you enter. The out of office email response is automatically sent to anyone messaging you through eBay. You set the start and end date for the message to appear. The message area is a massive 5,000 characters long for the long-winded people out there. When crafting this customer note, add the date when you're coming back and how quickly you'll be responding. Include your phone number if you are handling calls, but not emails while you're away.

Everyone has the right to a little R&R now and then, including a busy eBay Store owner such as yourself. With Store vacation settings, you can tick a checkbox and voila. Your Store is on vacation hold. You can add a message for people to see when they visit your store and indicate the date of your return—all visible on your listings themselves. If you like, you can even tick another checkbox and prevent item purchases until your vacation is over. But why? You can always increase your handling time in bulk using the Mass Editor tool that I mentioned in Chapter 7. You can change your handling time to any number of dates, up to 30. Most customers don't want to wait that long, but depending on the goods you offer, many unhurried people are willing to wait, so long as they know when to expect their shipment. Remember to bulk edit your handling time back to your usual number of days after your vacation hold is disabled. The vacation hold feature needs to be manually switched off when you come back to work. Figure 11–6 on page 192 shows my Store vacation settings.

Getting the Most Out of Promotional Offers

I'm pretty sure everyone stands beside me when I yell (at the top of my lungs), "I love free stuff!" Who doesn't? You may recall that I mentioned in Chapter 7 that you'll see the free stuff eBay quietly offers you under the Seller Hub > Promotional Offers pane. Check this mini-announcement board frequently for deals on free insertion fees and reduced or free final value fees.

In Chapter 9, I provided a QR code that takes you quickly to the page where you can order free, co-branded eBay-USPS Priority Mail shipping supplies, but it's a federal offense to ship UPS, FedEx, or even First Class Mail with these complimentary boxes. I get that you want to save money, so be sure to cash in on your very own allocation of free eBay branded supplies that are included with a subscription to Basic, Premium, Anchor and Enterprise level eBay Stores. You'll discover this and other subscription privileges on the

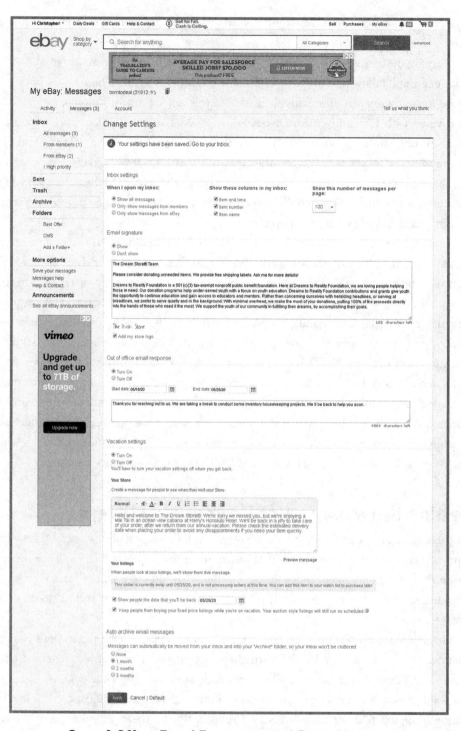

FIGURE 11-6 : **Out-of-Office Email Response and Store Vacation Settings**

Manage My Store page, by clicking the link Subscriber Discounts under the heading Store Design. Use the eBay shipping supplies coupon while shopping at the official eBay Shipping Supplies store located at https://www.ebay.com/str/ebayshippingsupplies (use the coupon code at checkout). While I simply love the free boxes, poly mailers, and packing tissue, the packaging tape has two, huge issues—it's flimsy (requiring more than one "pass" to seal the flaps of a box), and it has the eBay logo printed all over it, making it useless for protecting shipping labels. eBay also offers stickers and thank you cards that seem to be popular, but I feel are not a good use of my coupon allocation.

All Store levels (with the exception of the Starter) include a free subscription to the Terapeak Research tool that allows you to peer back in time and look at up to one full year of eBay sold item pricing data. You'll find Terapeak by going to the Research tab in the Seller Hub.

Spreading the Love with the Promotions Manager

In Chapter 7, I explained how you can convert watchers into buyers by using the little-known eBay feature that allows you to extend a special price to folks who have officially "watched" your listing (using the button on your item, shown in Figure 11–7 on page 194). This tool generates a solid percentage of my sales—people love to save money.

Store subscribers can ignite retail excitement like a marketing guru (without an expensive marketing degree) by using eBay's free Promotions Manager included with Store subscriptions. This simple tool provides you with five types of promotions, which I describe below.

Order-Size Discounts

Motivate customers to spend more in your Store using an order-size discount. There are multiple ways to configure this feature, which are:

▶ A dollar amount or percentage discount based on the total amount spent

▶ A dollar amount or percentage discount based on the total quantity of items purchased

▶ A buy one, get one deal where a free or discounted item is offered with purchase (you can make the number required higher than one in order to qualify for a free or discounted item)

▶ A dollar amount or percentage discount with no minimum purchase required

The Promotions Manager permits you to enable the promotion by selecting up to 500 items, entering SKUs or item IDs, or setting up rules and filters—the latter has a 10,000

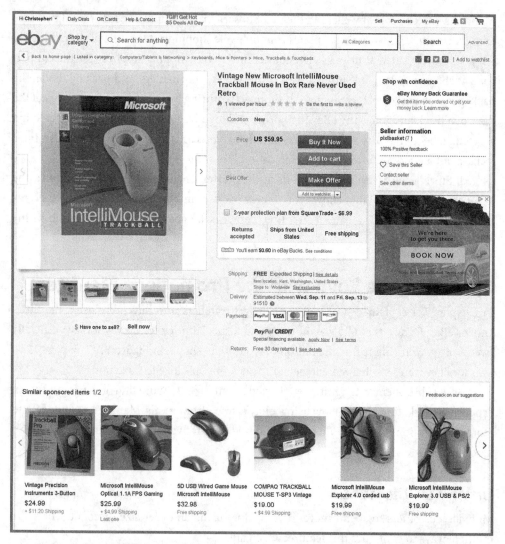

FIGURE 11–7: **Send Offers to Anyone Who Clicks the Add to Watchlist Link on Your Listings**

item limit. Rules could be something as simple as enabling the promotion to include only new items in the eBay Art category. You can select inventory one-by-one, filter by eBay categories, filter by Store categories, or include everything in your Store within any particular promotion. You can even filter by price range.

Your offers must be compelling though. Buy one, get one free is *way more compelling* than buy ten, get one free. Asking someone to spend $500 to save $10 won't captivate as much interest as $10 off $50 in purchases. Make it an offer they can't refuse. Capisce?

Markdown Sale Events

Everyone loves sale events, right? I sure do. Launch a markdown sale event with up to ten levels of discounts in one event (e.g., save 12 percent on men's ties or take $5 off each automotive tire purchased). But wait. There's more. You can optionally offer free shipping for all discounted items (which only applies to the first domestic shipping service offered). Items for markdown sales events can be selected by SKUs, item IDs, or through rules and filters.

Shipping Discounts

We live in a culture of free shipping. Everyone knows that free shipping isn't truly free because the purchase price has to include the cost of moving goods around—we simply love that we don't have to keep pulling up the calculator on our phone to determine if our purchase fits snugly in the budget we've set.

The Promotions Manager allows you to offer free or flat rate shipping that's triggered by either a minimum order size, a minimum quantity of items added to the buyer's shopping cart, or if you prefer, just free or flat rate shipping without conditions (another kind of sales event). You can schedule the offer and upload a picture for visual appeal. Figure 11–8 is an example of how you can include your own graphic when you're configuring promotional

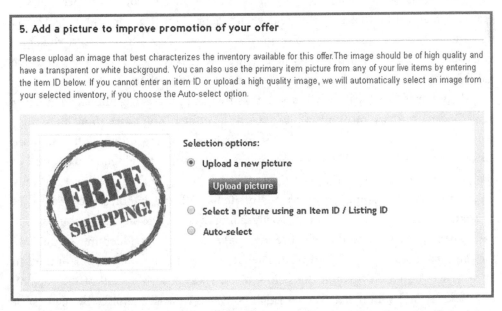

FIGURE 11–8: **Example of an eBay Free Shipping Promotion Custom Graphic**

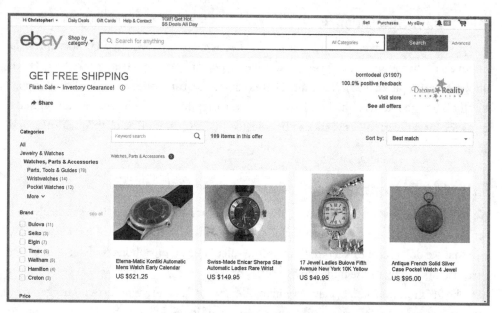

FIGURE 11–9: **A Promotion from the Buyer's View**

offers; Figure 11–9 is an example of an eBay promotion from the buyer's vantage point. Multiple offers can be prioritized by numbering them.

Free or discounted shipping is a concession you offer to your customer, but you bear an actual cost for this. It works great when freight is low (e.g., for light items). Scroll through all your sale items when you're on your first few rodeos—to make sure you don't lose your shirt on a particularly heavy item. The great news is that you can always exclude individual item IDs from a sale to cover these exceptional situations.

Many hardheaded sellers will argue that free shipping is a gimmick they never need to lean on. "I sell rare collectibles, and my customers don't care about shipping," they insist. eBay allows buyers to filter items that specify free shipping, free in-store pickup, as well as free local pickup. For some reason, even the high-end buyers scoff at shipping charges. I don't offer free shipping on everything in my store, but I certainly do promote free shipping on thousands of items. When I handled a collection of consignment artwork, I'd have buyers bellyaching over the freight. You see, it cost me $40 to box up the art, and that's before the freight expense was added in. "I think $65 for shipping is way too high," I'd read. The fact is, I was only entering $25 of the $40 into the handling cost field on the selling form. I was absorbing $15 of the packing costs already and still, there were complaints. When I raised the price by the cost of shipping and handling and offered free shipping, I would sell more. While I am no expert on psychology, I do recognize the wisdom of herd mentality when it comes to offering free shipping.

Codeless Coupons

It's not easy to make a buck. Attracting customers is a challenge, and for as long as I've been in business, acquiring new customers has always been expensive. Elon Musk has devoted many words to extol the success of Tesla while reminding the world that his electric car company has never had to advertise. Not everyone is Tesla. For the rest of us, we must promote ourselves. The most successful companies have a sales culture.

> **tip** ⓘ
>
> Why not share codeless coupons *everywhere* in order to discover new buyers? Anyone can buy on eBay as a guest *without registration* as long as the item is being purchased using Buy It Now and is less than $5,000. eBay guests can pay with PayPal, credit card, debit card, Apple Pay, or Google Pay.

You can set up codeless coupons (targeted offers) and share the URL for these promotions on social media, in emails, on your website, or my current favorite—by using a QR code (I generate my QR codes at https://www.qrstuff.com). These deals are private until you share the link. They are never visible on the general eBay site. Anyone clicking the link you provide will receive the discount automatically and without additional effort.

These special offers can work with a conditional minimum spend amount or item quantity. The offer can be either a fixed discount amount or a percentage off. As with all other Promotions Manager tools, you can focus the discount on SKUs or item IDs, or by setting up rules and filters. Items can also be excluded. After you set up the codeless coupon, eBay will generate a clean, short URL that you can share with anyone—even non-eBayers.

Volume Discounts

Consider a seller of high-margin, low-price phone cases. The wonderful thing about these cases is that people replace their cases all the time, which means ample repeat business. The downside is that cases are a low-ticket sale. The case peddler has to carry a wide variety and lots of SKUs in order to attract buyers. Add to this all the variations (i.e., the many different model numbers the cases must fit). Given the opportunity to save money, the owner of the latest-and-greatest smartphone will gladly invest in a selection of fashionable, yet affordable cases.

You can enable volume pricing on SKUs or item IDs, or by setting up rules and filters. The neat trick with rules and filters is that these volume discount options will appear not only on existing inventory that matches the criteria, but all future items will acquire the discount, as long as they match the rules and/or filters. So, let's use this example:

- ▶ Buy one item, no discount.
- ▶ Buy two items and save 12 percent off each item (you can make these percentages whatever you want).
- ▶ Buy three items and save 18 percent off each item.
- ▶ Buy four or more items and save 23 percent off each item.
- ▶ Filter to limit the discounts to Cell Phones & Accessories category.

The above volume discount plan will take immediate effect on what is currently listed and will apply itself automatically to all new listings, provided they are within the Cell Phones & Accessories category. The volume pricing tool in Promotions Manager should not be confused with the volume pricing option that appears at the tail end of the listing form. The individual listing volume discount option applies to the listing alone, and the Promotions Manager applies to listings in bulk. Figure 11–10 on page 199 displays the customer point of view of a seller promotion.

Sales promotions retain existing customers, attract new customers, and satisfy customers' demands for deals. Your Store success hinges on your ability to maintain long-term relationships with buyers and to encourage repeat visits to your store. Periodic, varied and exciting sales promotions will accomplish this.

Promotions Manager is super intuitive. You can even exclude items by SKUs, item IDs, eBay categories, or Store categories. Now that's flexible marketing. I like being able to quickly put low-priced, used inventory items on sale with steep discounts so that I can put some wings on these items and make room for more attractive and lucrative stock.

Use Promotions Manager to elevate your store and help it stand out. Promotions Manager allows you to creatively build retail excitement.

You'll find the Promotions Manager by starting at the Manage My Store page and then clicking the Manage Promotions link under the heading Item Promotion.

Branding Product Listings with the Listing Frame

Store sellers can deploy some really neat tricks, and using the listing frame is one of them. The listing frame is an optional section that can be placed below the item specifics area on your listings—only available to Store sellers. It's an all-or-nothing situation because the

FIGURE 11–10: **Customer Point-of-View of Seller Promotion**

listing frame will be applied to every listing. This additional concession is free, and you can turn it on and off instantly. The listing frame may contain any of these elements:

▶ Your Store header

▶ Left-hand navigation category list—as long as they contain items

▶ The Store logo

▶ A link to allow buyers to add you to their favorite sellers

- ▶ A Store newsletter signup link (more on this in a bit)
- ▶ A link to the items you've placed on sale with Promotions Manager
- ▶ A search box to query just your Store items
- ▶ A personalized message for buyers
- ▶ Links to your store pages

Sometimes too much of a good thing isn't a good thing, and I caution you to keep the listing frame clean and simple. Buyers open the listing page to read item details and look at your pretty pictures, so you don't want to overload their visual senses and distract them so they forget why they were looking in the first place. You should tinker with the listing frame until it looks just right. It's like cream in your coffee—not too much and not too little.

Access the listing frame setup by starting at the Manage My Store page; then click the Manage Promotions link under the heading Item Promotion.

Maximizing Sales with VIP Access to Email Marketing

Just when you thought the party was over—you guessed it—there's more fun in store for you. Store sellers can manage mailing lists consisting of attentive, interested buyers. We're not talking about spammy lists you buy from a broker; these are eBayers who asked to receive your emails. Buyers are prompted to sign up for email newsletters when they save you as a seller. This is no trivial business opportunity—building mailing lists is a cornerstone of every customer-centric business in the world. Your wallet will be the beneficiary of the additional customer touchpoints that blossom through email newsletters—available exclusively to eBay Store sellers (note the allocations represented in Figure 11–11).

Store Type	Monthly Free Email Allocation	Additional Cost per Recipient (Over Allocation)
Basic	5,000	$0.01 per email
Premium	7,500	$0.01 per email
Anchor	10,000	$0.01 per email

FIGURE 11–11: **Free Emails Allocated per Store Type**

The eBay police supervise your email activities, and per eBay policy, your emails can't include:

▶ Offers to sell items outside of eBay
▶ Phone numbers or email addresses
▶ Links or image references to items not located on an eBay site
▶ More than 100 eBay HTML tags
▶ JavaScript or other active scripting

My first subscriber joined my mailing list on November 25, 2004, and has remained with me ever since—now, that's loyalty! When sending emails, you'll select from a template or make your own layout and you can limit emails to eBayers who have made purchases in the recent past while excluding the idle subscribers who haven't bought in a while. This lets you focus on active buyers and preserve your free emails for individuals who are more likely to buy something. Here are some more features to pique your interest:

▶ Emails can be sent to select or all lists at once.
▶ You can add and remove mailing lists and provide them with informative names.
▶ You can opt to limit the recipients to subscribers who have opened your emails in the past.
▶ Emails can be made recurring—with frequencies between weekly and every eight weeks.
▶ An item showcase can be added featuring up to four of your listings.
▶ You can display a gallery view of up to 50 items.
▶ You can showcase your recent feedback to build buyer confidence.

You can check the status of pending and sent emails. You can even block eBayers on your list who have caused headaches in the past.

Access email marketing for Store sellers by starting at the Manage My Store page; then click the Email Marketing link under the heading Store Marketing.

The kind folks at eBay have provided beautiful savings with stores and with Terapeak pricing and sales intel. You'll be ahead of the competition the instant you subscribe. And here's the scorecard for all the goodies:

▶ Unlimited insertion fee credits for successful auctions
▶ Discounts of up to 60 percent off final value fees
▶ $25 per quarter of free shipping supplies for Basic Store subscriptions; $50 per quarter for Premium Store subscriptions
▶ Promotions Manager (this is huge)

▶ Discounts on business services

Anchor Store subscribers (that's me) score these VIP luxuries:

▶ White-glove customer support

▶ Deeper insertion fee discounts

▶ $150 per quarter of free shipping supplies

▶ $25 per quarter of free Promoted Listings

Everyone who lists in volume will need a Store—you'll save money on insertion fees, final value fees, and you will receive the red carpet treatment in so many other ways. As an eBay VIP, your listings will be marketed to more buyers and your increased sales will be the byproduct of your smart decision to subscribe to a Store. Go for the month-to-month deal when you're a newbie. You can always upgrade your subscription, but downgrading or ending an annual Store contract involves early termination fees, so take it slow and feel things out.

In the next chapter, I'll dive into the benefits of working with teams, so grab a cold beverage, relax, and let's get right into it.

Scaling Your eBay Business

Throughout this book, I have alluded to the possibility of your becoming successful not only with your eBay business, but achieving great wealth following proven methods for success. This is no storied myth—indeed there is a pot of gold at the end of the eBay rainbow. My eBay business has generated millions of dollars and continues to reap consistent rewards. I have the unshakable conviction that anyone with sufficient grit and a lack of chronic pessimism can achieve similar (or higher) results than I do. Fortunately, Entrepreneur Press never publishes "get rich quick" materials—and I never evangelize overnight success. Success is the product of smart, hard work. You can grow rich as long as you maintain the required stick-to-itiveness needed to become an eBay MVP. Let's use this chapter to explore how you can achieve the "big time" status for your eBay business.

Transitioning from Part-Time eBay Seller to Full-Time Business Owner

Seasoned businesspeople take decisive, swift action when expanding operations because they have loads of experience. Newbies must proceed with extreme caution. Expand too quickly, and your eBay business will collapse on itself because you'll be unable to manage uncontrolled growth. A high bar for the customer experience must be maintained. Grow too carefully, and you'll lose market share and opportunity. Start your focus on the customer and work backward. If trends tell you that a product is selling at a steady clip and the future looks bright, go deep on inventory. Test endlessly and keep adding steady winners. Dump bad products as quickly as you acquire good ones.

Before adding storage or a warehouse, look at scalable rental space. Flexible warehouse and personal storage allow for a long engagement before you get married to a particular location or idea. Contact the local Chamber of Commerce or look online for these business locations that offer complete turnkey warehouse solutions. A desire to keep this book evergreen compels me to avoid talking about firms that are titans today and could be gone tomorrow. Look no further than local business leaders in your city—they are easily found through the local government community development office (or persons designated to attend to these matchmaking moments).

If you can further delegate the pick, pack, and ship process, all the better. Big companies that handle this on scale (some use robots) are suitable for the task. The smaller the third-party company, (usually) the higher the per-box cost of handling your orders. The best, fully-automated, staffed fulfillment warehouses (sometimes called *logistics companies*) offer direct integration with your eBay account using eBay's selling APIs. The APIs allow big retailers and third-party developers (who make solutions for retailers), to programmatically integrate with eBay's selling system so that order processing and management is seamlessly connected—no human hands are required from the time an eBayer places an order to the point at which the person shipping the order has to pull it off the shelf, pack it, and hand the box to the shipping carrier. The largest sellers have hybrid (custom) systems in which some goods are fulfilled from in-house inventory and the rest sit in contract warehouse—the software determines order routing based on systematic rules created by the inventory manager.

I have always advised businesspeople to live and work in the same community. Time is our most precious commodity. If your commute to work is a lengthy one, then rent out your current home and rent or buy one near your new business. It would be genius if your warehouse had legally-permitted living quarters. A location must be evaluated from multiple angles. Compare the low cost of leasing or purchasing a building off the beaten path against all other factors.

When exploring business locations (e.g., warehouse, office, etc.), keep these five points at the top of your mind:

1. Proximity to your home (think about the daily commute)
2. Storage needs (now and years from now as your business grows)
3. Access to shipping carrier services
4. Workforce availability
5. Costs related to startup and ongoing costs such as utilities and maintenance

For anyone experiencing phenomenal business growth, temporary and scalable contract storage is ideal. Sustained, predictable sales evaluation through a few annual retail cycles will guide you with accurate enough data to select a permanent home for your "big" business. Setting up your own shop is expensive, and the initial outlay may include:

▶ Security deposit and first (and possibly last) month's rent, if you're leasing
▶ Business formation costs (for example, incorporation fees)
▶ Licensing fees
▶ Exterior building signage
▶ Furniture and fixtures
▶ Office supplies
▶ Warehouse equipment (shelving, forklift, etc.)
▶ Insurance
▶ Website setup
▶ Computers and software (or cloud licenses)
▶ Marketing expenses
▶ Payroll funds sufficient for launch and continued operations until you become profitable
▶ Inventory

Something that I cannot emphasize enough is the value of a good attitude. A prospective landlord who doesn't know you from Adam will feel at ease when dealing with you is a breeze. You enrich their day by smiling and being a positive person. A first impression happens in a flash, and the memory of it lasts forever. Your smile and friendly nature will score you better lease terms and more favorable opportunities with building owners, improvement contractors, vendors (and customers). As your eBay business expands, your smile will enrich and elevate every relationship and each opportunity will float right to the top like cream.

I'd like to share a recap with you from my enlightening conversation with Sam Doria, the founder and owner of Premier Shipping and Fulfillment (https://shipwithpremier.com/). This is along the lines of my earlier mention of scalable rental space, flexible warehouses, and pick, pack, and ship vendors. I spent many hours evaluating firms that offer warehousing and individual order fulfillment for eBay sellers. Premier Shipping and Fulfillment caught my eye because of their excellent reputation and low prices. I demand complete price transparency from vendors, and Premier Shipping and Fulfillment has clear, upfront pricing—no painful sales process or complicated forms to fill out before receiving a quote. Bravo.

Sam is an industrious entrepreneur who set up shop in the small town of Mickleton, New Jersey—a community of only a few thousand residents. Sam provides third-party logistics (also referred to as 3PL or TPL) to tiny eBay sellers shipping five orders per week all the way up to huge corporations shipping entire truckloads at a time. Sam's most prolific customer is shipping 1,200 orders per week out of Sam's warehouse. Premier Shipping and Fulfillment offers climate-controlled inventory management and will pick, pack, and ship an order for a fee as little as $1.95 per box. Sam's company offers dozens of marketplace integrations including eBay. Premier Shipping and Fulfillment will be expanding with a California warehouse to address the growing thirst for 3PL services. Premier Shipping and Fulfillment is one of the many 3PL firms that allow e-commerce moguls-to-be an opportunity to grow fast without having to invest in expensive infrastructure.

When you're a small business, working out of a garage or a home office, using an à la carte warehouse or a 3PL vendor is essential to eliminate the anxiety of setting up your own facility and to rapidly growing your company to the big size you want it to become.

Optimism Wins the Day

What are eBayers seeking? eBay is a site, like any retail shopping destination, where buyers demand:

▶ Known brands, quality emerging brands, and interesting products

▶ Prices that are very attractive

▶ A listing presented in a way that is reassuring

▶ Sellers who are trustworthy (e.g., great feedback)

▶ Zero or low risk of fraud (e.g., eBay's Money Back Guarantee)

Are you a pessimist or a serial optimist? Imagination is what separates a human worker bee from a big-time CEO. Not all CEOs come from fancy schools, but every successful leader makes smart decisions, is highly adaptable, and engages honestly with customers and employees. To play and win at the top of this game, you must wake up every morning with gratitude. You should work in a field that has you jumping out of bed just excited to be in business. The *American Dream* is alive and well. We are given the opportunity to make something big of ourselves in America. You can be born into absolute poverty, receive a free public education, work hard, and become successful in whatever you decide to do.

I perused eBay's Community Boards and curated some interesting remarks that I'd like to share with you:

Pessimist: *"There are a lot more sellers here than when we started in 1998."*

Optimist: *"On the other hand, there are a lot more buyers here now."*

Pessimist: *"Competition is tougher now."*

Optimist: *"There are buyers from a lot more countries now and millions of more people on eBay, so the opportunities are greater."*

Pessimist: *"eBay and PayPal fees are so high."*

Optimist: *"Not really that high when you compare them to the high cost of retail rents, losses due to shoplifting, and high payroll and turnover retailers have to deal with. Sellers have to learn from real-world businesses. There are expenses."*

See how optimism can change the conversation?

Brad Korb sees the difference. Since 1979, The Brad Korb Real Estate Group has been serving the real estate needs of people in the beautiful city of Burbank. Brad Korb is the #4 real estate agent in Los Angeles County and has reached the "billion-dollar club" in his business. I have purchased millions of dollars' worth of real estate from Brad using my eBay profits. Brad recommends eBay to his clients as a means to clear the clutter before selling a home. Everyone has unwanted things of value that fill closets, attics, and garages. Realtors like Brad find it easier to sell a home that's tidy and beautifully presented. eBay is a fantastic alternative to holding garage sales and generates far better results. I asked Brad to share his "secret sauce," and he said that gratitude plays a major part in his success and optimism as a business owner. Brad says he is happy because:

1. He woke up this morning.
2. He has his health.
3. He has a beautiful, loving, and committed spouse.
4. He has two beautiful children he loves very much.
5. He lives in a wonderful city—Burbank.
6. He is happy to have today and the time to get things accomplished.
7. He is happy for the opportunity to help others and those less fortunate.
8. He is happy that he has the opportunity to go "do it" and keep the good news coming.

Brad thinks eBay is a wonderful way to get started running your own business, and he agrees that Realtors all over the country need eBay experts to come to help home sellers get rid of unneeded stuff before they sell their home and move. Generating extra cash also helps defray the cost of moving. People with enough items can even generate money for their down payment. For him, the possibilities are endless, and staying focused and optimistic about your eBay business makes all the difference in the world.

Expanding Your Team as Your Business Grows

A business owner is a true superhero. You're juggling daily life, family duties, chores at home, social obligations, and of course, your company (possibly even a day job). Day one of operating a sole proprietorship means you'll be wearing every hat. You're the CEO, salesperson, marketing manager, purchasing agent, photographer, lister, customer service specialist, shipping clerk, returns manager, bookkeeper, PR guru, and morale officer (aka head cheerleader).

As your business grows, being a "jack of all trades" lowers the glass ceiling. Like Superman, you'll need to venture out of the Fortress of Solitude and become an employer to grow your business. Your need for additional help may become crystal clear to you immediately. It's also natural to be uncertain about the proper timing to hire employees. I have been on both ends of the spectrum. Experience allows me to make business decisions with crisp execution. In this chapter, I'll fill you in on hiring, managing, and retaining employees for your eBay business.

Knowing When You Need Help

Before you post a single help wanted ad, evaluate if you truly need to hire. Take a close look at your workday. Are you spending too much time distracted by personal calls and texts?

Do you engage in tasks that provide zero value to your business? Tasks gain more velocity when they are handled without interruption.

Before you hire anyone, take a week, a month, or even longer, and carefully scrutinize your actions. Unnecessary activities must be eliminated immediately. Trim off the fatty tasks that serve no purpose other than to fill time. Are you printing extra copies of your orders and keeping them in a file you never look at again? Do you have your phone set up to alert you when messages arrive in your personal social media inboxes? Are you answering personal calls during work hours? Are you surfing the web endlessly—attracted to interesting headlines and seductive ads? Are you piling papers instead of shredding them? Are you stymied by indecision (yes, decision making is a task)? Blogger Brandy Jensen has formed this hypothesis on productivity: "Twenty minutes is, objectively, the ideal amount of time—the Goldilocks number when it comes to doing things." I agree with her because I find that I am ferociously productive when I work on tasks in 20-minute stretches.

Clean up your task clutter and immediately end every unproductive moment. "A players" put their professional lives in the lead and focus on getting everything gone with the least friction and within the shortest amount of time. Once you have stopped updating your social media status multiple times a day and rehabilitated yourself from tabloid addiction—then look at how much you can get accomplished in a day without working yourself to the bone. If you've become a model of efficiency and laser focus but still see signs that you need backup, then it's time to start growing your team.

Here are the signs you need to hire employees:

▶ Customer messages are receiving slow responses or no reply at all.
▶ Your feedback is taking hits because of tardy handling of customer service problems.
▶ Order shipping is delayed, and you're struggling to meet order handling times.
▶ It takes you weeks or months to list the backlog of inventory you've purchased.
▶ Your family and friends complain you're spending too much time working.
▶ You've misplaced the joy and inspiration that brought you to self-employment in the first place.
▶ You're seriously contemplating quitting your business even though sales are great.

For a business neophyte, hiring people is a big step. The mere mention of payroll taxes and all that legal "stuff" is enough to frighten even the most courageous person. First of all, don't stress because it isn't that hard to hire. If your business is failing (we all must fail in order to learn and then later succeed), stop contemplating adding a payroll expense and figure out what is required to bring things back on track. You should not increase overhead unless you are already profitable or you can make a compelling case that you will be profitable in the near future and that adding more people will bring greater velocity to your profitability.

Deciding If You're Boss Material

If you work entirely by yourself, having another person around who is an asset to your business will brighten up your day, relieve many of the pressures of running a business, and grow profits. A poorly screened, hastily selected helper will resist your culture and goals. A demanding, drama-filled, unreliable employee is worse than having no employee at all. If you employ more than one person, a bad employee drags down the entire team. Lazy people inspire laziness and spark resentment in others. High standards are highly contagious, just as low standards spread faster than a wildfire after a season of drought.

Your business must persistently focus on outstanding customer service and a sense of urgency. Employees must align with your goals, be vigilant, and maintain a steady sense of urgency in their actions. No human being can be on their "best" every single day, but a dream team achieves stellar results, which is only possible when your team really clicks. If you expect everyone to be a clone of you—forget it. That's never going to happen. Compelling team purpose requires a vision, clear responsibilities, and a positive team culture.

People love to complain about their bosses when they feel alienated or unheard.

Magic happens when employees enjoy the work, expectations are realistic, and they feel heard and supported. Here are some things all successful bosses do:

- ► Keep the communication flowing
- ► Avoid the "big boss" attitude
- ► Develop a sense of teamwork and camaraderie
- ► Praise good work incessantly
- ► Provide honest feedback that never attacks the person
- ► Allow independent thought
- ► Give more responsibility
- ► Avoid being too rigid
- ► Allow for regular two-way feedback
- ► Promptly address employee complaints
- ► Pay people fairly and on time
- ► Never threaten someone with firing or use money to bend people to your will

As a successful leader, you will recognize that people are independent human beings with emotions and personal lives to attend to. When you take these into consideration and show true care for your employees, not only will work relations improve, but your employees will also feel better about themselves and their work.

Getting the Word Out About Hiring

Mastering the hiring process takes practice. It's critical that you keep an eye out for talented people everywhere you go. eBay is not "rocket science," and a sharp learner will pick up the knowledge needed to support your eBay business in a short amount of time. Spread the word to family and friends. Consider new job seekers (i.e., applicants without job experience). Avoid the job hoppers, i.e., people whose resumes show they can't sit still for very long.

You can post ads on job sites, promote your jobs on social media, and post notices on community bulletin boards. Mention your job openings at every opportunity. Everyone knows someone who is looking for a job. Both students and seniors are great candidates. These two categories of workers are more likely to be interested in part-time positions, which is great for eBay work. What makes your job more attractive than most is that it's completely flexible. As long as the work gets done, you can do it at any time of the day. Students appreciate evening jobs, and you'll be more than happy to accommodate flexibility in working hours and days. Seniors also often have a desire to work and stay active while bringing loads of experience and wisdom to the job. You'll also discover that shorter, more intense work shifts are far more attractive than long, boring ones.

Knowing What to Delegate

Once you make a hire, know what you want to delegate to your new employee. Do not delegate anything that is boring, an emergency, vaguely defined, highly confidential, or requires boatloads of planning. That said, delegating mindless tasks is a surefire way to have your best and brightest employees heading out the door for good. Once you have completely eliminated all unnecessary busywork, then think about what you'd like to delegate. Sellers of commodity items find it easy to hire employees to type up listings. Antique dealers find it very difficult to delegate this task because it requires specialized knowledge. These same dealers can train a qualified person to pack fragile items for safe delivery of those throwback items.

Presentation matters a lot in online retail. Dirty items and dark photos raise eyebrows and generate doubt. Buyers wonder if that's simply dirt or if the product is damaged in some way. Let's take car parts as an example. I consulted for a major vehicle recycling company (aka wrecking yards), and they wondered why their eBay sales were lackluster.

The business, run by two brothers, was listing a lot but selling very little. Grease and grime is a way of life for these guys, and auto mechanics generally don't care so long as the part works. For decades, they would pick parts off vehicles and have a delivery truck drop them off at the repair shops (their customers). The customer would clean up the parts before installing them on their customers' vehicles. The thing is, many eBayers who buy car parts are DIYers. These customers compare price and condition across many sellers, so it's important to put your best foot forward. At my recommendation, the brothers hired a team to clean the thousands of parts and take new photos. The sales took off immediately. Sometimes adding an employee-related expense increases your profits instead of gobbling them up.

While it makes total sense to delegate routine tasks such as cleaning and prepping merchandise, and you should offer interesting tasks that your workers might enjoy, use your team members' expertise and skill, and delegate jobs that someone else might do better (e.g., a handy person can restore and polish leather shoes, fix the "fixable" electronics or replace watch batteries, etc.). Many (if not most) company owners are the sales engines in their companies. Delegate time-sucking tasks so that you can focus on wooing new business and schmoozing existing customers (to score even more business).

Let's circle back to the task of typing up listings. Adding users to your eBay account is a snap. Here are the steps to follow in order to add authorized users:

1. Hover over "My eBay" at the top-right-hand corner of most eBay pages
2. Click "Summary"
3. Click "Account"
4. Click "Switch to classic view" if the link appears
5. Under the section "My eBay Views" click "Permissions"
6. Click "Add user"
7. Enter the trusted new user's name and email
8. Tick the appropriate permissions box(es)
9. Click "Add User"

Workers can create and edit drafts, or you can also allow them to publish and revise listings. With so much at stake in your business, newbies should be limited to creating and editing drafts that you later review and approve to ensure they comply with eBay policies. As your helpers sharpen their skills, trusted workers can be allowed to go all the way and post items.

You can view the Activity Log on the Permissions page to catch up on what your workers are doing. You can also instantly remove users when they should no longer have access.

eBay sellers can delegate these jobs:

- ▶ Merchandise sorting, cleaning, and prepping
- ▶ Photography
- ▶ Item research*
- ▶ Listing*
- ▶ Customer service (answering emails or calls and handling issues that arise)*
- ▶ Packing and shipping
- ▶ Processing and restocking returns
- ▶ Bookkeeping*
- ▶ Marketing (promoting the business, e.g., making offers to watchers, launching eBay promotional campaigns, social media marketing, etc.)*

*These jobs can be managed remotely by virtual assistants (aka independent contractors), without having to set up a payroll service.

Paying Your Staff While Obeying the Law

While there is no standard method of paying people and every situation is unique, you'll need to decide how you will pay helpers for the work they perform. If a worker is being paid on payroll (with taxes taken out), then use a payroll service. I use Patriot Software to prepare payroll checks and pay workers' compensation insurance. It takes seconds to print checks on blank check stock or schedule direct deposit. Taxes are all handled seamlessly— on time with no headaches. I used to struggle with all the forms and file them myself. What a mess.

But, do you need to add the high cost of payroll? Some workers are not considered employees. What if your family extends their helping hands? It is interesting to know that the IRS has an annual gift tax exclusion ($15,000 annually as of 2019). Payments of less than $600 during the year made to someone who is not your employee don't need to be reported. Per the IRS, whether an individual is an employee or an independent contractor depends on the "behavioral control, financial control, and relationship of the parties." IRS publication number 1779 assists in determining a person's status. Scan the QR code in Figure 12–1 on page 214 to pull up the publication.

You don't want to misclassify an employee as an independent contractor, so be sure you ask a tax professional or an IRS employee for help with worker classification.

There are a ton of gig sites where you can hire freelancers, and I'm of the opinion that you'd be safe classifying remote helpers as independent contractors. Payroll can take a significant bite into your budget and very small entrepreneurs would be wise to

FIGURE 12–1: **IRS Publication 1779–*Independent Contractor or Employee, Which Are You?***

legally avoid hiring employees if the same work can be delegated to a freelancer. If you pay independent contractors, you may still have to file tax forms (1099-MISC for the IRS), but you won't have to tack on the substantial additional cost of payroll taxes, workers compensation insurance, and payroll processing fees. While I have never done so (I asked a professional), you can file an IRS Form SS-8 requesting a "worker status" determination to have the government establish if the services someone is providing to you are considered those of a contractor or an employee.

If you become an employer, the IRS requires you to apply for an Employer Identification Number, also referred to as an EIN. You can apply for this online at the IRS website (if you are located in the U.S. or a U.S. territory. The state will have a similar registration requirement if you conduct business in a state that imposes a personal income tax. Most states do; however, the following states do not:

- ▶ Alaska
- ▶ Florida
- ▶ Nevada
- ▶ New Hampshire
- ▶ South Dakota
- ▶ Tennessee
- ▶ Texas
- ▶ Washington
- ▶ Wyoming

I did some sleuthing on eBay's Community Boards and found that some eBay sellers pay by "piecework," which would provide you with a known cost per item listed, packed, etc. An eBayer who sells antique silver items pays a freelancer per tarnished item to polish them up to a beautiful shine. He doesn't pay salary or hourly, and if the item isn't right, the worker has to resolve it without additional compensation. You could also pay a packer by the box for pick, pack, and ship work. Anyone who is legally an employee must receive no less than minimum wage, but if you offer the piecework option with a guarantee of *no less* than the minimum wage, your worker will have a strong incentive to increase output, which generates greater profits for you.

> **tip** ⓘ
>
> Hiring someone through an agency will cost a little more but will lift the pressure of dealing with payroll entirely off your shoulders. Employment agencies are a solution for rapidly adding skilled helpers when the need arises, such as during the holiday shopping season.

In the next chapter, I'll share my views on moving from "helping hands at home" and into the boardroom (yes, you can become "big time" selling on eBay).

In the next chapter, I'll educate you on what can go wrong and how to avoid the landmines of being in business. There's no need to experience my pain. I've done so many things wrong on eBay and want to guide you away from them. Why have an avoidable, bad experience? I'll help you step over these puddles.

Handling Unexpected Challenges Like a Pro

Statistically speaking, if you live a long enough life then you will experience adversity many times—challenges with family, friends, health, money, and a plethora of other possibilities. The same is true in business. Even though I was once homeless, I always knew I'd be rich. Facing even the most ferocious financial woes, I knew that money would be easy to acquire because there is so much of it readily available to be earned by the focused and hard-working. I'd like to ask you to follow a list of very reasonable rules that we can call the "Golden Rules" for your eBay business. I genuinely believe this brief guide will keep the money flowing and your troubles to a minimum and maintain a low-stress environment. My unbreakable rules are:

- ▶ Find happiness, peace, and joy in life.
- ▶ Have policies but never allow them to take precedence over common sense.
- ▶ Trade honestly—act at all times with integrity.
- ▶ Trade fairly.
- ▶ Ship only to the address on the order unless the buyer is a family member, friend, or someone well-known (because not doing so may forfeit all seller protections offered by eBay and/or PayPal).
- ▶ Pack better than is required for safe arrival (double-box very fragile items).
- ▶ Ship exactly what was promised.
- ▶ Obtain a signature on shipments valued over $750.
- ▶ Insure and use tracking unless suffering a total loss is either actuarial or tolerable (e.g., self-insured or very low-value items that are easily replaced).
- ▶ Use only the shipping method paid for in the listing (i.e., never ship by a slower and cheaper method than promised).
- ▶ Respect even the most demanding customer (e.g., the hard-to-please, the miser, the anger ball, etc.).
- ▶ Offer liberal returns (even a "no returns" item can be returned under the right set of circumstances).
- ▶ Be patient in dealing with everyone—family, friends, customers, vendors, and eBay customer support.

I embrace rules in my own life because having formal structure is a steady framework from which I can build *everything*. Growth and accomplishment is the byproduct of focus and effort—and rules, both explicit and implied. The way you approach your eBay business determines the outcome. What do you practice every day? What you practice, you will get good at. Do you practice happiness, peace, and joy in your life? Or, do you complain? If you complain, you will get very good at it.

In this chapter, we will go over common issues that may arise at some point along your eBay journey. We will also discuss time management and other minor tweaks that you can use to minimize trouble and maximize your profits.

Don't Sweat the Small Stuff
(But Handle the Big Stuff)

The most valuable resource in the universe is *time*. For businesspeople such as yourself, you can't squander your precious time. You'll earn substantially more money on eBay if you follow some simple and obvious rules that very few businesspeople seem to understand instinctively. Catapult your sales productivity by following these simple rules:

▶ Handle the tasks of greatest importance first.

▶ Banish social media distractions unless they are part of your sales marketing strategy.

▶ Get customer service right the first time (eliminate inefficient and incomplete communication).

▶ Never multitask (check out Dave Crenshaw's book *The Myth of Multitasking: How "Doing It All" Gets Nothing Done,* Jossey-Bass, 2008).

▶ Be prepared for problems so they are dealt with professionally but never emotionally.

▶ Organize tasks into bite-size moments rather than long, boring ones.

▶ Make fewer decisions—except those that have a deeper impact.

▶ Run away from "busy work" and focus on "big work."

▶ If you work from home, ask the family to respect work time and allow you to treat it like a real job; if you work at a business location, ask coworkers to avoid "drive-by" meetings and schedule a time to speak with you unless it's urgent.

Let's say you're sailing along smoothly and a message comes in. The box arrived crushed, and the item is unrecognizable. What is your time worth? If that item is $20, just issue a refund and move on with your day. I don't even insure items of low value because my time is so precious that I can't afford to waste the minutes required to fill out an insurance claim form. While I'm *not* dealing with that trivial insurance claim, I have the time to talk up my latest arrivals to a buyer, and they added another four items to their order worth ten times what I just lost on the damaged package.

Being always connected has changed the way we work and play. It's hard to know where to draw the line. Nonbusiness emails and other personal distractions are an anchor on your success and productivity. Maintain a separate business email to avoid personal distractions. Make it harder for friends to contact you *during work hours*. The family should always have your ear, but phone and email chitchat will draw you away from handling your orders and helping your customers. Encourage your loved ones to honor and respect your work time by texting or calling you during specific break times. Set boundaries so that other people value your time as much as you do—at work, you must deliver obsessive customer service. Turn off push notifications on your smartphone for apps and activities that are unrelated to your business.

Authentication and Grading Services

When your item is suffering the "cold shoulder" and you've given it plenty of time and exposure on eBay, it may be time to formally prove its worth. Certain items benefit from authentication and grading. An authentication expert uses skill and experience to certify that an item is genuine, while a grading service develops and applies a scorecard relating to the item's condition. See the Resources section for a listing of official eBay partners who provide this service.

Protections

Rest assured that the vast majority of eBay transactions go without a hitch. The more you sell, the more likely you'll run into a bad apple. eBay is generally a safe place to trade because users have to provide information about themselves and a form of payment in order to trade on the site. In Chapter 9, I explained how eBay protects you against abusive buyer practices, and how in some instances, negative and neutral feedback will be removed when a buyer is acting naughty. You can always ask that a bad remark be taken off when it relates to shipping delays caused by miserable weather or carrier delays (or if the tracking shows you shipped on-time. but the item arrived late).

Buyers also cannot double-dip their protection plans. If a customer initiates a PayPal Purchase Protection case, they can't also ask for help under the eBay Money Back Guarantee for the same order. You'll be covered if you have proof of delivery to the same address on the order and a signature on any order amounting to $750 or more. It is possible for someone to also initiate a payment dispute with PayPal or their financial institution if they paid another way. Common reasons include a buyer forgetting what they ordered, claiming nonreceipt, and even attempting to dispute a charge when they are outside your published returns grace period. When this occurs, remain calm and respond to eBay (or PayPal) with the information that is requested. I always call eBay for advice on how to handle the situation (they are very helpful).

There's a special Vehicle Purchase Protection that kicks in when someone completes a vehicle purchase on the eBay site (never when it's an "off eBay" deal). Scan the QR code in Figure 13–1 on page 221 to learn about the full details of this program.

FIGURE 13–1: **Vehicle Purchase Protection**

Cyber Security

In years past, I would recommend frequent password changes to stay ahead of hackers and account takeovers. I no longer believe it's required, and I've utilized the same password for a very long time. I don't use the same password twice. The passwords I use are highly complex and managed by my favorite password manager (not a person following me around taking notes, but a computer program). *LastPass* stores encrypted passwords and notes online. I can generate virtually unbreakable, highly-complex passwords with this free utility and store them to be automatically filled into the sites I visit. The passwords are so complex, no one could guess them, and I never have to remember them. I have watched with empathy as friends and colleagues spend literally hours trying to remember a password for a rarely-used website. A password manager grants you the memory of an elephant and further allows you to store notes, PIN numbers, the answers to site security questions, and even super-secret stuff you never want anyone to find out. Password managers have browser plug-ins and phone apps that you can install to streamline automatically logging into websites. LastPass has been around since 2008, and I have never (knock on wood) forgotten or lost a password, nor have any of my accounts been hacked. I even use LastPass to store the combinations to padlocks—it's that versatile, and it's free to use. Apple device users can utilize *iCloud Keychain,* which operates much the same as LastPass and allows you access across all of your Apple devices.

From time to time, you will receive emails that appear to be from eBay, PayPal, or your bank—or perhaps a noble prince in a faraway land (who needs your help escaping their war-torn country), but these fake emails are from fraudsters. These con artists send convincing and official-looking emails that include links or ask you to reply. Providing any sensitive information in response to these "spoof" or "phishing" emails will result in something bad happening to you (e.g., an account take-over, your money being siphoned out of your bank account, or worse). Legit emails from eBay will contain your eBay username, will never ask you to provide confidential information by email or phone, and will contain no link that requires you to submit confidential information.

Here's what eBay says are some typical traits of spoof emails and websites:

▶ Asking for confidential information

▶ An urgent tone that asks you to act quickly

▶ Unsolicited attachments

▶ A generic greeting, like "Attention eBay member"

▶ A web address that looks like eBay, but which may have a typo or extra numbers and letters (like http://signin-ebay.com or http://signin.ebay.com@10.19.32.4)

When you encounter a suspicious email, promptly forward it to spoof@ebay.com.

Protect your online passwords just like you would protect a newborn child. If you're ever in doubt about password security, immediately change it. While all banks and card companies have fraud protocols, dealing with unauthorized activity must be swift to mitigate potential issues.

Spam

There's an email going around offering processed pork, gelatin, and salt in a can. If you get this email, don't open it. It's spam. Any time my day is dragging or I'm feeling a bit down (not very often to be candid), I simply open my Gmail Spam inbox folder, and I see the great news:

▶ A dozen banks are offering me easy loans.

▶ A credit card company I've never used says I need to verify my social security number and date of birth to avoid having the card canceled (the one I was never issued).

▶ Dr. Sharleten has been arrested by a terrorist faction in his war torn motherland and needs me to handle his $5 million estate for a reasonable fee of 10 percent.

▶ My eBay (or PayPal) account has been "limited" until I verify my financial data to "reinstate" it.

Watch out for these and other dramatic communications. They are likely to lead to heartache. Please protect yourself by using an email service that detects most fraudulent spam. Gmail is among the most widely-used and best at detecting both nefarious emails and malicious code in attachments. Gmail scans billions of emails and traps the obvious offenders.

The simple way for you to remain secure within the "eBay World" is to communicate via the eBay message system. Hover over My eBay at the top-right of most eBay pages and then click Messages. *Legitimate* eBay messages and those from trading partners are readily seen in the messages area. You can filter messages, flag important ones, and create folders for better organization. You can always reach out to an eBayer by clicking Contact on their profile. While the messages system is fully self-contained, an email alert is always sent to the registered eBay user's email address.

eBay retains the right to review messages sent through the site, and they never allow the following message content:

▶ Offers to buy and sell outside of eBay

▶ Spam (advertising unrelated to eBay or an eBay transaction)

▶ Threats, profanity and hate speech

▶ Email addresses, phone numbers or other contact information, web addresses or links

For a deeper dive into this subject, click on Help & Contact at the top of most eBay pages, then type "member-to-member contact policy" into the search box.

I use AVG Antivirus to detect online threats and malicious code. Be sure that your computer has a reputable spyware and antivirus program actively providing a "moat" around your computer activity.

Internet Privacy

Why doesn't Cookie Monster have good internet privacy? He always accepts the cookies! A web cookie is very different than those lovely Toll House® cookies grandma used to make. Cookies are small text files placed in the memory of your browser or device. They are installed automatically when you visit a website such as eBay. There are different types of cookies eBay uses:

▶ Session cookies, also known as session-based cookies, that expire immediately when you close your browser

▶ Persistent cookies, which remain stored on your device between sessions and track things like settings and activities—these are the cookies that

> **tip** ⓘ
>
> Here's a "pro" tip. If you're a Chrome user, you can delete a single website's cookies by clicking the *padlock* icon in the browser, clicking *cookies* and then selecting and deleting or blocking the cookies manually.

FIGURE 13–2: **AVG Detects Malware and Tracking Cookies**

allow you to remain logged into certain websites and reduce that irritating need to keep entering your user ID and password

▶ Third-party cookies, which are set by a provider other than eBay (e.g., used by ad-serving services to tailor promotional messages based on your browsing habits)

Figure 13–2 is a prompt from a popular antivirus program, warning about cookie tracking.

Go Undercover

When using public or shared computers, you want to go *incognito*. It doesn't require you to don a disguise. If you don't want your browser to remember your activity, here's what you need to do:

For Chrome:

▶ Windows, Linux, or Chrome OS: Press Ctrl + Shift + n
▶ Mac: Press ⌘ + Shift + n

For Edge (Explorer) and Firefox:

▶ Press Ctrl + Shift + p
▶ Mac: Press ⌘ + Shift + p

For Safari:

▶ Go to File > New Private Window

The above instructions are for laptop and desktop browsers. If you've used an internet café or a shared computer and didn't go "incognito" then you must delete your browsing history and all cookies before you walk away. *You've been warned.* This is handled differently for phone/mobile browsers, so research this on your own. To delete your browsing activity and cookies in Chrome, you'd press Ctrl + H and click Clear browsing data and select the items you'd like to clear. For Firefox, click the gear cog icon (top-right) then click Privacy & Security and under Cookies and Site Data click Clear Data. For Edge/Explorer, press Ctrl + H and, then click Clear History. For Safari, go to Settings > Safari > Advanced > Website Data, and then click Remove All Website Data.

Check for a Certificate

Ever wonder why there's a little padlock popping up on the URL line in your browser for some websites and not for others? That cute graphic signals that the site you're on is using secure encryption. The encryption eBay uses (and requires) is referred to as Transport Layer Security (TLS). eBay uses TLS to encrypt these sessions. To guarantee that all financial data is protected, eBay (and most sites) require TLS for all HTTPS connections, and you should *never, never, never* enter sensitive information into any website unless you see the padlock. Clicking the padlock allows you to confirm the veracity of the security certificate (see Figure 13–3 on page 226) issued to the website—which allows you to differentiate between a fraudster site and a legitimate one.

Cover Your Bases

If your browsing experience has become slower than molasses, be sure to clean everything up (e.g., browsing history, cookies, and cached files). Use a private or incognito window when visiting sites you don't plan to use often. This prevents those sites from placing permanent files on your computer and that will speed up things a bit.

To further protect yourself and your privacy, set up a separate bank account within your current bank and ask the bank to issue a debit card for it. Keep a very low balance in this account to minimize financial exposure. If you need to make a purchase or use the card to cover eBay fees, you'll move funds into it from your other bank account using your bank's online transfer feature. If your passwords or account are ever compromised, you can instantly empty the money out of your "e-commerce" account to prevent any exposure.

FIGURE 13–3: **eBay's Security Certificate Issued by DigiCert**

Consider PO Box Services by USPS

Keep in mind that the information you share with eBay is stored, and eBay's employees and approved third-parties have access to it. Improve your privacy dramatically by obtaining a post office box at the USPS. Having an "official" government post office box is cheap and also allows you tremendous flexibility. Rent a box by visiting https://www.usps.com and hover over Track & Manage and click Rent or Renew PO Box.

USPS now offers a *real* street address so that you can order online and receive parcels from any shipper, even messenger companies. Sign up for this additional (and free) concession as well as the signature on file service add-on so you never have to sign for "signature-only" mail. Use the street address and box number as your registered mailing address on eBay and other websites. Porch pirates and nosey neighbors alike are now out of your ecommerce life forever. In Burbank, I also enjoy parcel locker service—whenever a package arrives, it's placed into a conveniently numbered locker and a key is dropped into my mailbox.

If you'd like your very own "mail valet" you can sign up for the Premium Mail Forwarding service. For a very low cost, the kind folks at the USPS will forward all mail (including) parcels to the address you choose. While they won't send things along to Kathmandu, you can receive your mail at your cabin in the Rockies or at your Santa Monica beach house. An official USPS post office box affords tremendous privacy and flexibility.

Blocking eBayers

Everyone starts somewhere, so please be kind to newbies. Someone who is a novice at buying or selling on eBay will be learning *as they go*—be gentle and kind. That said, there are some folks you'll want to avoid. When you encounter the worst of eBay, please promptly block them. In Chapter 1, I provided a QR code that takes you to the eBay site map where you will find the tools to block undesirable bidders.

What justifies the drastic measure of blocking another eBayer? Here are a few of the good reasons to pull the trigger on them:

- ▶ *Fee Avoidance.* An eBayer asks you to engage in prohibited activities, such as trading off-eBay or canceling a transaction to save eBay fees.
- ▶ *Deadbeats.* Failing to pay for their winnings—if they do it to you, they'll do it to others (also be sure to report the unpaid item in the Resolution Center—a black mark for them and a refund of your final value fees).
- ▶ *Duty Dodgers.* Cross-border customers who ask you to undervalue the shipment for customs purposes so they can save money on duties and taxes, but this also means if the parcel is lost or damaged, you'll end up eating it, and the loss will be all yours.
- ▶ *Squeaky Wheels.* Painful, annoying people who expect you to grade, certify, and guarantee your $1 item—or ask endless questions and request tons of additional pictures for a super cheap or as-is item.
- ▶ *Kids.* Minors who are not allowed to use eBay (a person under 18 can use an adult's account with permission, but that adult is fully responsible for everything that happens).

While it's not against the "eBay law" to be annoying, if someone is rude, threatening, or otherwise an unwelcome trading partner, it may not always be grounds for eBay to suspend them. But the power to block another member is always within your immediate reach. Block anyone you don't feel good about trading with.

The Egregious Abuses

There are some abuses that are considered the most serious of all and here are those that round out my list of most atrocious (that justify reporting the person to eBay):

► *Shill bidders.* While it is perfectly alright to buy an item from someone you know, you may never artificially increase the item price or desirability—shill bidding is a serious crime and involves collusion and manipulation of the bid process in order to ensure that an unsuspecting bidder pays top dollar. Sellers bidding on their own items with a separate account—no need to explain this right? Shame on them.

► *Bid manipulation.* A bidder places an exorbitant bid amount in order to determine the next highest bid, then retracts their bid and places a new one just above the current high bidder.

► *Bid shielding.* Two bidders work together with the first bidder placing their desired bid and the second bidder placing a very high bid that the second bidder retracts just prior to the 12-hour bid cancellation deadline, leaving the first bidder's lower bid (this "shielding" discourages others from placing bids).

► *Deadbeat buyers.* A person who places a bid or makes an offer to buy your item and never pays (P.S. eBay trades are real contracts, and it's not a video game).

► *Malicious feedback.* eBay has rules about what a buyer can and cannot say in their feedback remarks and some feedback can be removed.

► *Feedback extortion.* A buyer threatens negative feedback if you don't agree to something you never promised in the listing or demands a discount rather than simply returning the product—eBay will remove the feedback as long as the threat occurred within the eBay message system.

► *Threats.* An eBay member makes any type of personal threat, such as threats of violence or is inappropriate.

Promptly report and block offenders. Call (866) 540-3229 if you need a helping hand. You can also email customerhelp@ebay.com; however, the phone is the friend you'll like better. Easily and dramatically reduce your number of issues with other eBayers by setting the Buyer Requirements on your account. There are quite a few settings there. Stop bids and communication with undesirable people. To access Buyer Requirements, go to My eBay > Account > Site Preferences > Buyer requirements.

If you ever have login issues and you suspect your account has been subject to hijacking or a "take-over," then attempt to change your password immediately. If that isn't successful, call eBay for assistance right away to mitigate the damage that could occur with an unauthorized user masquerading as you. To help detect scammers, educate yourself with the knowledge found at eBay's Security Center. You'll find the link to the Security Center at the bottom of most eBay pages.

If you believe you have become the victim of an internet crime, you can file reports with the appropriate agency:

▶ Federal Bureau of Investigation Internet Crime Complaint Center (IC3) https://ic3.gov

▶ U.S. Postal Inspection Service (if the fraud involves the US mail, https://www.uspis.gov)

▶ Federal Trade Commission (https://www.ftc.gov)

▶ Your state's attorney general

▶ Your county's district attorney

▶ Your local police department (or if applicable, sheriff)

While no one can ever become inoculated against fraud, you can preempt issues by using common sense and following eBay and PayPal policies. Punctuality always pays dividends when dealing with any sort of shady person or criminal act—better safe than late.

Resolution Center

You may have noticed a bit of a somber tone in this chapter. Indeed, I take safe trading seriously. I'd like to close out the chapter by covering a few details about the Resolution Center. Chronically difficult buyers file an unusually high number of cases, and eBay has computer geniuses who write code to detect these naughty shoppers. The eBay staff then warn and sometimes restrict or banish the worst of the lot. Buyers and sellers can both utilize the Resolution Center which can be found by clicking the appropriate link at the bottom of most eBay pages.

While eBay offers all buyers its Money Back Guarantee, all good things come to an end, and there are time limits within which a buyer can gripe about a purchase. First, there is the designation of "Item not received." For most items, the limit is 30 days after the latest estimated delivery date (this appears on your listing based on the shipping method). For event tickets, the limit is no later than seven days after the event date or 30 days from the latest estimated delivery date, whichever is later.

A buyer may also select "Item not as described." A return must be requested no later than 30 days after the actual (or latest estimated) delivery date—or if the seller's return grace period is longer, within that returns period offered by the seller. For event tickets, a return must be requested no later than seven days after the event date or 30 days from the actual (or latest estimated) delivery date, whichever is later.

Buyers may also request replacement or exchange. It's best to check your messages frequently—even when on vacation because sellers have three days to respond to a case with a solution. For returns, the seller can ask the case to be closed if the item has not come back within ten days. Cases are automatically closed within 21 business days if the buyer doesn't ask eBay to step in and help. Neglectful and forgetful sellers who don't respond to cases will certainly have the case closed in favor of the buyer, and a refund will be issued, so it's critical that you pay attention and tend your eBay garden. Buyers can run to eBay for help later than the timelines I mentioned, and I encourage you to set limits—if a late-filed case is opened, ask eBay to close it in your favor for tardiness. The nice folks at eBay will only extend their published time limits for a really good reason (like a hurricane or national civil unrest).

Sellers can (and always should) open an unpaid item case. Unpaid items hit your pocketbook—eBay charges you a final value fee on sales, even those that remain unpaid. Report deadbeats by filing an unpaid item case in the Resolution Center as soon as two days after the listing ends (be kind and contact your buyer first to ask why the payment has not arrived) and immediately if the buyer is no longer a registered user. Promptly close the case within four days if payment still hasn't arrived, and eBay will place an unpaid item strike on the buyer's account, block them from leaving feedback for that listing, and credit back the final value fee. If you remain dissatisfied with the outcome of a case, you may appeal the decision. Please refer to the section in this chapter about arbitration. You can file the necessary paperwork yourself, or hire a high-powered attorney, by visiting the User Agreement link on the bottom of most eBay pages and heading over to the Agreement to Arbitrate page. While I have never personally initiated an arbitration proceeding against eBay, I caution you that you may wind up having your account limited if you get into a tussle with eBay's legal team. Like virtually any company (publicly-traded or private), eBay has no legal duty to allow you to use their services. Causing a ruckus may not be the best idea. All business owners have to carve out a percentage of their operating profits to cover losses due to damage, fraud, employee theft, and other unknown eventualities. For eBayers without a retail store, the silver lining is—you'll be limited to shrinkage caused by issues with buyers and employees (and when your cat tips over your Ming). Bricks-and-mortar retailers have to add in a substantial margin for shoplifting activity, but you'll be immune to such issues.

In the next chapter, I'll talk about how to take stock of your success and account for your profits (or lack thereof). So take "five" and when you're back, we can pick up where we left off.

tip

Enable the Unpaid Item Assistant to have eBay automatically report deadbeats and recover your final value fees if payment is never received. To enable this useful feature, head over to My eBay > Account > Site Preferences > Unpaid Item Assistant and configure the settings to your liking.

14

Keeping Your Finances in Order for Tax Day

Once you make your eBay fortune (or even if you just sell more than $600 worth of products), it's time to pay Uncle Sam. You *knew* this was coming.

For some reason, I am a math and accounting guru. I also absolutely hate math and accounting almost as much as I despise kale (and force myself to eat numbers while munching on my healthy kale salad). For the "little" guy, I recommend using a simple accounting system. If you are like me—still using a checking account—a One-Write system allows you to combine check-writing and record-keeping in one step. This only benefits you if you're paying bills by check. You have to keep your business and personal finances separate from each other so that when tax time arrives, your CPA isn't hiring a bookkeeper to clean everything up. Remember that a CPA (like an attorney) is a professional and won't want to get dirty hands doing all the detailed line-item book work.

For most businesses, even sole proprietorships, it pays to computerize. Get your accounting "act" together early or suffer extreme pain later. Trust me. I've made all the accounting mistakes. Sharpening your pencil may yield unexpected consequences—many taxpayers *overpay* when filing their 1040 return with the IRS and after learning the ins and outs of business taxes, realize that they may have enough tax deductions to exceed the IRS standard deduction. For each business entity type (mentioned in Chapter 3), the IRS requires a unique tax return form. For sole proprietors, you'll add an additional form to your annual tax return called the 1040-C. For other legal structures, an entirely separate return will be filed mutually exclusive of your personal return. Our tax system is honor-based, and while your friends might boast about not reporting cash tips at their service industry gig or pocketing all their garage sale loot, every dollar of business *profit* is reportable. The least expensive (free) tax advice is offered directly from the IRS and their numbers are (800) 829-1040 for individual taxpayers (including 1040-C filers) and (800) 829-4933 for business taxpayers.

Uncle Sam generally doesn't require a physical receipt for deductible business expenses that are less than $75. You never need to keep a pile of *de minimis* receipts. But, you must keep *good* records. A good record of a $2 parking meter expense or a $35 inkjet cartridge could be as simple as maintaining a spreadsheet. Dump the shoebox of receipts and use your phone to snap pictures (it will help you improve your photography skills), and store these images in a safe place—I use Google Drive (accessible anywhere I am) and have subfolders for each year.

Preparing for Tax Time All the Time

If eBay is your only business, tracking income is a breeze. You can generate sales insights in a few mouse clicks by going to the Reports tab within your PayPal account. If you don't deduct legitimate business expenses (like postage, packing supplies, rent, utilities, office supplies, etc.), then you'll end up paying taxes on all your income. That would be quite painful and unnecessary—you can legally deduct business expenses as well as the cost of what you sold (known as COGS or "Cost of Goods Sold"). I mentioned in Chapter 8 that I'm using QuickBooks to organize my finances—both business and personal. Some misguided accountants encourage clients to track endless expense categories, and I don't suggest following their lead if they do. You'll want to start looking for a new CPA if your current tax professional makes "brain surgery" out of bookkeeping. Take a signal from the IRS form you're required to file. Go to the "Expenses" section of the tax form you're required to file and work backward from there. There's a surprisingly small number of expense categories to keep tabs on, and QuickBooks or any good accounting software will have the same expense categories on the "chart of accounts." When entering expenses, always apply the correct expense category in real time rather than procrastinating until tax time. Doing this work *along the way* means you can press a few buttons and generate a simple report for your accountant.

If you're a business newbie, the most frequent rookie accounting mistakes are:

▶ Over-thinking and over-complicating the tracking of income and expenses
▶ Hiring expensive lawyers and tax people to provide advice the government gives out freely (well, technically not "freely" since this is a situation where your *tax dollars are at work*)
▶ Over-reporting or under-reporting income
▶ Failing to separate business and personal expenses (the government dislikes blurred lines)
▶ Missing out on deductions
▶ Treating an employee as an independent contractor
▶ Filing and paying taxes late (ask your accountant or the IRS about *quarterly estimated tax payments*)

While the never-got-paid-back loans you made to your brother-in-law aren't considered charitable deductions, if you give to any of the following organizations, you can deduct the contribution from your taxes (cash or a tangible item of value):

▶ A state, U.S. possession, or District of Columbia if the donation is made for "public" purposes
▶ An organization operated for charitable, religious, educational, scientific, literary purposes, or for the prevention of cruelty to children or animals
▶ A religious organization (e.g., church, synagogue, etc.)
▶ A war veterans' organization
▶ A nonprofit volunteer fire company
▶ A civil defense organization

▶ A charitable contribution made to a fraternal society

▶ A nonprofit cemetery

Who knew that even giving something to the government is considered "charitable?"

Those of us who are "older" have filed quite a few tax returns. You may not fully appreciate the time savings of preparing (at minimum) quarterly or monthly profit and loss statements ("P&Ls")—start looking at this now. A well-organized plan means you can hand your tax preparer your P&Ls, and they shouldn't require much more than that to get your taxes on the road. If you're like me and have substantial real estate and investments, taxes can get a bit more complex (my returns are 40 to 70 pages per year and sometimes more). I used to prepare my own taxes and that went well—however, the software required to do so costs a few bucks, and my time is so precious, I just prefer to delegate this task nowadays.

State Taxes

There are a few places that have no state income tax (good for you), which is even better when you aren't required to file a state-level tax return. California is my home, and it's not one of them. Tax preparation software is so good now that once your IRS return is prepared, your tax professional can rapidly pump out your state return along with it *automatically*. For the very rare few of us with complex taxes, it pays to have another tax professional review the work, and when my taxes are high enough to bother my sleep, I ask for a second opinion.

While eBay is legally required to collect state and local sales taxes in many jurisdictions, some sellers are still required to collect and remit sales tax. Check with eBay and the appropriate agency in your state to see what's required. I am of the opinion that eBay will be collecting 100 percent of sales taxes across the U.S. within the coming years as a matter of law, as more governments realize that being your "partner" is easier if eBay does the bean-counting.

States issue permits that extend organizations the right to sell goods to the public. These permits may go by different names, depending on the state. A seller's permit allows wholesale purchases without paying taxes and requires permit holders to collect and pay sales tax on retail sales (unless the goods are exempt from tax).

Figure 14–1 on page 235 will launch eBay's page for claiming tax exemption.

1099-K

No, a 1099 K isn't a high tech vitamin shot. It's the important tax form that the IRS receives each year to report your total eBay income; if a) your annual gross payments exceeded

FIGURE 14-1: **Visit this Page to Claim Sales Tax Exemption for Your eBay Purchases (and Upload the Required Forms)**

$20,000 and b) you had more than 200 transactions, then the IRS will be privy to the information. While all business income is reportable by you, even without someone else tipping off the government, only income above the aforementioned thresholds will be formally reported. You'll receive multiple income-related tax forms if you use more than one online selling marketplace and sell above the IRS reporting cutoff point. New to all this tax stuff? Accidentally threw away the form thinking it

> **tip** ⓘ
>
> The 1099-K shows income *by month*. This is super helpful if you want to evaluate sales trends or if you operate on a fiscal (rather than calendar) year.

was "junk mail?" You can always secure an IRS transcript. Request one online or by snail mail. Visit https://www.irs.gov/individuals/get-transcript to obtain one.

Remember to KISS

I'd like to close this chapter up by reminding you to enjoy life—including your business life, by using the KISS principle (keep it simple, stupid). William of Ockham, a wise Franciscan friar and student of logic said, "Entia non sunt multiplicanda praeter necessitatem," which means that more things should not be used than are necessary. Question everything you do and eliminate everything you do not need to do. Never, ever do anything "just because." In the next and last chapter, I'll explain how to connect, network, schmooze (and increase profits) by using the eBay Community.

CHAPTER 15

Connecting with the eBay Community

We're social creatures—when people run into each other and engage in conversation, great things happen. A shared mindset leads to better communities on eBay. You can network with other eBayers and eBay staff through the Community section of the site. You'll find the Community section at the bottom line (of eBay's homepage, that is). Finding like-minded souls who share your goals isn't always easy. Friends that relish their 9-to-5 don't understand why you're still cranking away at work into the night. eBayers are a unique breed—entrepreneurs with grit who are determined to make something great happen for themselves. You can't make *real* lemonade without *real* lemons. Success is elusive working in a vacuum. Discover the highest level of achievement by connecting with a variety of interesting people with similar values and interests. Professional excellence demands constant fertilizer.

The eBay Community functions as a peer-to-peer support "neighborhood" and is mostly self-managed, with eBay staff moderating and contributing content occasionally. Most community content is posted by people like you and me—eBay won't offer customer support through this area of the site (call (866) 540-3229 or visit the Help & Contact link if you require assistance).

eBay publishes the following tips for using the Community (for more on this, scan the QR code in Figure 15–1):

▶ Search for your question first—there may already be an answer in the Community.
▶ Find the right board for your question.
▶ Be respectful of others.
▶ Stay on topic and keep conversations flowing.
▶ Be collaborative by sharing your ideas and best practices.
▶ Stay safe. Never share personal information on our boards.
▶ Have fun, and enjoy your Community experience.

You must be at least 18 to post on the Community's boards, even when the account you're using is owned by an adult—this protects minors from online predators and

FIGURE 15–1: **More Information about the eBay Community**

inappropriate interactions with adults. eBay also forbids rude, abusive and shameful posts. Never post private information (such as another member's full name, address, phone, or other sensitive content). While it's tempting to engage in self-promotion, you're never allowed to spam the Community with listing links and ads.

There are a few ways you can use the Community to benefit your eBay business. You can check the pulse of what's going on with eBay (refer to Figure 15–2) and other sellers and buyers. You can query the Knowledge Base to glean quick answers to the most commonly-asked eBay questions. Community is great for engaging in discussions about topics that interest you (as shown in Figure 15–3 on page 240), and you can absorb wisdom

FIGURE 15–2: **eBay Community Section for Announcements**

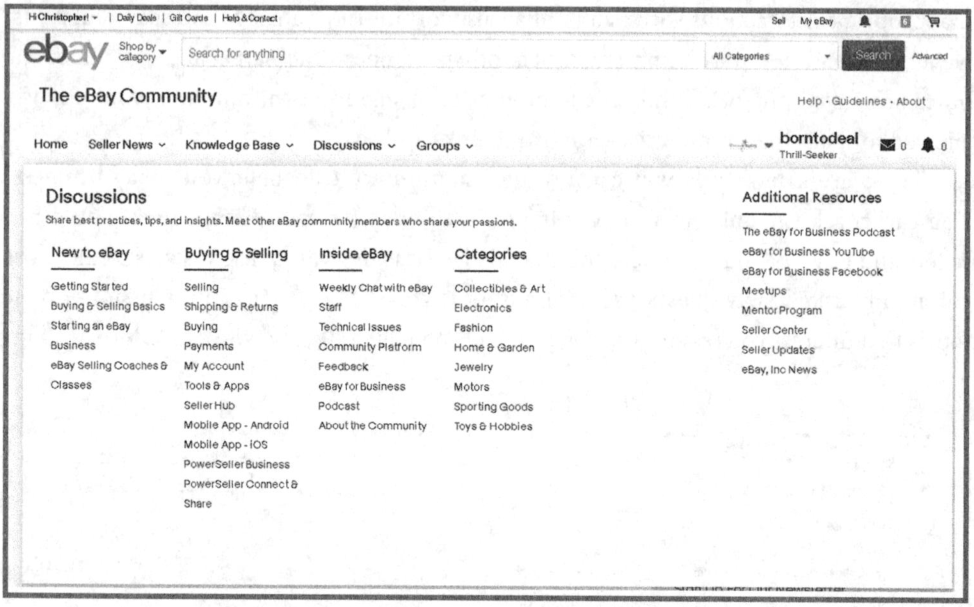

FIGURE 15–3: **eBay Discussion Boards**

from successful eBayers. Finally, you can check eBay's official system status if you're having technical issues with the eBay site (rare but it happens—save a call and look here first).

Preen Your Community Profile

Primp your Community profile before you commence your eBay Community safari hunting for eBay savvy. To manage your Community profile, you'll need to be signed in, then follow these steps:

1. Scroll to the bottom of the eBay home page
2. Click "Community"
3. Click your user ID
4. Click "My Settings"
5. Click the "PERSONAL" tab
6. Click "Personal Information"
7. Fill in everything to your heart's delight (the signature allows HTML code)
8. Click "Save"

tip

Suffering email overload? If you'd like to be a Community "interloper," you can prevent eBay from releasing email alerts to you related to your Community activity. Simply tick the checkbox under the Email section of My Settings on your eBay Community profile.

There are a plethora of Community profile settings you can adjust. While the default settings work great for most people, if you'd like to personalize your Community experience further, click the Preferences tab and modify things until you've achieved the settings that suit you. Explore these tabs and options on your own. However, it's worth mentioning that the Home Page tab allows you to show only the community boards that interest you. And, if you'd like to close the "curtains" to enjoy a little more privacy, the Privacy tab allows you to show your Community profile information, email address, and online status to no one (the default), eBay Community friends only, or the public eBay community.

Always Think about the ROI

Whether you're a bigtime CEO or a small-business owner struggling to keep the bills paid, social networks can become a weighty anchor on your time. As a serial entrepreneur and master of my own daily destiny, like crop farmers, I focus on spending the minimal amount of time to produce the highest yields. I'm also a persistent optimist—finding a silver lining in everything, everywhere I go. While you'll find many eBayers using the Community boards for social interaction, there are plenty of sellers leveraging this important eBay resource to:

▶ Promote their items for sale (every post includes a link back to your items)
▶ Seek help identifying rare and unique items
▶ Ask for price guidance on obscure products
▶ Weigh in with other sellers on the state of affairs in the marketplace

Imagine the benefit of being able to post a question on a discussion board and quickly receive a response from Takashi in Tokyo and Mehdi in Morocco—who both share your love of ancient Roman coins and help you identify and value yours (before listing them on eBay).

To get the most out of the eBay Community by following my simple rules:

▶ Have a business purpose in mind.
▶ Maintain a professional tone in all your posts.
▶ Avoid engaging with "trolls" who spew unhappy messages or "doom and gloom" regarding eBay.
▶ Use plenty of visual aids—pictures say it best and the discussion boards support posting of text *and* images.
▶ Be sure to "follow" your posts and enable alerts so that you'll know when your questions are answered.

▶ Get in and get out—don't allow yourself to slide into endless browsing for the mere sake of curiosity.

▶ If someone is mean to you, don't return the favor (no answer *is* an answer).

You'll find the eBay Community bursting from the seams with great information and wonderful ideas from official eBay staff and fellow eBayers. Enhance and elevate your eBay sales by sharing ideas there.

Become an eBay Celebrity

Now that you're an eBay expert, why not maximize your brand? The eBay for Business Podcast is the perfect hangout spot for sellers seeking sage advice from sellers. You'll find the link to this official eBay podcast on the Community page. You can become a famous eBay seller and join the fun by calling and becoming a guest. Email the team at podcast@ ebay.com for more information.

That wraps up our look into the world of starting an eBay business. I hope that you will find the journey as rewarding as I have. I look forward to seeing you around the eBay community!

eBay Resources

They say you can never be rich enough or thin enough. While that's arguable, I firmly believe you can never have enough resources. Therefore, I'm giving you a wealth of sources to check into, check out, and harness for your own personal information blitz.

These sources are tidbits—ideas to get you started on your research. They are by no means the only sources out there, and they should not be taken as the ultimate answer. I have done our research, but businesses tend to move, change, fold, and expand. As I have repeatedly stressed, do your homework. Get out there and start investigating!

Password and Identity Registration and Protection

LastPass: http://www.lastpass.com

Namechk: http://www.namechk.com

Legal Assistance

Avvo: http://www.avvo.com

Shipping

Freightquote: http://www.freightquote.com

U.S. Postal Service: http://www.usps.com

U.S. Postal Inspection Service: http://www.uspis.gov

Government Business Mentorship and General Resources

Service Corps of Retired Executives (SCORE): http://www.score.org

U.S. Small Business Administration (SBA): http://www.sba.gov

Federal Trade Commission (FTC): http://www.ftc.gov

QR Code Generator

QR Stuff: http://www.qrstuff.com

Philanthropy

eBay for Charity: http://www.ebayforcharity.org

Selling Research

Terapeak: http://www.terapeak.com

Authentication and Grading Services

Here are the official eBay partners (sanctioned but completely independent of eBay) that provide these services:

Sports Autographs and Memorabilia

James Spence Authentication: http://www.spenceloa.com

PSA/DNA: http://psadna.com/ebay/welcome.xhtml

Beckett Authentication: http://www.beckett-authentication.com

Sportscard Guaranty: http://www.sgccard.com

Pre-Certified Autographs

Fanatics Authentic: http://www.fanaticsauthentic.com

Sports Memorabilia: https://www.sportsmemorabilia.com

Steiner Sports: https://www.steinersports.com

Tristar Productions: http://www.tristarproductions.com

Upper Deck: http://www.upperdeck.com

Beanie Babies

Peggy Gallagher Enterprises: http://www.peggyg.com

Coins

Numismatic Guaranty Corporation (NGC): http://www.ngccoin.com

Professional Coin Grading Service (PCGS): http://www.pcgs.com

Independent Coin Graders (ICG): http://www.icgcoin.com

American Numismatic Association Certification Service (ANACS): http://www.anacs.com

Comics

CGC: http://www.cgccomics.com

CBCS: https://www.cbcscomics.com

Jewelry, Diamonds, and Other Gemstones

International Gemological Institute (IGI): http://igionline.org

Gemological Institute of America (GIA): https://www.gia.edu

Political Memorabilia

American Political Items Collectors (APIC): http://www.apic.us

Stamps

American Philatelic Expertizing Service (APEX): http://stamps.org/Home

Philatelic Foundation (PF): http://www.philatelicfoundation.org

Professional Stamp Experts (PSE): http://www.psestamp.com

Trading Cards

Beckett Grading Services (BGS): http://www.beckett.com/grading/ebay

Professional Sports Authenticator (PSA): http://www.psacard.com

Sportscard Guaranty (SGC): http://www.sgccard.com

Glossary

Acquisition cost. The all-in cost of purchasing inventory.

AdChoice. eBay's advertising methodology that uses your tidbits of activity data curated from eBay to tailor-make ads.

Analytics. The performance metrics of your listing(s).

API (application programming interface). A means for third-party developers to access a computer system using a protocol to build apps.

Arbitration. A legally binding means of settling disputes without the involvement of a court (including class action lawsuits which you are also agreeing never to file).

Aspect ratio. The relationship between an image's width and height.

Auction-style listings. Listings that allow you to receive competitive bids from multiple people and sell to the highest bidder.

AuctionWeb. The first iteration of what is now known as eBay, coded in 1995 by Pierre Omidyar, the founder of eBay.

Bespoke. Custom-made.

Best match. eBay's search algorithm based on listing quality, price, popularity, etc.

Boolean search. Keywords with operators/modifiers to give more relevant search results.

Classified ad format. A way to advertise where the seller and buyer complete the transaction off eBay.

COGS (cost of goods sold). The cost of the product, freight, storage, labor, and overhead.

Consignment. An agreement to pay for goods after they sell.

Copyright. Protection for works of authorship including photos, video, songs, written works, software, and more.

Corporations. Legal entities that are separate from their owners. Most corporations issue stock, are taxed separately, and can be held legally liable for the corporation's actions while shielding the stockholders and management from lawsuits, in most situations.

CSV (comma separated values file). A popular file format for sharing data.

De minimis. Low value.

Detailed seller ratings. Known as DSRs for short, these are anonymous and optional ways to leave detailed ratings for sellers on four aspects of the transaction.

Drop-shipping. A supply method in which you don't hold physical inventory, but transmit orders to the wholesaler or supplier who then ships the products directly to the customer.

EAN (European article number). Same as a UPC, except it has a country code prefixed to it.

eBay arbitrage. A technique used by eBay sellers to cash in on others' listing mistakes.

eBay for Charity. A program that allows users to support their favorite eBay-registered nonprofit causes.

Fast 'n Free. Listings that meet certain criteria and are likely to arrive in 4 business days.

Feedback. eBay's rating system for sold items.

Final value fee. Fee that are only assessed when an item sells.

Fixed-price listings. Listings that satisfy a buyer's urge for immediate gratification. There is no bidding, and the buyer doesn't have to wait until the end of an auction.

Good 'til Cancelled. A duration that keeps renewing every 30 days.

GTIN (global trade item number). An identifier use for trade items and are used to look up product information in a database.

Hallmark. Marks certifying the standard of purity of the precious metal in an item.

Incognito window. A private browser window.

Insertion fee. eBay's fee for starting a listing.

Item specifics. Descriptive keywords that tell a buyer about your item. They may include brand, size, length, width, height, type, color or style, and many more, and vary depending on what you're selling.

Limited liability company (LLC). An entity that protects you from liability in most situations in the event of lawsuits or business failures.

International Standard Book Number (ISBN). Every published book is assigned an ISBN. The ISBN identifies a book's edition and publisher.

Maker's mark. A mark that tracks back to the manufacturer.

Manufacturer's part number (MPN). An identifier of a specific part design used to provide a pinpoint reference to that part that is unique to the manufacturer.

MIND patterns. Ecommerce web components. MIND stands for Messaging, Input, Navigation, and Design.

Notice fee. Fee paid once the sale occurs in eBay's Real Estate/Timeshares category.

OATMEAL. Accessibility testing methods. OATMEAL refers to Open Accessibility Testing Methods for Experts and Layfolk.

P&L (profit and loss statement). Income and expenses for a particular period.

Partnership. The simplest way for two or more people to own a business together. Partnerships are a good way to manage a business when you aren't the only owner and you'd like to test things out before advancing to a more formal business structure.

Patent. A license that gives an inventor the sole right to exclude others from making, using, or selling an invention.

Philately. The study and collection of postage stamps.

Promoted listings. An eBay service providing favorable search placement.

Purity mark. Denotes precious metal purity, e.g. 14K, 18K, 800, 925, etc.

QR code. A barcode that stores URLs, addresses, or just about anything.

Retail arbitrage. A technique used by eBay sellers who buy high-demand, sale, and clearance merchandise from local retail stores or their online sites (where purchases can be delivered to the local store) and then sell those products on eBay for a profit.

Seller Hub. A dashboard for managing listings and linking to resources.

Shrinkage. Occurs when items are lost due to damage, loss, or theft.

SKU (stock keeping unit). A value used to identify an inventory item.

Sole proprietorship. The most common business structure for someone just getting started in business. You'll be considered a sole proprietorship if you don't register any other form of business entity.

Successful listing fee. Fee paid when you sell vehicles on eBay Motors.

Top-rated seller. A seller with great shipping statistics, low order defects, 100+ transactions, $1,000 sold within a year to US buyers, and on eBay for at least 90 days.

Trademark. Protection for a symbol, slogan, or word(s) registered or established by use as representing a company or product.

Turnkey. Ready for immediate use.

Universal Product Code (UPC). A barcode system used in the US and Canada, as well as some other countries, for tracking merchandise in stores.

VeRO (Verified Rights Owner program). eBay's team that allows owners of intellectual property rights to report eBay listings that may infringe on those rights.

Acknowledgments

would like to extend my most sincere gratitude to Matt Wagner, my longtime literary agent; Jen Dorsey, the editorial director for Entrepreneur Press, for giving me this opportunity; Ben Akrish, the technical editor for this book and my mentee, who has consistently kept me honest and on course; and my employees for helping me become a man.

—C.M.S.

About
the Author

Christopher Matthew Spencer is a Burbank, California-based businessperson, author, and public speaker. He owns wholesale, retail, hospitality, real estate, and publishing companies. Experienced in the field of consulting, he has worked for and advised businesses of different sizes, from startups to companies listed in The Fortune 100. Christopher Matthew is an eight-year veteran of the U.S. Navy. He volunteers at least 10 percent of his time and income to nonprofit causes and takes immense pride in helping entrepreneurs to achieve their dreams and score big in business.

Index